THE GREAT PYRAMID
Your Personal Guide

By the same author

THE ARMAGEDDON SCRIPT
BEYOND ALL BELIEF
THE COSMIC EYE
GOSPEL OF THE STARS
THE GREAT PYRAMID DECODED

THE GREAT PYRAMID

Your Personal Guide

From Exploration to Initiation

☆

PETER LEMESURIER

Element Books

First published 1987 by
Element Books Limited
Longmead, Shaftesbury, Dorset

Printed and bound in Great Britain by
Billings, Hylton Road, Worcester

Typeset in Linotron Palatino by
Character Graphic, Taunton, Somerset

Designed by Humphrey Stone

Cover design and diagrams by Ray Smith

Cover photo: The Ancient Art & Architecture Collection

British Library Cataloguing in Publication Data

Lemesurier, Peter
The Great Pyramid : your personal guide
1. Great Pyramid
I. Title
932 DT63

ISBN 1-85230-016-7

Contents

Acknowledgements

I am indebted to the following for permission to reprint copyright material: Peter A. Clayton for generously supplying the photograph on p. 16; Feature Pix for that on pp. 4-5; the Institute of Pyramidology, of 31 Station Road, Harpenden, Herts., for the pictures on pp. 15 and 69, which are taken from Dr Adam Rutherford's *Pyramidology* (Institute of Pyramidology, 1957 onwards); and the University of Chicago Press for the map on p. 2, from Ahmed Fakhry's *The Pyramids* (University of Chicago Press, 1969).

The pen-and-ink drawings, along with the photos on pp. 12, 36 and 39, the diagrams on pp. 30 and 187 and the map on p. 224, are taken from the Edgar brothers' *The Great Pyramid Passages and Chambers* and *The Great Pyramid: Its Scientific Features*. The diagrams on pp. 24, 60, 98, 127, 128, 203 and 231 are from David Davidson's *The Great Pyramid: Its Divine Message* and *The Judgement of the Nations in the Great Pyramid's Prophecy*. Those on pp. 88 and 137 are from Prof. C. Piazzi Smyth's *Our Inheritance in the Great Pyramid*. (See bibliography for publishing details.) The aerial photo on p. 21 is of unknown provenance. Any copyright entitlements inadvertently misattributed or omitted will be gratefully acknowledged in future editions.

I should like to acknowledge the impartial help of Peter Clayton, Dr I. E. S. Edwards, the Royal Greenwich Observatory at Herstmonceux and especially the late Dr Adam Rutherford, who was a major source of facts, figures and sound general advice. I am also grateful to Michael Mann for 'spotting' the manuscript in the first place, to Pam Price and Frank Ward for reading it, to Simon Franklin, John Moore and Annie Walton for their editorial skills, to Ray Smith for his immaculate artwork – and to all those involved in the book's production for their immense care and patience.

P.L.

PART I
GUIDEBOOK TO GIZA

'Soldiers, consider that from the summit
of these pyramids, forty centuries
look down upon you.'

NAPOLEON BONAPARTE,
before the Battle of the Pyramids,
1798

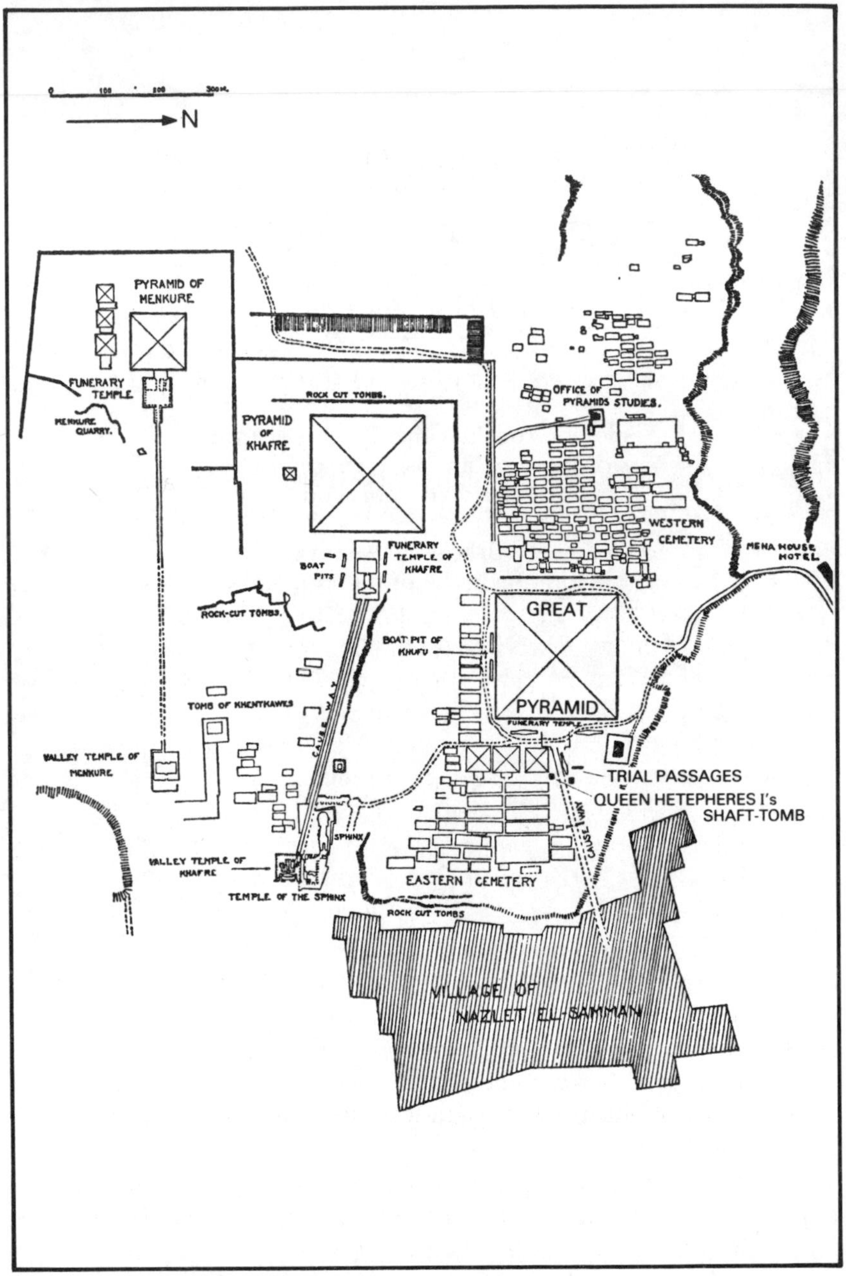

Plan of the Giza Plateau, showing the Sphinx, the three major and seven subsidiary pyramids. The site is approached from the north via the Cairo road, shown here entering the picture from the right.

1
The Lie of the Land

If you have made it in person to Cairo and the Giza Plateau, let this book serve as your guide to the Great Pyramid. Even if you can get there only in imagination, come with me now on a tour of the first, and the sole surviving, of the Seven Wonders of the ancient world.

The straight, broad avenue that slices south-westwards through the Cairo suburbs finally peters out by the entrance to the Mena House Hotel amid a noisy throng of expectant beggars and camels and turning buses. From here on the road narrows, transforming itself into something more like a ceremonial driveway. Skirting the camel-park, it sweeps southward in a great curve as it climbs from the lush fields and waving palms of the delta, up a steep, sandy escarpment and onto the very rim of the desert.

As you near the top, your eyes are full of sunshine and empty sky. To your left, the distant view of the hazy flatlands of the delta is much as it has been for centuries past. The confused clamour of distant bazaars and market-places, the amplified call of the muezzin to the faithful, float up to you on the gentle breeze. Up here, some two hundred feet above sea level, you feel in a different world – a world of silence and calm, blissful, sterile emptiness.

But as you breast the summit you are suddenly aware that you are not alone. Even without looking, you are aware of enormous presences rising out of the ground to your right. You turn, and there, clawing their way gauntly into the sky, are the craggy summits of two of the most stupendous monuments that the world has ever known.

The serrated pile nearest you is the gigantic, crumbling stoneheap of the Great Pyramid itself. Beyond it, and to the right, looms the Second Pyramid of Giza, the remnants of its original outer casing still clinging precariously to its top, and gleaming like a snow-swathed mountain-peak in the sunlight.

There they stand, silent and immovable. There they have stood

now for over forty centuries, the frozen testimony of some teeming, ancient past awaiting the dawn of some distant, unknown future.

Their scale is cyclopean, their sheer bulk awe-inspiring. What ancient mind, you ask yourself, can have conceived so audacious a project? What titanic forces of will must have been at work? What demon can have driven the unknown designer of the Great Pyramid to set the mighty project in motion in the first place?

And can it really be that its whole, enormous bulk – still, even today, by far the heaviest stone building in the world – was raised to cover the body of a single, microscopic man?

As you buy your ticket for 'Cheops' at the little kiosk opposite the Great Pyramid's north face, the contrast is immediately rammed home. 'Cheops' is the Greek version of the name of the king who allegedly built the monument. His Egyptian name was HWFW, which we generally transliterate as 'Khufu'. But can there ever, you wonder, have been anything in common between this lordly pharaoh and the harassed little official who takes your dirty Egyptian pound notes and issues you with your ticket? Are we talking about the same race of beings at all?

True, the throng of cotton-robed guides who cluster eagerly about you have a certain dignity, an expansive and friendly self-confidence about them. You are welcome to employ them if you wish. Virtually none of them can read or write, but what they tell you they have on good authority from their fathers and grandfathers, and they will tell you it fluently in any one of half-a-dozen different languages.

Certainly it will be a colourful account. But you must not expect the results of up-to-the-minute research to fall from their lips. They have their living to earn, and a quick turnover of contented customers whose preconceived notions have been confirmed has much to recommend it in their eyes.

Whereas you, with the most awesome monument in the world staring you in the face, have much to gain from careful attention to the facts.

And they, as it happens, are every bit as colourful ...

The north face of the Great Pyramid dwarfs the visitor as he or she climbs the curving approach road that leads up onto the Giza Plateau. The modern entrance, dimly visible in the shadow cast by the late afternoon sun, is situated directly opposite the two kiosks. (*Photo overleaf*)

Beyond the crumbling north-west corner of the Great Pyramid, the limestone-clad summit of the Second Pyramid of Khafre (Chephren) gleams in the morning sunlight.

Now that you have your ticket, you resist the temptation to rush straight for the entrance and 'do' the inside of the Pyramid first. Many tourists, hungry for delicate Egyptian reliefs and hieroglyphic inscriptions, do just that. Intent on their fixed idea, they miss what is really there, and quickly re-emerge disappointed.

For the Great Pyramid's interior contains none of either.

Instead, first consider the building from the outside.

What you see now, as you walk slowly towards it with a distinct and growing sense of awe, is the Pyramid's core-masonry only. Those two hundred and three courses of limestone blocks were once covered with polished, white, limestone casing-stones from the Moqattam Hills on the far side of the Nile, much like those still clinging to the top of the Great Pyramid's mighty neighbour. If you want to see them today, you could do worse than visit some of the older Cairo mosques. For that is where most of them have finished up – unmercifully quarried from the pyramids for use as building stone, as has so often happened with other ancient buildings.

The Pyramid's apex also seems to be missing. Certainly, the 454 foot high building is flat-topped today. The present summit platform, which is over a hundred yards further away from you than the base, looks much smaller than it really is. But if, while you are at Giza you keep an eye on the summit, you may see some agile young visitor manage to avoid the watching police and make it to the top. That will give you a much better idea of the platform's real size, which is actually some twenty feet in each direction.

Meanwhile the mast on the summit is not a radio mast or flagpole. It was put up by the astronomers Gill and Watson in 1874 to indicate where the Pyramid's actual apex would have been. But then it is by no means certain that the building ever had one. Even historians living as far back as the time of Christ described it as both perfect and topless.

The fact is memorialised, astonishingly, on the reverse side of the Seal of the United States of America, as reproduced for many years on the common-or-garden dollar bill.

For the designer of the 1782 official seal of the USA, the Great Pyramid's capstone was obviously of special significance. Indeed, his representation of it here is highly reminiscent of the medieval alchemical symbol for the divine tetragrammaton YHWH (or 'Jehovah') – whence, no doubt, the upper inscription which apparently means 'He has looked with favour on the beginnings'. Meanwhile, the capstone's final installation atop the thirteen courses of stones depicted is clearly taken to represent, in the designer's own words, 'a new order of ages' (NOVUS ORDO SECLORUM). Whether the number 13 is intended to be significant here is unknown. For an examination of the possible links between the divine tetragrammaton and Khufu's tetragrammaton (HWFW) see *The Great Pyramid Decoded* pp. 249-60.

But why build a pyramid without a top?

There are two further points that catch your eye before you reach the base of the Pyramid itself. Running from top to bottom down the centre of the north face you notice a rough groove, or hollow, in the masonry. The same is true of all four faces. Nobody has ever succeeded in explaining satisfactorily why they are there, though they seem to be deliberate.

What might a hollowing of the face suggest to you?

You have scarcely started to think about that one, when you notice a course of stones about a fifth of the way up that is much thicker than those above and below it. This is the thirty-fifth course, and it does indeed mark a level exactly one-fifth of the way up from the base to the theoretical, designed apex of the Pyramid.

Why should the designer have wished to emphasise this particular level?

Then you notice that the course-thicknesses actually run in quite distinct waves – a thick one, followed by several courses of ever-decreasing thickness, then another thick one, and so on. Clearly it would have been easier to maintain a constant angle of slope if all the courses had been of the same thickness.

So why the constant variation?

Incidentally, that angle of slope is virtually unique – and perhaps the best known of all the strange facts about the Great Pyramid. The best estimates give it an angle of 51°51′14.3″. That may not seem especially remarkable to you, apart from the fact that the figure is extraordinarily precise. But actually there is an astonishing consequence.

On that basis, the height of the Pyramid's theoretical apex from the ground bears exactly the same relationship to the perimeter of the building's designed base as the radius of a circle does to its circumference. Divide the distance around the base by the height, in other words, and the answer is 2π.

This fact may seem mind-boggling in constructional terms alone. But in a building that dates from the very edge of prehistory it can be distinctly disturbing, if you were brought up on conventional ideas of man's early history.

It also poses a further question.

Why go to such incredible lengths to produce this unique and special angle of slope in a mere royal grave-mound?

You may feel it unfair that you should be asked such questions. In a purported guide-book, after all, you expect to find all the answers. In the case of the Great Pyramid, however, the answers are by no means so easy to come by. Yet there is no need to worry. We shall be coming back to most of these points in due course, when you have had a chance to digest your experience of the Pyramid and to consider the facts at your leisure.

Indeed, there will be many more such questions to come. And the answers that I shall go on to suggest may well prove even more overwhelming than the physical reality of the Great Pyramid itself.

Eventually, then, you reach the base of the Pyramid. Now you can begin to appreciate the sheer bulk of the rectangular blocks of its core-masonry. From further back, they may not have looked particularly big. Now you realise that the stones of the bottom course are literally neck high. Can you imagine the weight of such blocks, the sheer difficulty of transporting them and cementing them accurately into position even today?

It has been estimated that the Pyramid contains no less than *two and a third million* such blocks, each averaging around two and a half tons in weight. On the evidence of other sites, the archaeologists tell us that the builders can have worked with nothing more complicated than ropes, levers, ramps, sleds and rollers. On the other hand Herodotus, the ancient Greek historian who is the first writer known to have described the Pyramid, claims – on the authority of the Egyptian priesthood of his day – that the blocks were raised from course to course with the aid of wooden machines. But then he also says that the Pyramid took a hundred thousand men only twenty years to build.

Now that is some claim. Certainly it is one that is well worth checking. Should you have your pocket calculator with you, in fact, now is your chance to use it.

It seems probable that building operations took place mainly during the ancient, three-month time of High Nile, when the delta was flooded and the peasants were consequently freed from their agricultural work to participate. However, let us generously ignore even this probability, and assume that the work went on unabated for an average of twelve hours of daylight every day for twenty years. No strikes, no holidays, no sandstorms or inclement weather. And no modern arc-lights either.

Key in the figures.

2,300,000 blocks, divided by 20 years, divided by 365.242 days, divided again by 12 hours. How many blocks does that give you

A World
of Books
for
Young
and Old
Recycle Bookstore
1066 the Alamada
San Jose, CA 95126
(408) 286-6275
MADE IN U.S.A.

Until J. H. Cole's official Egyptian government survey of 1925, the only significant clearing of the Pyramid's base of the enormous mounds of sand and rubble encumbering it was that undertaken by Colonel R. Howard-Vyse in 1837. In his search for an additional, underground entrance similar to that in the Second Pyramid, he discovered the partially preserved lowest course of casing stones, the limestone foundation-platform, fragments of the basalt pavement and the carefully levelled natural rock beneath. It was in the course of this work that the ninth-century Arab forced entry and the present tourist entrance known as Al-Mamun's Hole was rediscovered in the masonry above. A drawing by Vyse's assistant Perring memorialises the event.

per hour? No, it's all right – your calculator hasn't gone wrong. The answer is just over twenty-six.

But that's almost one block every two minutes!

Is it possible that these enormous stones were really handled by primitive labour at such a rate, and with the obvious accuracy that you now see around you?

Perhaps, after all, you should bear in mind that, to Herodotus, the building of the Great Pyramid was already almost as remote in time as Herodotus himself is to you . . .

Somewhat shaken, perhaps, you now decide to take a closer look at just what standards of accuracy were involved. Just along from where you are standing, and below the main entrance, some of the ancient casing-blocks have actually survived. Thanks to centuries of concealment beneath the desert sands, they are still cemented firmly in place against the bottom course of core-masonry, their outer slope still displaying accurately the original slope of the Pyramid.

You examine them closely.

All except a few of the casing-stones that survived the Arab despoliation during the early Middle Ages were to become severely sand-blasted over the centuries, as was the newly exposed core-masonry of much softer limestone above. The figure in the foreground gives some idea of their size and of the thicknesses of the lower courses of masonry (compare chart p. 226).

Clearly, they are made of a finer grade of limestone than the core-blocks. Originally their white, outer surface was polished. In fact, investigations have suggested that the whole surface of the Pyramid must have been levelled and honed to a standard of accuracy equivalent to that now normal in optical work. The result was a gigantic, blazing, four-way mirror reflecting the sun's rays onto the desert around.

No wonder the ancient Egyptians called the Pyramid *Ta Khut* – 'The Light'.

Above where you are now standing, the north face was a single *five-acre* mirror in its own right. Which means that, in all, some twenty-one acres of casing were finished to the same standards of accuracy as the stones that you now see before you.

Just look at the joints. Do you see how incredibly fine they are? In fact, they average less than a fiftieth of an inch in thickness. You would be lucky to get a penknife blade between the stones. And yet in that minute gap there is a layer of cement so strong that the stones will often break before the cement does.

Why was such incredible accuracy demanded? How was it achieved? And how can it be squared with the primitive tools that the builders are supposed to have used, including jewelled saws, stone pounders and scrapers?

At this point you have a decision to make. If you prefer to visit the interior of the Pyramid straight away, you should turn to page (27). If you can wait, however, may I invite you to come on a tour of the outside of the building first?

If you wish to follow the best magical practice, you will of course turn left now and make the half-mile tour in a clockwise direction. And while you are making your way towards the north-east corner, you will have a chance to take a closer look at the bare rock on which you are walking. Originally this was covered by an artificial pavement of basalt slabs. This in turn came up to the level of the thin rock-platform on which, as you can see, the bottom course of masonry rests. This platform doesn't pass all the way under the Pyramid, though what there is of it is certainly levelled with truly astonishing precision. In fact, the native rock at the centre of the original building-site seems to have been left proud, in the shape of a low knoll. There were, as we shall see, good reasons for this.

Around the outer edge of the pavement there was originally a so-called *temenos* wall. Fragments of this have actually been discovered. It served as a boundary, and marked off the whole area around the Pyramid as a sacred enclosure.

Having reached the north-east corner of the Pyramid, you now take a closer look at the rock a yard or so away from it. Do you see a roughly rectangular hollowing of the rock, some twelve feet across and several inches deep? This is one of the Pyramid's four foundation-sockets. Their outer corners seem originally to have been used to establish the building's base-diagonals. However, the building itself never actually reached those corners. A metal pin within the socket represents one surveyor's estimate of where the north-east corner might have come.

Perhaps this shortfall was just as well. For the four sockets are all at different distances from the centre. The lower the level of the socket-floors, the further out they are. No doubt this is inevitable in a building with sloping sides. But the consequence would still have been a base that wasn't square.

'Who cares?' you may ask.

Well, the builders cared. For a start, they managed to align this whole, gigantic pile to true north with an accuracy of *better than a twelfth of a degree.* That must have been difficult enough. With a non-square base, it might have proved even more so. Either way, the accuracy of their work is little short of incredible.

How could the builders possibly have achieved such precision? And, more to the point, why would they have wished to do so?

Then again, even if you project the original slope of the casing-stones down into the sockets, it *still* falls short of the four outer corners. In the case of this north-east socket, the shortfall is as much as eight inches.

What is the point of having foundation-sockets that lie beyond the limits of your building?

Before proceeding on your clockwise tour, you now look up at the Pyramid's north-east slope-edge. This is one of four traditional routes to the summit. It is a long, hard climb. Nowadays it is made even more difficult by having to avoid the notice of the Egyptian police. If you wish to attempt it, then you will probably have to do so either at night (which would be foolish) or very early in the morning.

The building, after all, is ancient and crumbling. Any route other than via the four corners is nowadays liable to prove fatal. And each time the Pyramid crumbles a little more. If this were England, it is likely that the whole building would long ago have been declared unsafe and roped off completely from the public.

Here in Egypt there are still some things to be thankful for.

On passing around the north-east corner, you come to the modern road. You walk along it past the restaurant and the Farouk museum. On your left, you pass the filled-in site of what was orignally a long, deep pit in the rock.

This was one of five great pits that have so far been discovered around the Pyramid. At an early stage it was deduced that they once contained ceremonial wooden boats for the use of the dead pharaoh's soul. The divine sun-god Ra (so the ancient Egyptians believed) rode daily across the sky in a series of boats, and nightly through the underworld in yet more of them, and in this way the pharaoh, who was nothing less than Ra's earthly manifestation, could hope to join the god in his eternal journey.

The ancients were nothing if not thorough in the practice of their religion.

Opposite the centre of the Pyramid's east face, you stop and

The minute size of the visitors contrasts starkly with the massiveness of the bottom few of the Pyramid's 203 courses of core-masonry. After the two lowest courses, the thirty-fifth course from the bottom – visible in the picture – is the Pyramid's next thickest course, and marks one-fifth of the full-design building's total height. This view from the first of the three subsidiary pyramids shows about half of the Pyramid's eastern base-side. The now only vestigial ceremonial causeway runs away towards the bottom right.

look to your left. Here the ground slopes away from you gently towards the delta. Later on, it becomes more precipitous.

But it is not just a relatively flat slope of natural rock. Look more closely, and you will see that there, running down away from you just to the left of the mass of ruined tombs, are the indistinct remains of a causeway that once led all the way up from the delta to the Pyramid. Now, especially at this end, it is little more than a flattened stretch of ground. But originally, according to our friend Herodotus (who seems, on the whole, to have reported pretty accurately what he saw and heard), it was a magnificent, decorated roadway that took some ten years to construct. Up it, so the archaeologists assert, came the building materials for the Pyramid, off-loaded directly from the boats that brought them across the Nile at the time of the annual summer flood – to be followed, in due course, by the dead pharaoh himself.

At this point, if you have time, you should make a small detour.

Seen from the Great Pyramid's summit-platform the boat pits on its eastern side stand out starkly against the sand-strewn rock of the Giza plateau. The large pit at the lower right shows clearly how the underlying rock strata rise towards the Pyramid's centre, which lies more or less opposite the intersection of the axes of the two main pits. It is from this point that the original ceremonial causeway ran between the left-hand boat-pit and the first of the subsidiary pyramids (centre) towards the upper left-hand corner of the picture. The vertical arrow on the left marks the site of the Trial Passages (see text), the horizontal arrow the shaft-tomb of Queen Hetepheres I, Khufu's mother. The structures at top right are royal family mastabas.

Strolling about a hundred yards down the causeway, and directly away from the Pyramid, you come to a low wall surrounding the second of the five great boat-pits. This one has been excavated and left open for your inspection. Vaguely boat-shaped, it lies parallel to what was once the left-hand edge of the causeway, and so is not quite square-on to the Pyramid.

But this is not the only item of interest here.

To the left, on the far side of the boat-pit, and about its own width northward from it, you discover what appears to be the sloping entrance to a tomb, with rectangular ramps down either side-wall. A couple of yards further on, you see where two further surface-openings have been blocked up with stones and rubble.

Don't be fooled. Contrary to the belief of almost everyone who sees it, this is not a tomb. Known to Pyramid specialists as the 'Trial Passages', it is where the masons who built the Great Pyramid first tried out in the solid rock short sections of the proposed internal passageways to their correct dimensions. What you can

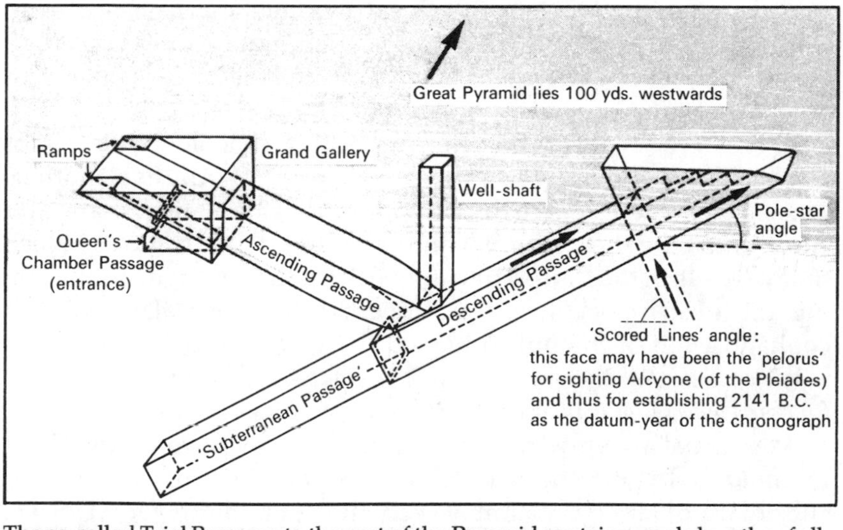

The so-called Trial Passages to the east of the Pyramid contain sample lengths of all the building's main passageways to their correct dimensions. The Subterranean Passage, however, is here cut on the slope, instead of horizontally as in the Pyramid; and the Well-Shaft leads upwards from the intersection of the Descending and Ascending Passages, instead of downwards from the bottom of the Grand Gallery. In addition, the bottom end of the Ascending Passage is tapered both horizontally and vertically, instead of only horizontally as in the Pyramid. These alterations suggest that the trial passages were a kind of prototype, rather than a later copy.

see from the outside is a section of the so-called Grand Gallery (which you will find described in chapter 3). Sections of the Ascending, Descending, and Subterranean Passages are to be found inside, though the last-mentioned, sloping here, is horizontal in the Pyramid. Also present is a section of the so-called Well-Shaft – though this, equally curiously, is misplaced entirely. Its narrow upper end is represented here by the nearest of the blocked entrances visible at ground level.

But this immediately poses further questions.

Why, if these passages were really a prototype for those in the Pyramid, do the archaeologists persist in claiming that the complexities of the Pyramid's passage-system are the result of continual changes of plan during building? Conversely, if the Pyramid's passageways had been constructed first, why would the position of the Well-Shaft and the slope of the Subterranean Passage have been changed here?

Leaving the boat-pit on your right, you now walk back directly across the causeway towards the nearest of the row of three small, ruined pyramids opposite the Great Pyramid's east face. A few yards to the left of this small pyramid's left-hand corner you come across the square entrance to a shaft in the rock – one of many in this part of the Giza necropolis.

It was here, in 1925, that the American archaeologist Professor George Reisner discovered the intact tomb of Khufu's mother, Queen Hetepheres I. At the bottom of its stone-filled shaft, and surrounded by her magnificent, gilded tomb-furniture (which today stands in the Cairo Museum) was the alabaster chest containing the dead queen's viscera, together with her alabaster sarcophagus. But of the queen herself there was no trace.

Why would the Egyptians go to the trouble of burying all the royal funerary objects, and then omit to include the queen herself?

As you make your way back up the causeway towards the Great Pyramid and rejoin the road that takes you past the three ruined subsidiary pyramids, you may well reflect upon this fact. For it is not an isolated case. Again and again we find royal tombs containing empty tomb-chambers. In the case of the known pyramids, there is not one whose sarcophagus has been found to contain the body of the person for whom it was built. All three of the pyramids to your left, for example – possibly built for Khufu's close relations – contain tomb-chambers, but all three have been found to be empty. So, indeed, was that of the Great Pyramid itself.

'Tomb-robbers,' you may say. And you would not be alone. We do know, after all, of tombs that have definitely been robbed.

But in such cases, the body was often dumped unceremoniously on the floor during the robbers' feverish search for hidden jewels. Here, on the other hand, there were simply no bodies.

'Stolen for the jewels wrapped inside the mummy's bandages,' you may suggest. Certainly jewels are known to have been secreted in this way.

Yet there are other pyramids to the south of here in which the alleged tomb-chambers are actually too small ever to have contained a body in the first place.

How logical, then, is it to assume that the pyramids once contained royal bodies, now stolen, if you cannot point to a single definite case of one that did? How can you label the pyramids 'royal burial mounds' when it is known that Khufu's own father, Snofru, had two pyramids at Dashur, and possibly a third at Meidum as well? Is it seriously suggested that he could have been buried in all three?

On the right of the road, as you approach the south-eastern corner of the Great Pyramid, you pass a third, walled boat-pit. Of particular interest here are the rock-strata revealed by its vertical sides. As you look across the pit towards the Pyramid, you realise that the strata at this point form a kind of dome of rock under the Pyramid itself. The designer seems to have chosen this feature deliberately, as a means of giving his building the firmest possible foundation. Hence, presumably, the low knoll of rock which (as we saw earlier) seems to have been left proud under the building's centre.

The Pyramid, after all, has been estimated to weigh over six million tons, or some thirty times as much as the Empire State Building. Even with such a helpful substratum of rock, the enormous pile has subsided by about a foot under its centre, while surviving at least two major earthquakes. Without this feature, it might have suffered even more serious damage than it has, and the internal passageways would probably have become either blocked or far too dangerous to enter today.

We have cause to be grateful for the architect's foresight.

As you turn the south-east corner of the Pyramid, the first sight that confronts your gaze is that of the soaring Second Pyramid, supposedly built by Khufu's second son, Khafre. It looks even bigger than Khufu's monument, but that is because it stands on slightly higher ground. Then again, it was built with slightly steeper sides, and still stands today complete almost to its apex, where it still retains some of its original limestone casing. From it you can gain some idea of what the Great Pyramid might once have looked like in all its glory.

The Third Pyramid, however, which stands next in line beyond it to the south-west, is much smaller. Supposedly built by Menkure, Khufu's grandson, it has only a tenth of the volume of the Great Pyramid and, though virtually complete, never received the intended final touches. Today it is surrounded by the partially-dressed granite blocks with which it was originally encased to a quarter of its height.

Down in the valley to your left, meanwhile, is the Great Sphinx, its grotesque, eroded form guarding the whole Giza necropolis. And between it and the Second Pyramid a large pit-tomb in the rock marks the spot where, according to some authorities, Khufu was really buried.

But, if that is the case, what was the point in building the Great Pyramid in the first place?

You are also struck at this point by a long, curiously modern-looking building alongside the Great Pyramid's south face.

This marks the site of a fourth boat-pit, which was discovered in 1955 under a series of forty-one stone slabs bearing the name Djedefre (reputedly Khufu's first son and successor). Unlike the boat-pits that you saw earlier, this one was found to be rectangular, not boat-shaped.

But the biggest surprise was that it was found to contain a complete do-it-yourself kit for one of the so-called solar boats long theorised about by the Egyptologists. Nearly fifty yards long, and built largely of cedarwood from Lebanon, it is the oldest ocean-going ship ever discovered.

The modern building, in fact, is a museum built especially to house this priceless artefact from the Egyptian Old Kingdom.

And beyond it, to the west, lies a further great boat-pit which is still unopened at the time of writing, though presently being probed with remote-sensing equipment.

What further caches of priceless objects, you wonder, still lie undiscovered under the rock and sand of the Giza plateau?

Until Cole's survey of 1925 the base of the Great Pyramid was never fully cleared of its mounds of rubble. In this early aerial photograph, however, the great gash blasted out by Colonel Howard-Vyse in the Pyramid's south side is clearly visible, as is the prominent thirty-fifth course of masonry running across the top of it. The uppermost 'hole' marks the approximate site of the top end of the King's Chamber's south airshaft (see chapter 3). In the background, beyond the Cairo road, the flatlands of the Delta stretch away into the distance.

Prominent on the south face of the Pyramid, you are intrigued to see an enormous gash in the masonry. At first sight you might take it for some kind of entrance. That, indeed, was what its creator, Colonel Richard Howard-Vyse, thought it might turn out to be back in 1836. Having thoroughly explored the interior from the north and found no secret burial-chamber, he seems to have been determined to blast the building apart, if need be, in order to discover one.

And not without some success.

For, with the aid of liberal quantities of gunpowder, he was to discover four hitherto unknown chambers above the so-called King's Chamber. He it was, too, who originally uncovered the magnificent casing-stones that we saw earlier, which had been hidden for centuries under a mound of sand and rubble on the north side of the Pyramid.

However, Vyse failed totally in his endeavour to find any actual burial. And so he decided to investigate whether there might not be a second set of passages opening on the south side of the

The author pays a visit to the pebble-strewn, sandy knoll to the south-west of Giza, from where the whole pyramid-complex can be seen. In front of the Third Pyramid (nearest camera), three of the six surviving subsidiary pyramids are visible; the remains of the other three lie just to the right of the Great Pyramid (furthest from camera). The Second Pyramid (centre) appears to be larger than its northern neighbour, partly because it stands on higher ground and still retains most of its apex.

Pyramid. Here explosives were used again, and the inevitable result was the damage to the ancient core-masonry that you now see before you. But of a second entrance there was not the slightest sign.

Oddly enough, the Second Pyramid, over to your left, *does* have two entrances. Both, however, open to the north, and are connected to the same subterranean passage-system, as you can verify for yourself. And, as with the Great Pyramid, the sarcophagus in its tomb-chamber was found to be empty.

The Third Pyramid, too, seems originally to have had two northern entrance-passages, though only one of these reached the exterior of the finished building. This pyramid, as it happens, *was* found by Vyse to contain a burial, with the mummy still in its basalt sarcophagus. The former is now in the British Museum, along with the wooden coffin-lid. The sarcophagus, however, was unfortunately lost at sea on its way to England.

Equally unfortunately, radio-carbon dating has shown that both body and coffin-lid date from early Christian times, and so are over two thousand years too 'late' for the building itself. They are an example of a widespread phenomenon known as 'intrusive burial' – the taking-over of an already existing ancient monument for your own use, with all its possibly misleading consequences for later archaeology. We shall have more to say on this subject later.

To the south of the Third Pyramid are three further subsidiary pyramids – all of which were likewise found to be empty – while the Second Pyramid, too, at one time had a small satellite pyramid on its south side. Two of these subsidiary piles reveal a feature typical of the older Egyptian pyramids – a definite, stepped core. Whether the Great Pyramid itself contains such a core is unknown at present.

This makes a total of ten pyramids at Giza, of which nine still survive today. Should you wish to see and photograph all nine at once, then your best plan is to walk (or to take a camel-ride) to the far side of the valley on your left and to climb the ridge beyond it. At the western, or right-hand end of this ridge there is a large mound, and it is only from around here, over three-quarters of a mile from the Great Pyramid, that you are likely to be able to get all nine pyramids in your viewfinder at once.

Such is the sheer scale of the Giza complex.

It is also from here that you may be lucky enough to see an extraordinary phenomenon. Near dawn and sunset at the time of the equinoxes (i.e. around 21 March and 22 September) a ghostly shadow suddenly appears on the south face of the Great Pyramid, apparently dividing it vertically exactly in half, with the shaded side nearest the sun.

There is, of course, nothing supernatural about it. The phenomenon occurs because the Pyramid's core-masonry is actually hollowed, or concave, on all four faces. Since the concavity is only a yard deep, it is virtually invisible under normal circumstances on a face that is all of two hundred and fifty yards long at the base. Only when the sun is almost exactly edge-on to the face does the hollowness show up as the famous shadow.

In a celebrated early aerial picture taken at the equinoctial sunset, Brigadier P. R. C. Groves was to succeed in capturing the Great Pyramid in shadow-phase. Note the simultaneous absence of this feature on the other two pyramids. The apparent two-lane highway (top left) is merely part of Groves's aircraft.

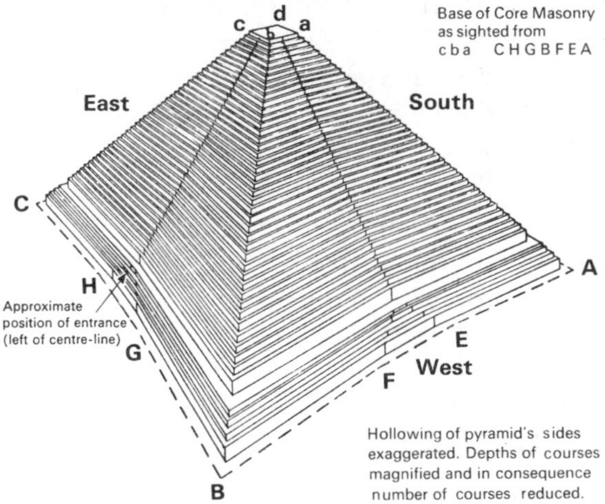

This symbolic reconstruction by David Davidson of the Great Pyramid's core-masonry shows clearly the concave shape of each of the Great Pyramid's four faces and the curious inset triangles at the centres of their bases. The prominent thirty-fifth course of masonry (here shown as the fifth) marks the tops of all four triangles.

But why go to great lengths to build such a concavity into the design of a pyramid, if it is so small as to be virtually unnoticeable for most of the year?

Stand at the foot of the centre of the north face at noon on the same day, incidentally, and the sun will appear to rest on the summit of the Pyramid itself.

Could it be, then, that the design of the Pyramid is directly connected with the equinoxes in some way – and that the missing capstone is meant to be associated with the sun?

Rounding the south-western corner of the Great Pyramid, you are almost on the home straight. Here you pass between the west face of the Pyramid on your right and the ruined tombs of the western cemetery on your left.

These tombs have provided a happy hunting-ground for generations of archaeologists. Many of them were allegedly built for the members of Khufu's family and the nobles of his court. For people of rank it was, it seems, unthinkable to be buried anywhere but in the great desert necropolis which stretches for hundreds of miles down the western side of the Nile. The west, after all, was the direction of the dead, the direction of the setting sun. Even, as some sources suggest, the direction of the land of the ancestors.

And so all down the edge of the western desert we find tombs and pyramids. Of known pyramids there are nearly ninety; of tombs possibly thousands.

And where better to be buried than in the very shadow of the mightiest 'tomb' of all? What better guarantee of sharing in the immortality of Khufu, the great god-king himself?

Once again, then, you reach the north side of the Pyramid. You pause, though, for a moment at its north-western corner to locate the north-west socket with its tell-tale metal pin. Then you look along at those casing-stones that you examined so carefully earlier. Extending the line of their base towards you, you get the distinct impression that it can never have reached northwards as far as this – unless, that is, the finished casing of the Pyramid was also concave on each face.

That, after all, is what you might expect, in view of the concavity of the core-masonry.

Oddly enough, however, such casing-stones as survive show quite clearly that the finished surface *wasn't* concave. The original

Pyramid, in other words, cast no equinox shadow. The line of the casing-stones ran straight to left and right of where you now see them. Consequently the building, as we saw earlier, never reached the corner of the socket where you are now standing. And so, in view of the concavity of the core-masonry beneath it, the casing must have been a yard thinner at the corners than in the middle – a very odd arrangement indeed.

Unless, that is, you expect your building to be rebuilt and extended at some future date.

But why construct a building on this assumption? Why conceal within your casing the concavity that you have so carefully built into the core-masonry in the first place?

And why, as a result, put up a building that is not only apexless, but also around twenty-four feet shorter around the base than you apparently intended it to be?

Ponder this, if you will. For it is by no means the least of the Great Pyramid's many mysteries.

Moreover, as it happens, it turns out to be the key to finding your way inside.

2

The Forbidden Passageways

The Caliph Al-Mamun of Baghdad, son of Harun Al-Rashid of *Arabian Nights* fame, was a prince of vast learning and resplendent intellect. Succeeding to the throne in AD 813, his special fascination was astronomy, whose navigational value to the maritime traders of the growing Muslim empire was, of course, inestimable.

One day the rumour came to his ears that the Great Pyramid of Giza contained a secret chamber in which were stored not only celestial maps and tables, but a vast hoard of treasures as well. There, too, it was reported, were to be found semi-magical artefacts, weapons which would not rust and glass which could be bent.

The temptation was altogether too great for him. A great army of workmen, engineers, architects and masons was duly assembled. For days they scoured the polished surface of the Pyramid for an entrance, only to draw a complete blank, and so force was decided upon.

But where should the attack be mounted?

Being of a logical turn of mind, Al-Mamun decided – no doubt on the evidence of such other pyramids as were already open in his day – that the entrance must lie in the middle of the north face. This suggests, incidentally, that he knew nothing of the twin entrances to the neighbouring Second Pyramid, which are offset well to the left of centre.

Possibly because it happened simply to be the level reached by the drifting sand of his day, he also decided to attack the casing at the level of the seventh course of masonry. Hammer and chisels alone proving unequal to the task, his workmen attacked the stones alternately with fire and vinegar. And gradually the masonry started to yield.

The result was the cave-like entrance which you see before you today.

As it happens, however, those ninth-century Arabs missed their target. The internal passages and chambers were not where they thought they were. Indeed, but for an extraordinary slice of luck – or providence – the Pyramid's upper passageways might still be undiscovered today.

If the Caliph had been more familiar with the typical ancient Egyptian cast of thought he might not have made his mistake. For the Egyptians were obsessed, much like their later Mayan counterparts in Central America, with numerology. Numbers, in other words, and their possible symbolic meanings, fascinated them. Furthermore, their addiction to the numbers-game seems to have had close connections with Al-Mamun's own special hobby-horse – the study of the heavens.

And so the influence both of numerology and of astronomy duly figured prominently in the symbolic arts and architecture of Egypt, and not least in the Great Pyramid.

The Caliph, as we saw, decided to attempt his forced entry at the level of the seventh course of masonry. Now the number seven has a long history of associated esoteric meanings and symbolisms. Most of them have to do with the idea of perfection, or completion – and often a perfection of a particularly 'spiritual' kind, at that. Examples of this are plentiful in the ancient Hebrew Bible, for example, where the 'sacred' seventh day marks the completion of the very week around which our whole society still revolves today. To the Egyptians, too, we may assume that seven was no less auspicious and magical a number.

So that it actually appears unlikely, on the face of it, that the architect would have chosen the seventh course to symbolise the *beginning* of what was ostensibly the 'path of the dead' through his equally ostensible 'royal tomb'. In view of what we have just said, it seems much more likely that this number would appear in connection with that path's *culmination* or *completion*. Possibly, in other words, we might find the burial-chamber floor mounted on a course-level divisible by seven, or discover that it actually formed a seven-sided shape.

Both, in fact, are true, as we now know, of the so-called King's Chamber and Queen's Chamber respectively.

For the entrance, however, it seems much more likely that the architect would have chosen a course-number such as *nineteen*, which has long had death-laden connotations. Not that there is anything particularly magical about the fact. The reason is purely astronomical. It just so happens that the moon's eclipse-cycle lasts some nineteen years. Fairly regular total eclipses result, so that both sun and moon appear to undergo a sudden and dramatic 'death' every nineteen years or so, as the astronomically minded Caliph was no doubt fully aware.

And so, if he had thought of applying this knowledge to his search for the entrance of the Great Pyramid, he might have concluded that the fairly prominent nineteenth course was a more promising one to attack.

For that, in fact, was where the entrance was.

Again, we discovered in the first chapter that the length of the base-perimeter of the Great Pyramid *as built* actually falls some twenty-four feet short of the distance apparently intended. The building, in other words, seems to have been left not only minus its capstone at the top, but also minus twenty-four feet of perimeter at the bottom.

Now there is a long symbolic tradition whereby negativity is associated with the human left hand, and positivity with the right. As in today's use by airline pilots of the magnetic compass, left corresponds to 'minus', right to 'plus'.

If the Caliph had realised, in other words, that the building was actually 'minus twenty-four feet' of base-perimeter, he might have deduced that this was actually a clue to the position of the entrance – the key to opening the can, so to speak.

For that, in effect, is what it is.

Move up to the nineteenth course, measure a distance of twenty-four feet to the left of centre, and you will discover what Al-Mamun would have discovered if he had done the same.

The entrance.

And so, not without a certain sense of awe and anticipation, you make your way up the modern pathway to Al-Mamun's forced entry on the Pyramid's centre-line – the modern tourists' entrance. But before going inside, you first walk on past it a little to the left. Here the pathway narrows and steepens as it climbs further up the north face of the Pyramid, then makes a dog-leg back to the right.

Until eventually, some fifty feet above the base, and twenty-four feet to the left of Al-Mamun's Hole, as it is now known, you find yourself standing before the original entrance.

From time to time the Egyptian authorities have seen fit to barricade this entrance. This is because it gives direct access to the Pyramid's lower passageways, which have been held to be too dangerous for the general public. Depending, then, on present policy in this regard, your visit to this part of the passage-system may have to be purely imaginary.

Not that there is anything particularly dangerous about the Descending Passage itself. This rectangular shaft – some three and a half feet wide and four feet high – bores directly down into the Pyramid on a slope of roughly 1 in 2. For well over a hundred yards it cuts downwards and southwards with deadly accuracy, first through the Pyramid's masonry, and then through the rock beneath, deviating no more than a quarter of an inch in all that distance. At the bottom, the long descent ends in a squared-off wall of rock, into which a second, horizontal passage of rather smaller bore has been cut. This leads on even further southwards beneath the Pyramid.

Before going on to discover where this underground passage leads, there are various striking details to be noticed.

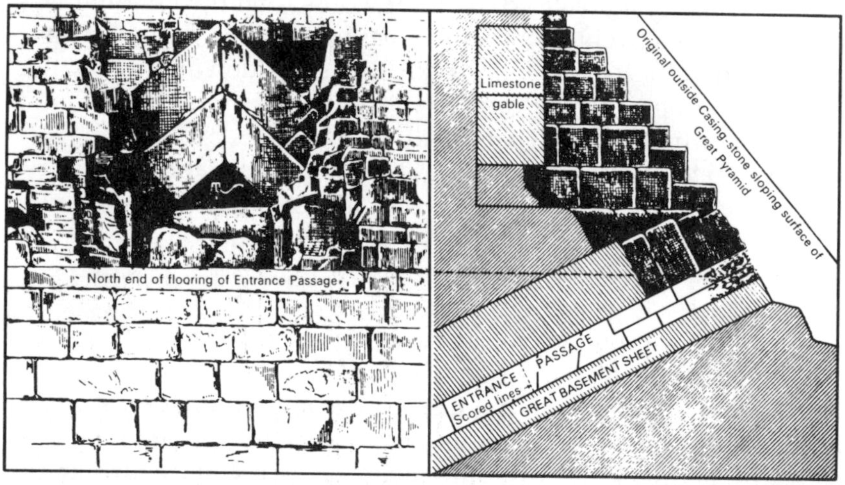

The great double limestone gable over the original entrance-passage originally had other gables in front of it – apparently indicating some kind of entrance-chamber to house the original stone swing-door. The curious 'scored lines' in the walls of the narrow entrance passage (here shown dotted) mark a point directly beneath the gable. The hard, limestone flooring of the passage, known as the Great Basement Sheet, is no less than thirty-three feet wide.

A number of further questions, too, demand to be answered.

The present flooring of the Descending Passage, as you can see, consists of a sloping layer of limestone some two and a half feet thick. Known as the Great Basement Sheet, this is all of thirty-three feet wide. It is on this that the sloping walls of the passage were originally built. On top of these, in turn, the roofing-blocks are fully twelve feet wide and eight and a half feet thick.

But why make the floor masonry so absurdly wide, when the passage itself, like all the Pyramid's main passageways, measures only three and a half feet in width?

Meanwhile, on either side of the entrance, and some three courses of stones above the end of the Basement Sheet, you now notice an extra-thick course of masonry. This is in fact the nineteenth course to which we referred earlier. It is almost exactly thirty-eight inches thick.

It may, of course, be pure coincidence, but how interesting that the nineteenth course should itself be 2 x 19 inches thick!

Now project the angle of the Basement Sheet upwards and outwards from the present north face to where it meets the baseline of the nineteenth course. Visualise the point of intersection. That is where the entrance would have come in the outer casing of the Pyramid as designed. The passage, in fact, would have 'fitted' the nineteenth course exactly.

The entrance too, in other words, would have been thirty-eight inches high.

Having established this theoretical point of departure, you now turn your attention to the masonry surrounding the entrance. And the feature you notice at once is, of course, the great double limestone gable half-hidden in the masonry above the entrance-passage. Originally, it seems, there were further gables in front of this one, each leaning backwards more and more until the Pyramid's sloping outer casing was reached.

Now there are two possible reasons for this extraordinary series of gables. Since they were originally totally invisible from the outside, their purpose cannot have been decorative. The impressive Egyptian hieroglyphs on the upper right-hand block are there only because the nineteenth-century German Egyptologist Lepsius saw fit to carve them on the already exposed gable in honour of the Emperor Friedrich-Wilhelm IV of Prussia. What looks like a much older, more primitive inscription in unknown characters in the small niche just below the apex of the gable may mean anything or nothing. But even if it is genuine, it hardly seems designed for prominent display.

This curious carving in the stonework of the rough niche beneath the point of the entrance gable is generally ignored by Egyptologists and Pyramidologists alike. Could it be a tetragrammaton written in some ancient, unknown script – and possibly standing for a name such as *HWFW*? Compare pp. 71 and 105-9.

Consequently the gables' function must have been either structural or purely symbolic. If it was structural, then this would argue the existence of some kind of open space beneath them – a space which needed protecting from the enormous weight and thrust of the masonry above.

Now the Descending Passage itself clearly doesn't qualify in this respect. It is so narrow as to be perfectly well protected by its own massive roofing-blocks, as the designer himself clearly realised – for behind the gable that you now see in front of you there are, it seems, no others. And so there would seem originally to have been a small chamber of some kind at the entrance to the passage. Its most likely purpose would have been to house the mechanism of the horizontally pivoted stone door which, it has been suggested on the evidence of other sites, originally sealed the entrance.

Certainly *something* did, or Caliph Al-Mamun would have spotted the opening at once.

But we should not forget the possibility of a symbolic meaning, too. The Pyramid itself, after all, is clearly a symbolic structure of some kind, so that it would not be at all surprising if the entrance-gable, too, had a symbolic, as well as a structural function. Look at it from a distance, for example, and you get the clear impression of an upward-pointing arrowhead.

Is it, perhaps, pointing at something of importance in the masonry above it? Or does the 'arrow' symbolically emanate from something directly below it – some feature in the Descending Passage itself, possibly?

Let us, even if only in imagination, go down in and see.

Certainly, there *is* an odd feature at this point. Nearly forty feet down the passage from the original entrance, you find that the sloping masonry-joints of the passage walls on either side are suddenly replaced by two almost vertical ones. Immediately after

Pyramidologist John Edgar demonstrates the discomfort involved in descending the Pyramid's entrance-passage. The drawings supplied by the brothers Edgar in the 1920s provide an invaluable record of the Pyramid as it was before the installation of gangways, handrails, electric light and other modern refinements for the benefit of visitors. This view is from the bottom of the Well-Shaft (see p. 38).

From the sloping bottom of the Descending Passage, a smaller passage is cut horizontally beneath the Pyramid. This is known as the Subterranean Chamber Passage.

these, at a point that is in fact directly underneath the gable, you discover that two perfectly straight lines have been scored in either wall, exactly perpendicular to the slope of the passage.

What could they mean? Do they in turn point at something? Could they possibly be a kind of 'starter's grid', the 'go'-mark on the sacred snakes-and-ladders game that the soul of the deceased was expected to play in the Pyramid's labyrinthine interior? Or could they have some other, equally unexpected purpose?

Now the masonry-joints revert to normal, as the passage plunges ever deeper, first into the Pyramid's interior and then into the living rock beneath it. It is a hundred yards yet before, stooping uncomfortably as you shuffle down the surprisingly steep slope, you at last reach the bottom, only to be confronted by a further, horizontal passage even lower and narrower than the first one.

Virtually on all fours now, you cross the Subterranean Passage's low threshold and scramble along it, still in a southerly direction. Above you there is a hundred feet of rock, and on top of that the gigantic mass of the Pyramid itself.

After some eighteen feet, you suddenly realise that the passage wall has suddenly receded to your right. You are in a kind of minor chamber some six feet square, whose roof is exceedingly rough and irregular. You might think that it had simply been left unfinished, but for one fact. The irregular undulations are so prominent as to suggest that the rough appearance is *deliberate.* The maximum height of this Lesser Subterranean Chamber, after all, is only some four and a half feet, yet the roof height varies by over a foot.

But what would be the point of leaving a chamber deliberately 'unfinished'? What symbolic message, if any, could that possibly convey to anybody?

You will have time to ponder that question further as you continue your journey through the underworld. The Subterranean Passage itself has a further five feet to run before you suddenly find yourself emerging into a great open space. But take care – don't look up!

For as you enter the Great Subterranean Chamber, the floor of the passage drops away beneath you.

Admittedly, though, the drop is only a two-foot one. Negotiating it, you find yourself standing on the rough, uneven rock-floor of a gigantic, rectangular chamber some forty-six feet long and twenty-seven feet wide – the largest of all the Pyramid's chambers.

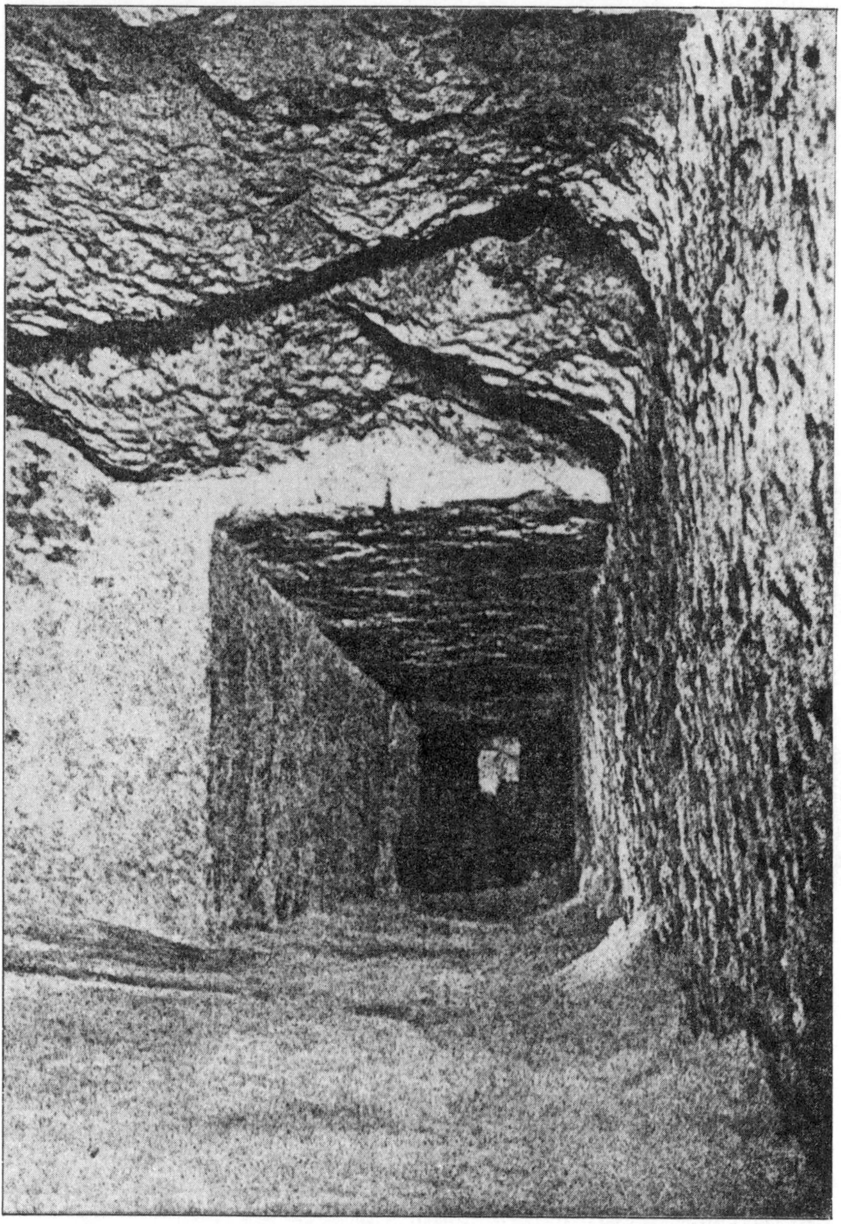

The Subterranean Passage suddenly widens to form the square Lesser Subterranean Chamber. Though its sand-strewn floor is flat, its roof has been left in the form of an extraordinary series of rough waves. The distant legs of the Edgar brothers' Arab assistant show where the lower end of the Descending Passage terminates.

The horizontal tunnel leading from the bottom of the Descending Passage and through the Lesser Subterranean Chamber finally debouches into the north-eastern corner of the Great Subterranean Chamber with a sudden drop in floor-level.

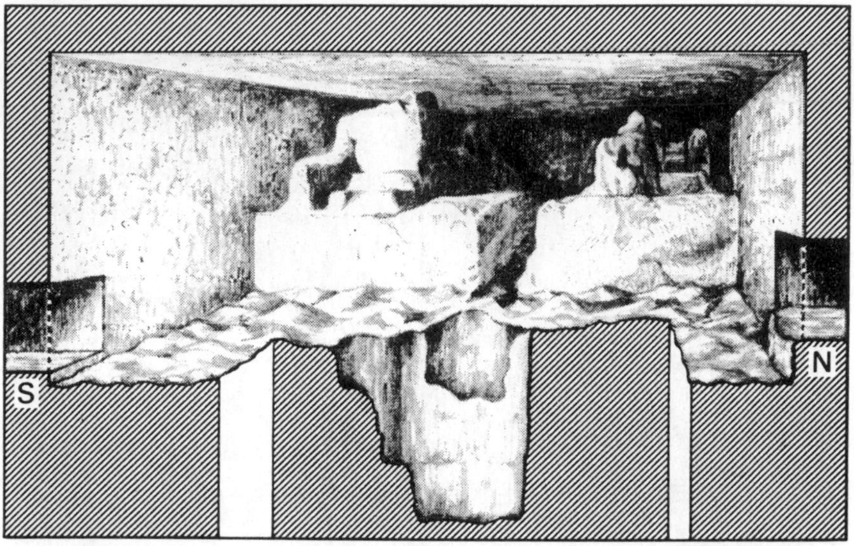

The direct route (from right to left) across the Great Subterranean Chamber leads the unwary visitor into a deep, yawning pit. Skirting it to the right, he finds a gulley leading towards the western wall of the chamber between extraordinary rock-outcrops on either side. A small recess has been cut into the western wall near the north-west corner. To the south, a narrow entrance only two and a half feet wide and high marks the beginning of the final, Dead-End Passage.

Like the Lesser Subterranean Chamber – indeed, like all the Pyramid's chambers – it stretches to the right, or west, of the passage-system itself. But this time wall and roof are alike more or less flat.

It is the floor that is so extraordinary.

Straight ahead of you, it dips uncertainly to the south for about four yards, before tumbling into a kind of ravine some four feet deep. Starting at the left-hand (i.e. east) wall of the chamber, this ravine cuts diagonally across the uneven floor in front of you, to end in a gaping pit some seven feet square and nine feet deep.

But to the right the floor slopes gradually upwards until, about half-way to the west wall of the chamber, it suddenly rises steeply to form a kind of rocky plateau. Atop this plateau, a series of steep ridges, or walls of rock, stretch in parallel lines towards you, with deep gulleys between them.

Only opposite the pit is there any break in the rocky plateau. At this point a steep gulley, corresponding to the ravine on the other side of the pit, allows you easy access to the far west wall

In the western wall of the Great Subterranean Chamber a small recess has been cut at a point just beyond where the parallel rock ridges nearly reach the roof.

of the chamber. And here, at the top of the wall to your right, you find that a small, blind recess has been cut into the rock just below roof-level.

What does it all mean? Is this merely, as most Egyptologists maintain, an 'unfinished chamber'? Have its original contents perhaps been removed at some time in the past? Or was it deliberately designed as a kind of 'chamber of horrors', with some special role to play in ancient initiation-rites?

Certainly the ancients knew about this chamber. At least one classical smoke-inscription on the roof testifies to the fact. And in view of this they must have known, too, about the further passageway which bores yet further under the Pyramid on the far side of the chamber.

Only some two and a half feet square, this is no place for claustrophobes. It is a case of hands-and-knees for a further eighteen yards of rough-hewn rock and ancient mould. And then...? A dead end – a solid wall of rock.

Once again, what is the point? Why dig a passage beyond the intended 'burial chamber', especially if this was to be left 'unfinished'? Could it have been cut to probe the rock foundations, to point to some hidden chamber beyond it, to house hidden jewels or artefacts? Or could it, once again, have had some deeper, symbolic purpose?

In particular, is there some special significance in the fact that the distance from the Pyramid's entrance to this final, blank wall is exactly the same as the vertical height of the Pyramid's summit-platform above its base?

And so you have come, even if only in imagination, to the end of the underground passage-system. Backing gingerly out again, you emerge from the Dead End Passage into the Great Subterranean Chamber and, picking your way carefully around the pit, re-enter the Subterranean Passage. Passing through the Lesser Subterranean Chamber, you re-emerge at the bottom of the Descending Passage.

Now you begin your long climb back towards the light.

This way around, the going is easier. Not being bent quite so low, you can see about you more easily.

And so it is that you suddenly notice a gaping hole on your left, in the west wall of the passage, just above the level of the roof of the Great Subterranean Chamber.

Looking more closely, you see that it is the entrance to a rough tunnel (compare illustration p. 33). To start with, this slopes slightly downwards, but then heads steeply upwards. Three further sections lead even further upwards, eventually ending in a regularly constructed, vertical shaft through the masonry of the Pyramid itself.

Where does it lead?

The ascent is difficult – indeed, almost impossible for anyone who is not a rock-climber. But were you to make it to the top, you would find yourself emerging eventually in the Pyramid's upper passageways.

So who dug this so-called Well-Shaft? And was it cut from the bottom upwards, or from the top downwards?

The structural evidence suggests that it was in fact dug downwards from the top. You don't start an upward-sloping tunnel from the bottom, after all, by boring downwards. You might well finish sinking a downward-sloping tunnel by boring upwards, however – if you happened to sink it a little too far.

But this, if true, would suggest that the shaft *wasn't* cut by tomb-robbers, as is often asserted. The evidence of the Trial Passages suggests quite clearly that it was in fact part of the original design.

But why? Was it, as the Egyptologists suggest, so that the workmen could escape after filling the Ascending Passage in the masonry above with plugging-blocks after the supposed royal funeral? Was it perhaps intended as an inspection-shaft for later checks on possible damage by subsidence and earthquake?

Or was it intended, once again, to have some special symbolic significance?

Certainly the Pyramid's designer must have thought it highly important. It may or may not be that the lower entrance that you have just come across was originally left sealed. But it has to be admitted that, either way, it still posed a serious risk to the supposed 'burial' upstairs – if burial it was. The mere knowledge by unauthorised persons of this secret 'back door' to the Pyramid's interior could, after all, set at risk the whole complex of massive security-precautions in the upper passageways.

Did the ancient Egyptian priesthood, then, who are known to have been familiar with the lower passageways already know of the existence of the Well-Shaft? Had they already entered the upper passageways, the supposed upper 'burial-chamber', long before Al-Mamun?

Was the Well-Shaft, indeed, always *known about?*

Perhaps you will never know all the answers to these questions. The best that you can do for the present is simply to note the fact that the Well-Shaft is undubitably *there*. And also the fact that the distance from where the Subterranean Chamber's roof-level cuts the Descending Passage floor (just below the Well-Shaft's lower entrance) to the bottom of the Descending Passage's long slope is some twenty-four feet – the same twenty-four feet that helped you find the Pyramid's original entrance in the first place.

Was this distance, then, intended to act as the 'can-opener', not merely for the Pyramid itself, but also for the Well-Shaft?

Still pondering this point, you continue climbing up the entrance passage towards the bright pinhole of light that is the entrance. Were this night-time, the probability is that you would now see a particular star shining straight down the passage. Certainly this was intermittently the case (once in every twenty-four hours, in fact) at the time when the Pyramid is alleged to have been built.

For that star was the Pole Star.

In the third millennium BC, the Pole Star was not the present Polaris, but Alpha Draconis, chief star in the constellation of the Dragon. Earlier still, other stars would have fulfilled that role. In 10,000 BC, for example, it seems more likely that the star Theta

Herculis would have come nearest to marking the celestial North Pole, while around 13,000 to 14,000 BC it was Vega in the constellation of the Lyre.

Few of the so-called 'Pole Stars' ever mark the exact celestial pole, however. Alpha Draconis itself, for example, was circling at a distance of nearly four degrees from the Pole in the third millennium BC. What is remarkable is that the designer of the Great Pyramid seems to have recognised this fact.

For his entrance-passage, too, which points to within a twelfth of a degree of true north, 'undershot' the celestial pole – in this case by 3°41′. Alpha Draconis, in other words, would have shone directly down the passage only at the lowest point in its orbit of the Pole.

Where did the designer get his extraordinarily sophisticated knowledge of astronomy – if that is what it was? How did he manage to incorporate it so exactly in the design of the Pyramid? And why?

Eventually you leave the subterranean part of the entrance-passage behind, and are once again climbing up through the Pyramid's limestone masonry. Almost at once, however, you notice another anomaly. The headroom has suddenly increased. Standing up in the opening, you turn around.

There, sloping upwards and away from you, is the beginning of another passageway.

This passage, which is again rectangular in cross-section, looks as though it might lead up into the heart of the Pyramid itself. But there is a snag.

It is blocked.

Blocked, moreover, by at least one gigantic block of granite, wedged firmly into the tapering lower end of the new passage. And this plug itself was originally concealed by a further, prism-shaped block of limestone which once formed the roof of the Descending Passage at this point. That block fell just over a thousand years ago. Hence the fact that you can now stand up in the opening.

How did the Granite Plug get there? Was it slid down the passage which holds it, as archaeologists generally suggest? Or was it built-in from the beginning? And does the fact that it was concealed by a block of limestone until relatively modern times mean that the existence of the upper passageways remained completely unknown until then?

You may wonder. But what is quite certain is that there is no way up at this point. Even the comparatively recent hole in the

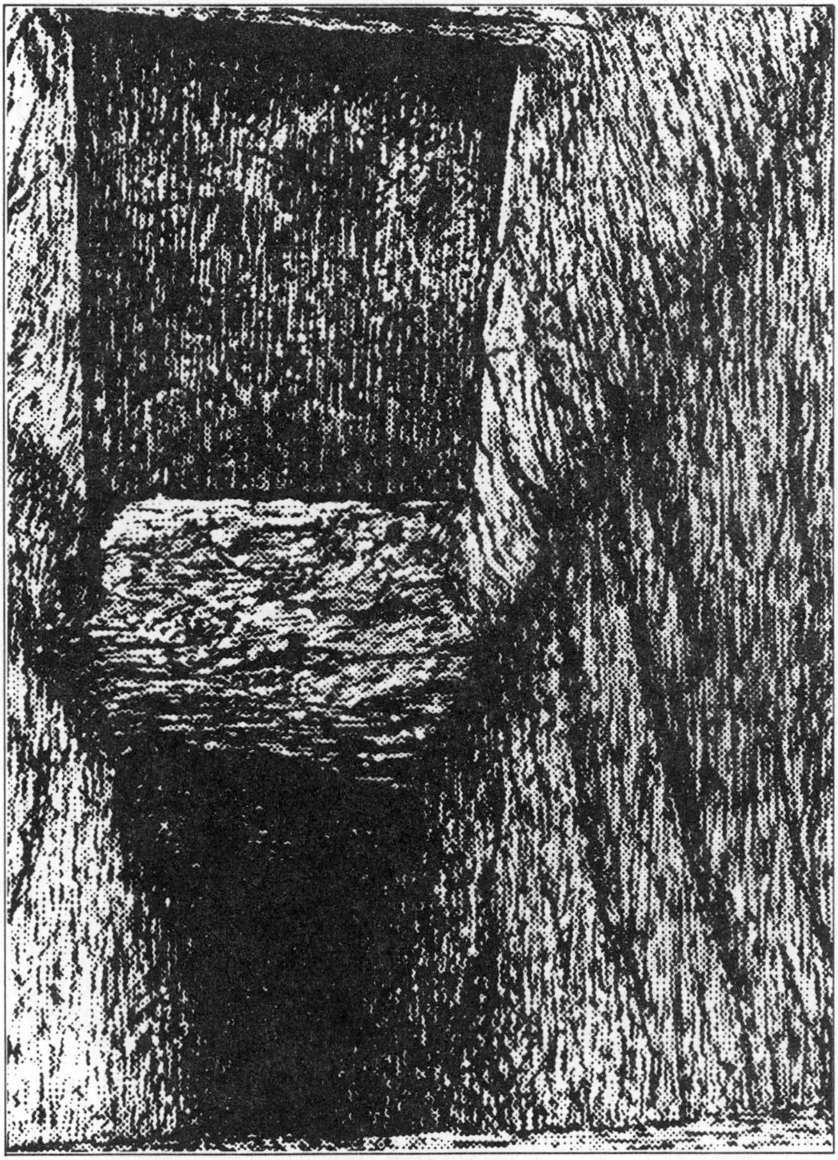

The Ascending Passage was originally bored upwards through the Pyramid's existing masonry from the roof of the entrance-passage. But three granite blocks – the so-called Granite Plug – were immovably jammed into its tapered lower end, apparently at the time of building. The picture shows the lower end of the bottom one. The remains of sockets on either side of the opening seem to represent an automatic latch-arrangement for locking into position a final limestone slab which concealed the opening and restored the passage-roof to its original smooth slope.

masonry just below the opening is nowadays generally barred and padlocked. And so you have no choice but to complete your climb back towards the original entrance.

Beneath your feet, the wooden gangway installed by the Egyptian authorities conceals a limestone floor into which a deep gulley has been worn by the passing feet of millennia. Elsewhere in the Pyramid, you can see what the passing feet of only a few hundred years can do. But the lower passageways were known even to the ancients. Up this slope, perhaps, have passed priests, acolytes and initiates without number, after undergoing strange and indescribable experiences in the horrific Subterranean Chamber.

Such, at least, is one view. But whatever went on down there eventually came to an end, and the last of the ancients, emerging from the entrance, carefully closed its secret door behind him.

3
Journey into the Interior

So it was, then, that the Caliph Al-Mamun, arriving at the Pyramid in AD 820, found himself confronted by a totally sealed structure. An enormous, white half-lozenge of shining stone, enigmatically embedded in the sand. Almost, you could say, an object from another world.

Yet wherever it might have come from, now it was firmly here on earth. And there was treasure inside. Somewhere in there were artefacts and manuscripts beyond price. So, at least, the rumour had it.

Entry was therefore paramount.

With unrestricted force at its command, will tends to take the direct route. Certainly Al-Mamun was no exception to the rule. In such pyramids as were already known to him in Egypt, the entrance was in the centre of the north side.

And it was therefore in the centre of the north side that, as we have seen, the Caliph struck.

So it is that, as you now enter the Pyramid by way of the modern tourists' entrance, you are actually following the route of Al-Mamun's workmen.

At once, you are in a kind of robbers' cave. Al-Mamun's Hole, as it is called today, is a dim cavern of enormous, rough-hewn boulders. Following it, you can see how his workmen first forced their way directly southwards through the Pyramid's masonry. For this they used hammer and chisel, fire and vinegar. As a result of their efforts, you now have an almost unique chance of examining the Pyramid's comparatively rough core-masonry from the inside.

Understandably, however, such niceties were of little interest to the Caliph's workforce. Their sole interest was the prospect of the treasures that awaited them further inside the Pyramid. Yet progress was agonisingly slow. By the time they had reached what is now the end of the first, straight section of the tunnel, they were already close to despair.

And it was while they were aiming what may well have been their last, few, desperate hammer-blows, something extraordinary happened.

From deep within the thickness of the masonry, some twenty-four feet to their left, there suddenly came the muffled, reverberating boom of a falling block of stone.

The Arabs were no fools. If a stone had fallen, then it must have had beneath it a space to fall into. And that space could only mean a chamber or a passageway.

At once, then, the workmen directed their demolition-efforts to the left-hand wall of their tunnel. And as you now round the resulting bend, you see what they discovered.

There before you is the side of the great Granite Plug which originally sealed the Pyramid's upper passageways. And below it you can catch a glimpse of the Descending Passage, as it runs away to your right into the depths. The block that had fallen into it was none other than the prismatic roof-block that had originally concealed from view the beginning of the Ascending Passage.

Can it be that the Pyramid was programmed to reveal its inner secrets at just such a moment? Could the roof-block in the Descending Passage have been designed to fall just as soon as the anticipated vibrations of future hammering disturbed it? Was it actually intended *that the existence of the upper passageways should be revealed only to some future age which could contemplate the building free from all considerations of religious awe?*

You may choose to think so. Yet consider what was now revealed. An Ascending Passage blocked by three huge, immovable blocks of granite brought especially from Aswan, some four hundred miles to the south. According to the historians, these were originally slid down the passage from its top end after the supposed funeral, to protect the pharaoh's final resting-place.

Now you can test the theory for yourself.

Look first at the fit of the blocks against walls, floor and roof. The fit is snug, even tight. You do not have to be an engineer to draw the obvious conclusion.

There is no significant clearance.

But with no clearance, there can be no slide, however slippery the floor (and certainly the original, highly-polished floors were slippery).

Now look again.

Insert your hand between the bottom block and the next one up. As you can see, there is plenty of room. You have no need to

Swinging their cavernous tunnel to the left, the ninth-century Arab intruders came upon the side of the threefold Granite Plug – the upper two of whose stones are visible here. Via a hole in the floor (left foreground) they were then able to enter the Descending Passage, and so to rediscover and reopen the Pyramid's long-lost secret entrance. After some further labour they were also able to enter and clear the Ascending Passage, which climbs away to the right. 'Al-Mamun's Hole', as this cavity is called, is nowadays the Pyramid's official entrance for tourists.

worry about whether the upper block will suddenly slide down and crush your hand. It is no more likely to move now than it was when it was first put there.

But if it was slid all the way down the passage, why did it jam just here? Why didn't the lowest block jam at the same point? Or, if we blame it all on a build-up of whatever lubricant was used, why did the third block nevertheless manage to collide with the second one?

The most obvious answer would appear to be a simple one. The three blocks of the Granite Plug were not slid down the passage at all.

They were built in when the Pyramid was constructed. Which might explain why, after burrowing all around them and clearing the Ascending Passage of further, limestone blocks, the Caliph's workmen found only an empty, lidless sarcophagus in the supposed tomb-chamber. No funeral, it seems, can ever have taken place.

But in that case, why block the passage in the first place?

'Security' may seem the obvious answer – even in the absence of a subsequent burial. Plans, after all, can change. And yet there are some curious hints that this might not have been the real purpose. After all, the whole of the Descending Passage was left open to anybody who knew where the door was – when it, too, could easily have been plugged from top to bottom. (The excellent condition of its walls and roof shows quite clearly that no plugging-blocks were ever slid into position.) Again, there is the so-called 'Well-Shaft' connecting this to the upper passageways – which is hardly calculated to ensure their security. And finally, no great intelligence is needed to realise that, while the Granite Plug itself is virtually impenetrable, the limestone masonry around it certainly isn't.

All of which would seem to suggest that installing a plug at this point, and lugging blocks of granite all the way from Aswan for the purpose, can have been intended only as a *token* security precaution. In other words, the role of the Granite Plug was always intended to be symbolic rather than practical.

Which is not the first time that we have suspected the existence of a purely symbolic purpose underlying the whole, gigantic project.

Climbing the modern steps to the right of the Granite Plug, you now enter the Pyramid's original Ascending Passage. There it stretches, away to your right – a mere three and a half feet wide and four feet high – for over forty yards up into the heart of the Pyramid. Today, thanks to the plug-clearing efforts of the Arabs and the passage of generations of later tourists, this mirror-image of the Descending Passage is dilapidated, much worn, smoke-blackened. Yet if you sight carefully along its walls and roof, you can still gain some idea of the straightness and precision with which it was originally constructed; or rather cut.

For there is a curious feature that becomes apparent only upon careful examination. The masonry-joints in the side walls are – to start with at any rate – vertical and horizontal, not aligned to the slope of the passage. This suggests that the lower part of the passage was in fact not built at all, but *bored through* the already existing core-masonry, rather after the style of its counterpart in the Trial Passages (see chapter 1). The Pyramid, in other words, seems to have been built up to a level some ten feet above the Granite Plug before the Ascending Passage was ever started. The fact naturally raises new doubts about how the Granite Plug was inserted.

Was the masonry assembled, bored through, taken apart, and then reassembled with the granite blocks inside it? Or was the passage bored in strict time with the raising of the masonry, and each plugging-block then rammed in by main force as far as it would go just as soon as there was room for it?

It is difficult to arrive at definite answers to these questions. A larger question does arise, however.

If the Ascending Passage was bored through the masonry, then surely this suggests that it was an afterthought, and that the upper passageways represent a change of thinking on the designer's part?

The historians, after all, constantly insist that the Great Subterranean Chamber represents an abandoned tomb-chamber – and thus the demise, you could say, of Plan A, as depicted in the diagram overleaf.

The putative Plan B is shown in the diagram on page 51. It involved cutting a new, ascending passage, building a further, horizontal passage, and constructing a second tomb-chamber (the so-called Queen's Chamber).

Then this plan, too, was abandoned and, under Plan C, the Grand Gallery was built, leading to a third, definitive tomb-chamber even further above ground, now known to us as the King's Chamber (see diagram, p. 52).

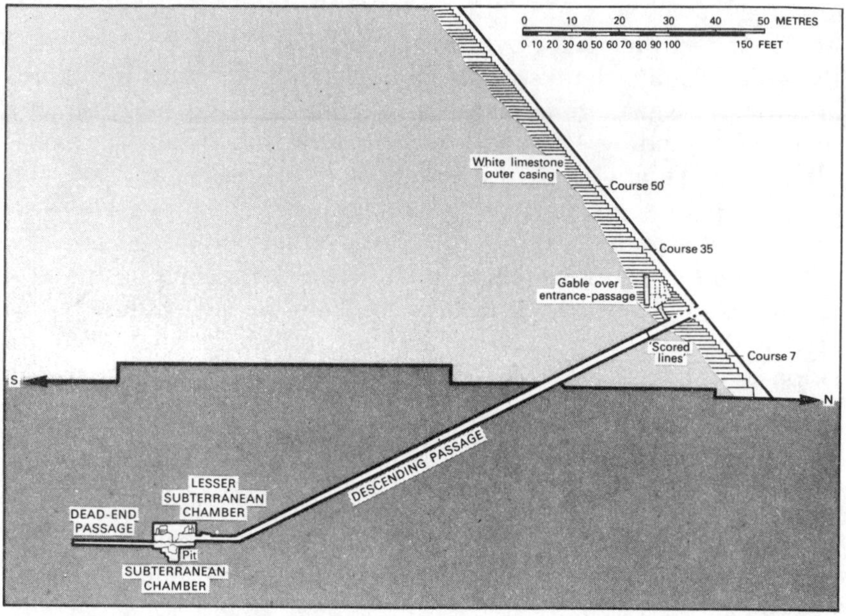

The traditional 'change of mind' theory – Plan A. This would result in a subterranean tomb-chamber and a passage-layout similar to that found in the other Giza pyramids.

And certainly this 'change-of-mind' theory seems quite consistent, at first sight, with the masonry at the lower end of the Ascending Passage. A few feet up the passage, after all, the wall-joints start to run parallel and perpendicular to its slope – suggesting that this represents the point at which the change of mind actually occurred. Yet within fourteen feet or so you once again come to a set of *vertical* joints, followed by further joints on the slope. Indeed, two further sets of vertical joints are to be found even further up the passage, the three sets of vertical joints having a spacing of some seventeen feet (or ten Egyptian royal cubits) between each pair.

It is these 'girdle stones', as they are known, that actually give the lie to the 'change-of-mind' theory. It is quite clear, after all, that the interruption of the sloping passage-masonry by further vertical blocks of stone at regular intervals must have been deliberate. Moreover, the reason is not too difficult to deduce. By boring the passage through enormous blocks of stone that were already firmly anchored in the Pyramid's masonry, the builders contrived

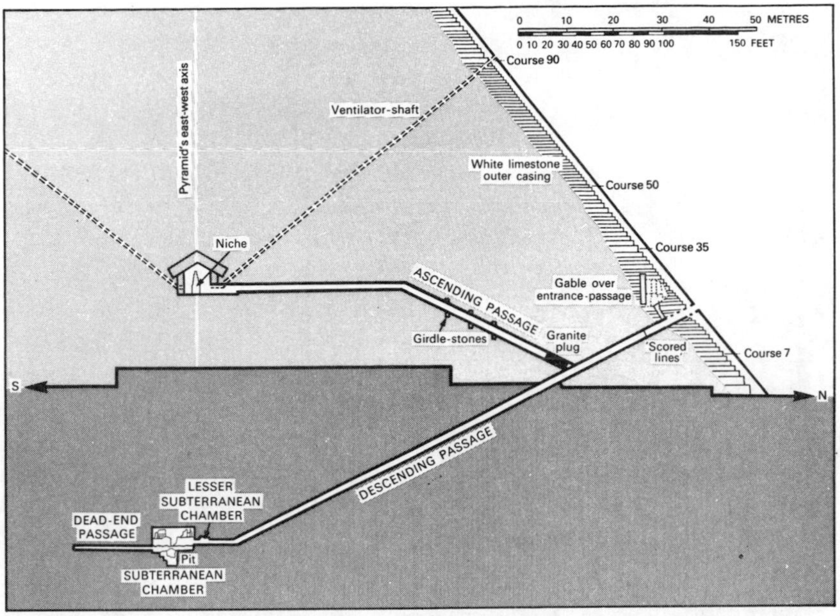

The traditional 'change of mind' theory – Plan B. A burial-chamber directly under the Pyramid's east-west centreline is now envisaged. The purpose of the ventilator-shafts is, however, uncertain, while the Granite Plug seems to pose insuperable problems to the supposed burial.

to ensure that there would be no tendency for the passage-masonry to avalanche downwards into the entrance-passage under conditions of stress, such as earthquake or subsidence. Hence the related decision – a deliberate one, as it now appears – to anchor the whole lower end of the passage by boring it through the Pyramid's masonry itself.

The quality of the limestone at the lower end of the passage seems to reinforce this conclusion. It is a much harder and finer stone than that visible in, say, Al-Mamun's Hole, and this would suggest that it was deliberately selected for the role that it was going to have to play in providing the walls, floor and roof of the already-planned Ascending Passage. A passage whose prototype, you will recall, was already present in the Trial Passages (see chapter 1).

Even so, the stone was still not hard enough. It has become worn and exfoliated through the centuries. And so perhaps it is just as well that the Egyptian Department of Antiquities has installed wooden gangways and metal handrails for your convenience.

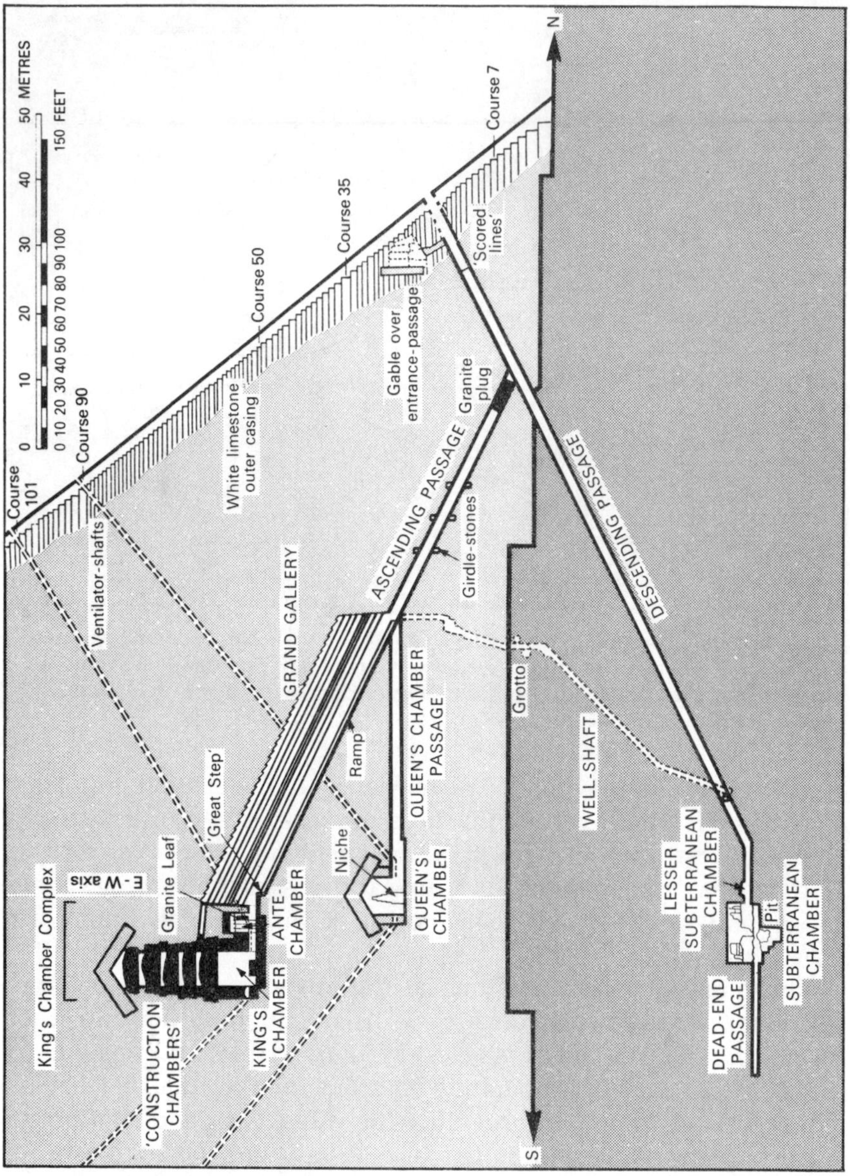

The traditional 'change of mind' theory – Plan C. The burial is now re-sited even higher in the masonry, beyond a yard-high step marking the building's east-west centreline. A unique, corbelled, sloping hallway is also incorporated, as is an antechamber containing three-and-a-half portcullises. Five further, relieving chambers are erected above the new, granite tomb-chamber.
(Black shading = granite)

It is these, and not the ancient masonry, that now take the bulk of the wear caused by the incessant stream of visitors.

And so, with the help of these modern fitments, you eventually make it, stooping, to the top of the Ascending Passage. Hitherto the way has been cramped, almost claustrophobic. Some four feet high and three and a half feet wide, the passage has allowed just room enough for one person at a time, and even so there are many who find the experience back-breaking.

Suddenly, however, you find that you can stand up straight. Even while you are still climbing the last two feet of the sloping Ascending Passage floor, the walls open up to either side, and the roof suddenly rises to a lofty height.

You have entered the Grand Gallery.

This great, sloping hallway is architecturally unique. Nothing quite like it has ever been found elsewhere. Over fifty yards long, and twenty-eight feet high, the whole structure is built on the same slope as the Ascending Passage itself, whose floor continues up the centre of the Gallery. As you can see, the first twenty feet or so of it was removed in Al-Mamun's day, or possibly even before, to reveal a further, horizontal passageway stretching away beneath it – the so-called Queen's Chamber Passage.

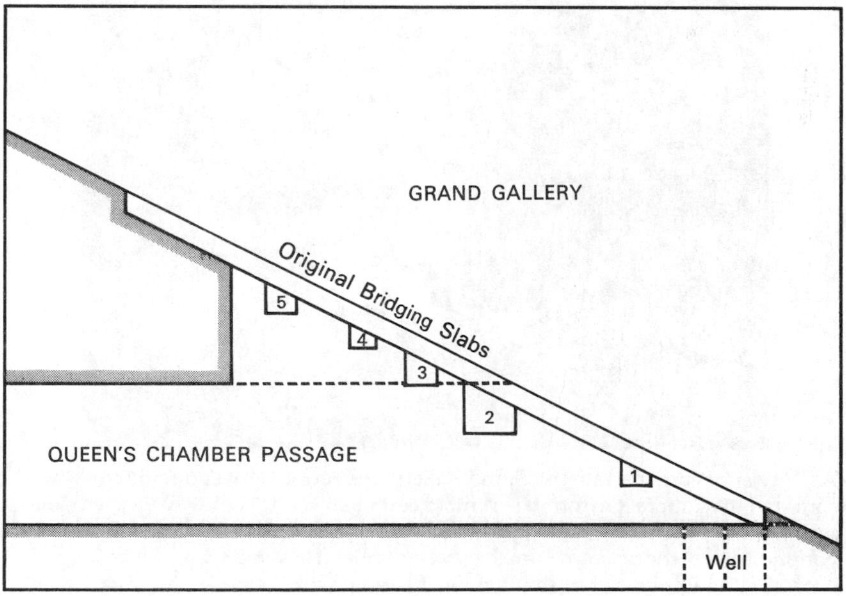

As the visitor emerges into the Grand Gallery, the roof-height suddenly rises by some twenty-four feet to form a sevenfold corbelled vault. Half-way up each side wall, a groove seems to indicate provision for some kind of sliding floor. The bottom stone of the western ramp has been removed at some stage to provide access to the upper end of the Well-Shaft (see p. 72).

Resisting the temptation to explore this first, however, you follow the route which the Caliph's workmen themselves eventually took. And this lay remorselessly up the Gallery, towards the culminating passage-complex whose entrance you can see at its distant upper end.

In view of the gap in the floor at the bottom end of the Gallery, the Egyptian authorities have thoughtfully provided gangplanks and handrails to enable you to use the side-ramps instead. And so, mounting the left-hand ramp, you start to climb the slope.

What the original purpose of the ramps was is unknown today. You will find similar ones in the downward-sloping entrance passages of some of the tombs in the Giza necropolis. It may be that, in such cases, they were lubricated and used for sliding the sarcophagus down into the interior, the central gangway being left unlubricated for the benefit of the mourners' feet. Here, however, the ramps are much further apart, and in any case that particular use is out of the question, as we shall see. There has to be some other purpose.

And so, once again, we may begin to suspect some special, symbolic role.

The rows of rectangular holes sunk into the ramps where they join the wall (compare the diagram on p. 199) pose similar problems. Numerous suggestions have been made as to how they *could* have been used. They originally could have held spacing-girders during construction, or stops for the plugging-blocks that are supposed to have been stored here, or even statues of Osiris. All we can say for certain, however, is that there were originally twenty-eight of them on each side of the Gallery – each some six inches wide and twenty-one inches long, this latter distance being measured alternately horizontally and on the slope.

Next to each of them, you notice an 'inset-stone' in the wall, crossed by a rectangular depression parallel to the slope of the Gallery. Only the two ramp-holes at the very top end of the Gallery lack this feature.

What these signify has to be, once again, a matter for conjecture.

Seven and a half feet above the ramps comes the first of seven corbellings, or overlaps, in the wall-masonry. On seven occasions, in other words, the width of the Gallery narrows suddenly by some six inches as it approaches roof-level. Consequently the width of the roof is some forty-two inches (or two Egyptian royal cubits) less than the total width over the ramps. But, since each ramp is

Prior to the installation of handrails and wooden gangways, ascending the Grand Gallery was a slippery and insecure business. True, the rectangular holes let into the side ramps, each with its corresponding inset-stone in the wall, at least provided something to hang on to. Yet both their spacing and their length, at one royal cubit horizontally and on the slope alternately, seem to indicate that their purpose was more than mere practical convenience. Beneath the Grand Gallery, the Queen's Chamber Passage runs away horizontally into the heart of the Pyramid some twenty-one inches wide, this can mean only one thing.

If you first imagine the whole Gallery as a telescopic structure,and then 'collapse' it downwards, top to bottom, in your mind, thc top section exactly fits the bottom section – to form a simple continuation of the Ascending Passage.

Once again, then, some symbolic process seems to be at work. It is as though you are meant to think of something extraordinary happening as you enter the Gallery – something 'explosive' enough to force the roof up to its present, dizzy height. Perhaps, then, that distance is significant?

Were you to measure it, you would soon confirm that suspicion.

For the distance involved is *twenty-four feet* – that same twenty-four feet that is missing from the Pyramid's base-perimeter, and that helped you discover the original entrance in the first place (see chapter 2).

Clearly, then, some kind of numbers-game is in progress. In which case, if the *twenty-four-foot* jump in the roof-height is significant, then so, too, may be the *sevenfold* decrease in the Gallery's width as it ascends towards roof-level. The meaning of the *fifty-six* original ramp-holes and inset-stones could similarly have something to do with the fact that fifty-six is eight times seven. And if you now look up at the roof and count the roof-stones (which stand out quite distinctly), you should find that there are exactly *forty* of them. Could five times eight, you wonder, somehow be significant too?

Actually, there is some disagreement about this number: counting from floor-level (which is not as easy as you might think) you may well finish up with a total of only thirty-nine. Nevertheless the official word from researchers who have examined the roof more closely is that the true figure is indeed forty. And so it seems to be up to you to decide whether to believe your own eyes or those of the experts.

There are good and practical reasons why the roof-stones should stand out so clearly. They were installed not flat, but ratchet-wise. As a result, there can now be no sliding, and thus no cumulative, downward pressure on the wall at the lower end of the Gallery. The structure, like that of the Ascending Passage, is stable. And the fact that you can count – or attempt to count – the roof-stones may thus have a purely practical explanation.

Yet there are some worrying anomalies.

Why, for example, does the north (i.e. lower-end) wall of the Gallery have only six, not seven overlaps? What is the purpose of the two six-inch-wide slots that run the whole length of the side walls, and that seem to mark the half-height of the Gallery? Could they indicate the presence of some kind of sliding floor? And if so, are we to think of that floor as real or as purely imaginary?

Possibly you may feel that I am overdoing the numbers and

The yard-high Great Step at the top end of the Grand Gallery marks the east-west centreline of the Pyramid. Now much broken and worn, it brings the visitor to the top of the fiftieth course of masonry, 153 courses below the summit-platform, and ushers him into the low passage leading to the King's Chamber beyond.

symbols. Possibly there is a simple, rational explanation for it all. Perhaps even the great, seven-foot-wide 'step' at the top end of the Gallery has a simple purpose – though not, presumably, as a simple step. For you, admittedly, approaching it via the side-ramps, it is only a foot or so high. But for anyone trying to scale it from floor-level it involves clambering over a considerable obstacle, a kind of 'altar stone' that is almost exactly a yard high.

A yard?

But in that case it seems, after all, to be back to the symbolic numbers-game.

For the original height of the so-called Great Step was exactly the same as the depth of the concavity on each face of the Pyramid's core-masonry; that same concavity which produced the twenty-four-foot shortfall in the Pyramid's actual base-perimeter that identified the entrance – and that consequently got you this far in the first place.

There is a sting in the tail, too. For the front of the Great Step lies exactly on the Pyramid's east-west axis.

From the top of the Great Step, a square entrance at the bottom of the Grand Gallery's south wall now leads you further southwards through a horizontal passageway. Since this has a height and width of only two Egyptian royal cubits, or some three and a half feet, you have to bend almost double. Perhaps as a result, you cannot help noticing the unevenness of the floor-blocks – a direct consequence of the earth-movements which have distorted the Pyramid during the course of its long history.

Still, the discomfort doesn't last long. Only four feet or so beyond the entrance, the roof-level suddenly rises at the start of what is known as the Antechamber. Now you are able to stand up straight in a small, twenty-one-inch space between the north wall of the Antechamber and what appears to be a suspended stone portcullis spanning the passageway.

This sixteen-inch-thick slab, the so-called Granite Leaf, is an extraordinary affair. As its name implies, it is made of granite, as are the floor, the roof and most of the walls from this point on. It consists of two blocks, one on top of the other, fitted and cemented into rectangular grooves in either side wall. These grooves descend no further than the roof-level of the low entrance-passage, however – which effectively means that the portcullis could never have been lowered to the floor.

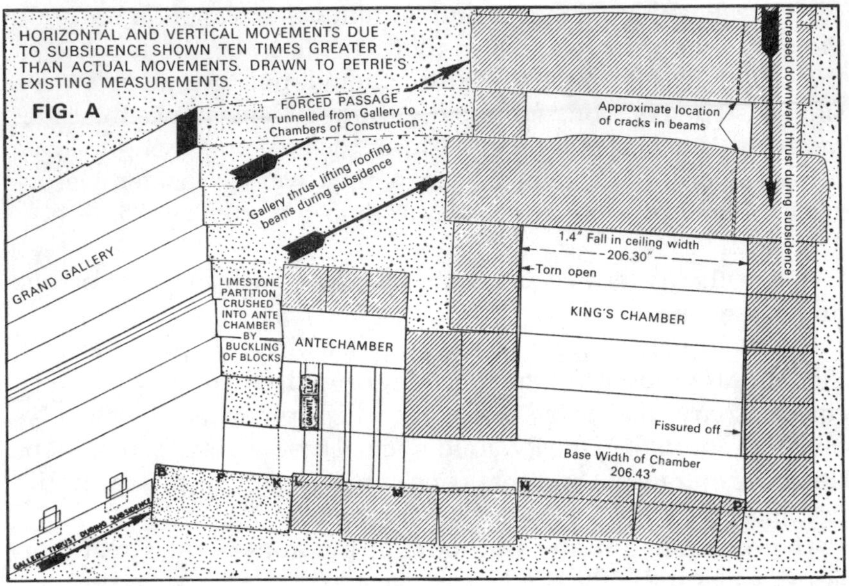

Thanks to two major earthquakes – in 908 and 1301 AD – and about a foot of subsidence under the building's centre, the King's Chamber complex in particular has become seriously distorted. On restoring the stones to their original positions, however, the extraordinarily refined mathematics of its construction start to become clear. In the diagrams, stippled areas represent limestone, hatched areas granite. P" = Pyramid or primitive inches: RC = royal cubits.

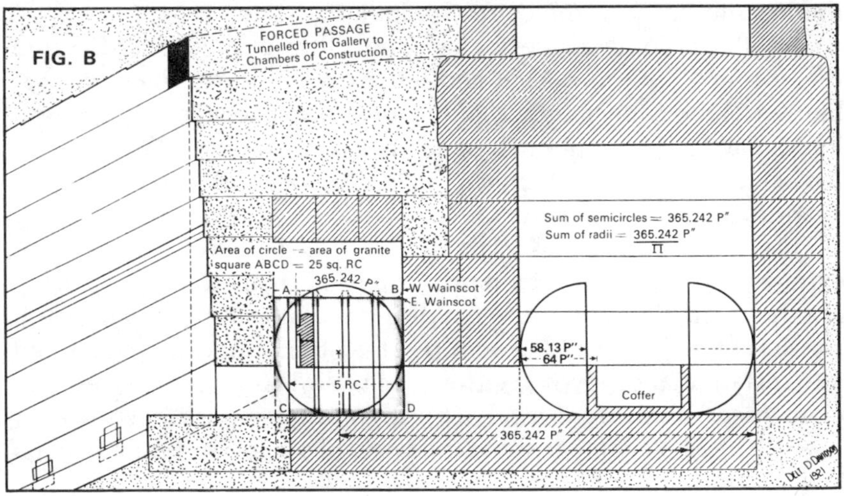

Pyramidologists such as John Edgar have made much of the fact that it is necessary to 'bow beneath' the Granite Leaf in order to enter the Antechamber proper. But in fact the passage beneath it has exactly the same height as the rest of the King's Chamber Passage. On the right, meanwhile, can be seen the remains of the pilasters designed to guide the three main portcullises down to a point some three inches below the present floor-level.

What is the point of installing a portcullis that cannot be lowered? Whom would that keep out? And why, in any case, the sudden switch to granite?

The entire north face of the Granite Leaf, you will observe, has been planed down by almost exactly one inch, with the exception of two side rebates – one in each of the grooves on either side – and a horseshoe-shaped 'boss' near the centre of the upper stone (compare diagram page 203). This boss, it has been suggested, was originally used as a purchase for the tackle with which the upper stone was originally lowered into position. Yet there is no corresponding boss on the other side of the stone, such as this arrangement would of course demand.

Once again we seem to have a hint of a purpose that goes beyond the purely utilitarian. The 'boss', or 'seal', in other words, may have an overriding symbolic function.

Meanwhile the top stone of the Granite Leaf is undressed and irregular at the top – apparently intentionally so. Somehow you get the distinct impression that the stone has been 'broken off from above'. Consequently this fact, too, may have a 'meaning' that goes far beyond the obvious physical explanation – in this case, perhaps, subsequent damage by intruders.

Ducking under the Granite Leaf, you are in the Antechamber proper. The roof-level is still a good six feet above your head, even though the passage width through the lower part of the chamber remains the same as before. In fact, were you to multiply the roof height by a hundred, you would arrive at a distance exactly equivalent to the full design Pyramid's overall height and base-side added together.

Could this fact mean that there is intended to be some symbolic connection between the Antechamber and an eventual re-completion of the Pyramid to its intended dimensions? Could both hold the key to some secret affecting not only the soul of the dead pharaoh, not only the ancient initiates who, thanks to the Well-Shaft, may have passed this way, but also you yourself?

In either side-wall of this ten-foot-long chamber, you can just detect the remains of three further pairs of portcullis grooves. The fact that the pilasters between them have been largely demolished – possibly by the Caliph's workmen – suggests that they, too, may originally have held stone portcullises which extended, unlike the Granite Leaf, right down to floor-level. Indeed, the side grooves actually extend three inches *below* the floor. Yet quite how these portcullises were intended to be lowered is not easy to understand. The lower section of the right-hand wall of the chamber is over eight inches higher than that of the left-hand wall, while each of the right-hand grooves terminates at the top, unlike those on the left, in a horizontal, semicircular cavity. Above this, the walls of the chamber then recede suddenly to produce an overall width of over six feet until roof-level is reached.

The problem is not made easier to solve by the presence of four vertical grooves running down the southern end-wall of the chamber, each originally terminating at the lower end in a kind of scoop just above the entrance to the next section of low passageway.

Within the Antechamber the now-dilapidated grooves for the three major portcullises can still be made out, as can the four grooves in the south wall, which originally terminated at their bottom ends in shallow, semi-rounded scoops. The twelve-inch layer of limestone at the top of the wall is easier to see in this illustration than it is in the Pyramid today. Over the years, both limestone and granite have become blackened to the point where they are almost indistinguishable. Through the low passage beyond, the King's Chamber opens, like all the Pyramid's chambers, to the west, or right.

Various mechanical systems have, of course, been suggested for handling the portcullises, given the design of the chamber, using a selection of ropes, beams and drums. Few of these suggestions, however, have proved very convincing. And none of them has managed to explain why the top twelve inches only of the chamber's south wall are built of limestone, not granite.

Was the Antechamber really intended to act merely as a strongroom door? Were the grooves in the south wall designed to permit stone wedges to be jammed down against the south face of the final portcullis? Or would all these precautions have been unnecessary, in view of the plugging-blocks in the Ascending Passage?

And could the Antechamber, apparently like so much else in the Pyramid, thus have some deeper meaning that goes beyond mere physical function?

Leaving the Antechamber, you pass on into a further section of low passageway. It is some eight and a half feet before you finally emerge in what historians regard as the Pyramid's definitive burial-vault, the magnificent King's Chamber.

Built entirely of granite, this superbly proportioned chamber, which now opens to your right, is a marvel both of construction and – you now have to face the fact – of esoteric number-symbolism. Even ignoring the finer mathematical points (see Appendix F of *The Great Pyramid Decoded*), the basic facts are astonishing. The chamber's length, at some thirty-four and a half feet (or twenty royal cubits), is exactly twice its breadth (ten royal cubits). Its height, at just over nineteen feet, is exactly half its floor-diagonal. As a result, the diagonals of its east and west walls each measure fifteen royal cubits, its cubic diagonal twenty-five royal cubits. Its walls consist of exactly one hundred polished granite blocks, arranged in five courses. The floor you are standing on coincides with the Pyramid's fiftieth course of masonry, which is nearly a hundred and fifty feet above the ground. And the level corresponding to a third of the height of the full-design Pyramid passes through the granite roof-beams above your head. And all this in a building at least as old as the earliest phase of Stonehenge.

Clearly, the number five has some special significance in this chamber – just as it seems to have in the Pyramid in general. The architect, you will recall, arranged for the thirty-fifth course of core masonry to be thicker than all those around it – and this marks exactly one-fifth of the height of the Pyramid. The Pyramid itself, if you include its base, has both five sides and five points.

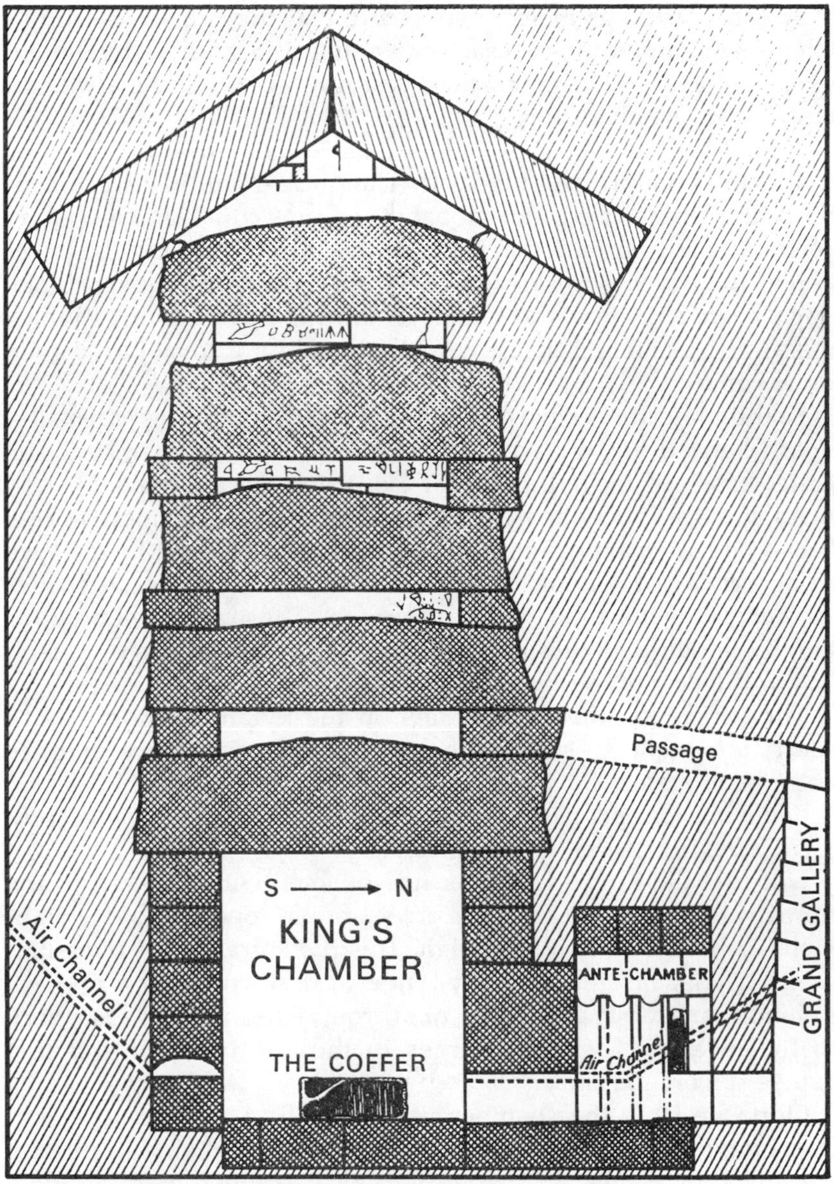

Vertical section of the King's Chamber Complex, looking west. Crossed lines indicate granite, single lines limestone. Note the south ventilator opening, the forced passage from the top of the Grand Gallery and the upside-down, painted hieroglyphs in the upper chambers.

So that it is no great surprise to find that the sum of the King's Chamber's dimensions is exactly five times the sum of the dimensions of the granite coffer which you now see standing at the far end of the chamber.

More than big enough to contain a six-foot man, the coffer was found to be empty and lidless by Caliph Al-Mamun's workmen. Since it is uninscribed, the probability seems considerable that no pharaoh was ever buried in it. Since it is also wider than the lower end of the Ascending Passage, it is quite clear that it must actually have been built into the chamber during construction – which makes the likelihood that it was ever used for a royal burial even more remote.

So the conjectures have multiplied. Perhaps there was a treasure-hoard beneath it, or a passage leading to another chamber? The coffer has been moved, the floor excavated, all to no avail.

As you see it now however, the coffer is probably more or less back in its original position – which is interesting. For the distance from the axis of the entrance-passageway to the axis of the coffer is – not for the first time – twenty-four feet. Those same twenty-four feet by which the entrance, and thus the whole passage-system, lies to the east of the Pyramid's axis.

The coffer, in other words, lies on the Pyramid's north-south centreline. In the King's Chamber, you could say, balance has once more been restored.

Could this idea of 'balance', then, have some direct connection with the overwhelming 'fiveness' of the chamber?

Not that the King's Chamber has finished with you yet. In the north wall, for a start, there is a rectangular opening some eight inches wide and five inches high. It is the entrance to an airshaft which leads, first horizontally, then at a steep angle – and via several sharp twists and turns – out through the Pyramid's masonry to the exterior. There it emerges in the one hundred and first course of core-masonry.

Opposite it, in the chamber's south wall, is another opening. This one, now much mutilated, is curiously curved, and its interior is remarkably similar in shape to an old-fashioned oven, or even to the abdomen of a pregnant woman (see diagram p. 65).

After some six feet it, too, leads to an airshaft, but this one is different. Not only can you feel the fresh air passing through it, but it is straight and roughly circular in cross-section, having a bore of roughly a foot.

What arcane significance can there be in the change of shape? Can we arrive at some clearer idea of the airshafts' meaning than the Egyptologists, who merely assign to them some unknown 'magic' function? Why are they found in no other Pyramid?

And what, in any case, does a dead body want with airshafts?

The south airshaft, incidentally, terminates in the one hundred and second course of core-masonry. Adding this figure to that of the terminal course of the north airshaft (101) we get the figure 203.

Yet the two hundred and third course is the level of the Pyramid's summit-platform!

Could there be a connection? Is one of the functions of the airshafts to emphasise the height and numerical value of the base of the missing capstone?

Above your head, every one of the nine massive granite roof-beams – one of which weighs some seventy-two tons – is cracked right across. For this you have the great earthquakes of AD 908 and 1301 to thank. Fortunately, however, the Pyramid's construction is such that you need fear no imminent collapse. While there is an enormous weight of masonry pressing down on the ends of the beams, there is – surprisingly, perhaps – no weight whatsoever on their centres. The reason for this is actually very simple.

You see, there are five more empty chambers above your head.

Possibly 'chambers' is not exactly the word to use. Perhaps 'spaces' would be better. Excavations have shown that the bottom four are, on average, some three and a half feet high, with very uneven floors of undressed granite, and flat roofs almost exactly the same as that of the King's Chamber. There are, in other words, five successive ceilings like the one above you, each dressed flat on the lower side and left proud and undressed on top.

But the top chamber is different. It is roofed by a great gable, each side of which consists of twelve blocks of limestone, set at an angle of thirty degrees to the horizontal. It is this gable which ultimately protects the King's Chamber from the enormous weight of masonry above it.

These five 'secret chambers', consequently, are known as the 'Relieving' or 'Construction' Chambers. The reason for this is plain. Together they serve as a kind of buffer standing between the King's Chamber and possible destruction as a result of earth movements.

But can this be their only function? Why does no other Pyramid have such Chambers? Is it purely fortuitous that here, once again, the number five comes clearly into prominence?

In the culminating King's Chamber, you have reached the second of the three terminal points of the Pyramid's passageways. The first – the end of the subterranean Dead-End Passage – we examined earlier, in chapter 2. The third is the so-called Queen's Chamber, and to reach it you now have to retrace your steps.

And so, bending low once again, you re-enter the King's Chamber Passage. After a brief chance to straighten your back in the Antechamber, you duck beneath the Granite Leaf and, with a brief, final glance at the curious boss on its other side, you make your way out through the second section of low passageway.

Just before you reach the end of it, however, you come across a cavity in the left-hand wall of the passage. This was excavated in the last century by an Italian pyramidologist called Caviglia, who was determined to discover whether or not the north airshaft of the the King's Chamber led to a second, unknown chamber. In the event, he found that it didn't.

But what Caviglia's excavation did reveal was the extraordinary series of twists and turns executed by this airshaft in the thickness of the masonry before it finally heads away at a steep angle towards the north.

What, you may ask, is their function?

Once again, your guess is as good as anybody's. The convolutions in question seem far more complicated than would be necessary if their purpose were merely to avoid the masonry of the Grand Gallery.

So should you once again suspect some symbolic meaning?

Pondering this question, you finally emerge from the King's Chamber Passage onto the Great Step. Now a magnificent sight greets your eyes. For suddenly you are, as it were, on a kind of open dais, from which the Grand Gallery now slopes dramatically down and away from you into the distance, and, beyond that, the long, rectangular tube of the Ascending Passage.

Before beginning the descent, however, you glance up to the masonry immediately above you and to your right. There, at the very top of the Grand Gallery's east wall, you notice that an entire block of masonry has been removed. Just inside the resulting black cavity, a rough-hewn passageway leads off to the right, i.e. back the way you have just come. After some twenty-five feet it emerges

Perhaps the most impressive view of the Grand Gallery is from the top of the Great Step at its upper end. With the whole of the visible world as it were 'on the slope', the visitor can easily experience an unsettling uncertainty as to which way is actually 'up-and-down'. The steel retaining brackets, handrails and electric lights – all absent in the Edgars' day – represent the Egyptian government's laudable efforts to preserve the monument and keep it open to the public.

in the lowest of the five Construction Chambers above the King's Chamber.

Whether the tunnel was dug by the Pyramid's original builders, by the later guardians of the Pyramid for inspection purposes, or by subsequent treasure-seekers, is unknown for certain today. But the directness with which it heads unerringly towards its goal suggests that whoever was responsible knew the details of the building's construction like the back of his hand.

Could even this feature of the Pyramid, then, have some ulterior significance?

It was the flatness of the ceiling of the lowest Construction Chamber (now known as Davison's Chamber) that helped to convince Colonel Howard-Vyse, back in the 1830s, that at least one other chamber must lie above it. Most non-subterranean pyramid tomb-chambers, after all, were known to be roofed with a protective gable or corbelled vault, to protect them from the weight of the Pyramid's masonry. The fact that this ceiling was flat therefore suggested that the crowning vault must lie somewhere even further above it. And when a reed, pushed through one of the cracks in the roofing-beams, penetrated to a considerable distance, this only helped to confirm the suspicion.

In the event, Vyse was proved right. Three and a half months of upward quarrying and blasting duly revealed not one, but four more chambers above Davison's Chamber, before the expected gable was finally reached at a height of some seventy feet above the King's Chamber floor. There in the Pyramid's interior, in other words, was what may well have been the world's first high-rise block.

All four chambers, of course, proved to be as empty as on the day when they were originally sealed – except for two curious features. The lowest of the four was found to be liberally coated with a black dust which proved to be the remains of ancient insects, apparently sealed in at the time of construction. (Provided that sufficient of these still remain to be vacuumed up, it should thus now be theoretically possible – as it was not possible in 1837 – definitively to date the building's construction by radio-carbon dating.)

All of the newly discovered chambers were found to contain hieroglyphs. Or so, at least, Vyse was to claim.

Not that these were careful, artistic figures of the kind that you will find in the later tombs. Instead, they were rough markings slapped on with red paint, and many of them upside-down. This latter fact made it seem that they were in fact quarry-markings, daubed on the building-stones before they were ever assembled. But what did they mean?

By no means all of the markings have been deciphered, but one recurrent marking is quite clear. It consists of a royal oval, or cartouche, containing the name 'Khufu'.

Cheops's principal vertical cartouche (left) reads, from top to bottom, 'HWFW'. Another cartouche (right) found in the Construction Chambers reads 'Hnum – HFW'. Whether the difference indicates any actual difference of identity is a question very much open to dispute.

Sometimes the name appears as 'Khnum-Khufu' – apparently the Egyptian for 'Khnum protects me'. The legend 'Year Seventeen' can also be made out.

Yet how you interpret this information is largely up to you.

It could mean that the stones were quarried in the seventeenth year of the reign of the historical fourth-dynasty pharaoh – in around 2606 BC, say, or simply during the seventeenth year of building. Or, indeed, during the reign of a much earlier king called Khufu.

Could it be, in fact, that the historical Khufu actually took his name from a much earlier, semi-legendary figure who had built the Great Pyramid – a building that was already an ancient monument in the third millennium BC?

This last point, after all, seems to be confirmed by Khufu's own so-called Inventory Stela, now in the Cairo Museum.

Could it even be that the name 'Khufu', which refers to the idea of protection, was the original name of the Pyramid itself – a reference to its supposed role in protecting the body and soul of its mighty occupant?

And could it be this name that is represented by the strange, unknown hieroglyphs that are to be found to this day in the so-called 'eye' of the Pyramid just below the entrance-gable (see diagram p. 32)?

Once again, you have much food for speculation. The most obvious answers may very well turn out to be the wrong ones. And so you would do well to keep an open mind as you now descend the left-hand ramp of the Grand Gallery.

At the bottom of the slope you come to a wooden cabinet projecting from the wall. This houses some of the Pyramid's present-day electrics. But it also conceals the fact that the bottom stone of the ramp is missing – apparently chiselled out by main force after the building's construction. Behind it, a low, rectangular conduit leads some four and a half feet horizontally westwards to the mouth of what looks like a bottomless pit. Some twenty-eight inches wide, this is a square shaft cut first through the Pyramid's masonry and then, via a kind of natural 'grotto', through the rock underneath it, until, after edging somewhat southwards, it eventually links up with the lower passageways.

It is, of course, the so-called Well-Shaft.

The precision of construction at the shaft's upper end contrasts strangely with the roughness of the excavation at its lower end. The apparently brutal disfigurement of the Grand Gallery's western ramp seems to argue for a last-minute improvisation, or even a later intrusion, yet the idea of the shaft seems to have been present in the architect's mind from the beginning, if the evidence of the Trial Passages (chapter 1) is to be believed.

Could the Well-Shaft really have been cut by intruders, especially when it seems to have been sunk from above (see chapter 2)? Yet, if it was excavated by the original builders, why was the Grand Gallery's masonry so disfigured in the process? Was the shaft perhaps cut by them but left sealed at either end, so that in the event of severe earth-movements the Pyramid's priestly guardians could open it up for use as an inspection-tunnel? (Petrie's discovery of plaster tell-tales on some of the cracks in the King's Chamber suggests that such checking may indeed have been carried out.) *Or was it, as historians generally suggest, simply an escape-route for the workmen who allegedly plugged the Ascending Passage after the supposed royal burial?*

And why does the shaft encounter the solid rock beneath the Pyramid at a point which is not twenty, not thirty, but twenty-four feet above the building's exterior baseline?

The top of the Well-Shaft, apparently cut and constructed with great care by the Pyramid's original builders, seems to have been roughly opened at a later date by chiselling out the bottom stone of the Grand Gallery's western ramp. From here a horizontal tunnel less then two feet high leads some four and a half feet westwards (i.e. away from the observer) to the lip of the main shaft.

Stepping down from the ramp, you are once again on level ground. And stretching back to your right is the horizontal Queen's Chamber Passage.

The fact that you can enter it at all is, of course, due entirely to the removal of the stone slabs which originally sealed the opening. These slabs formed a twenty-foot-long section of the floor of the Grand Gallery, and you can still see today not only where they fitted at either end, but also, in either side-wall, the sockets of the beams which originally supported them.

With their removal, however, the Grand Gallery's floor is, so to speak, 'undermined'. It is as though, once you enter the Queen's Chamber Passage, the Grand Gallery is symbolically 'closed' to you. Which suggests that exploring this section of passageway last is actually what the designer intended you to do.

At around four feet high and three and a half feet wide, the first part of the passage is, for all practical purposes, much the same size as the Ascending Passage which leads to it. To start with, the walls on either side are laid in two equal tiers of masonry, each wall having fifteen pairs of stones of uniform size. Then a set of

The twenty-one inch high downward step near the southern end of the Queen's Chamber Passage seems too high to escape the suspicion that it has some special symbolic meaning. Meanwhile, from around this point, the walls start to be covered with a thick, white, crystalline deposit.

longer stones leads to a section where the walls are built of one course of stones only.

Is there some special significance in this arrangement? Should we, in the number fifteen, once again see the presence of the now-familiar five?

After some sixteen yards you come to a downward step. This is not as high as the Grand Gallery's Great Step but, at some twenty-one inches, it is certainly too high to escape the distinct suspicion that there may be much more to it than a mere step.

Hence, of course, the intermediate step kindly placed in front of it by the Egyptian authorities for your convenience.

What might a 'step down' at this point signify?

The floor level having consequently dropped by the same amount, you now have more headroom. Now over five and a half feet high, the passage continues for a further six yards.

Using remote sensing equipment, French and Japanese researchers have recently discovered ten-foot-deep cavities in the masonry behind the wall on your right, i.e. towards the Pyramid's centre, though subsequent drilling suggested that they contained only sand.

Could these be significant, either symbolically or structurally, or are they merely evidence of shoddy workmanship by the workers responsible for the core-masonry – perhaps the earliest known case of jerry-building?

And now you finally enter the Queen's Chamber itself.

Understandable though it may be in the light of the Arabs' supposed ideas on the status of women, the name 'Queen's Chamber' is totally misleading. Doubly inferior the chamber may be when compared to the magnificent King's Chamber, but the ancient Egyptians were not noted for treating their queens as second-class royalty. Quite the reverse, in fact. It was actually Khufu's queen and sister, Merytyetes, who was regarded as the carrier of the royal blood, and you may therefore rest assured that she had a perfectly satisfactory tomb-monument of her own.

The chamber, as you see, is built entirely of limestone. Since, like the topmost Relieving Chamber over the King's Chamber, it is roofed with a gable – in this case consisting of twelve limestone blocks – you can be sure that no further chamber lies immediately above it. Curiously enough, however, something else does. For the apex of the gable lies directly below the riser of the Grand Gallery's Great Step (see diagram, p. 52). It, too, in other words, lies exactly on the Pyramid's east-west axis.

The gable is so constructed, incidentally, that more of each block lies behind the wall on either side than is visible over your head. As a result, the roof-blocks actually subtract from the weight of the masonry overhead, rather than adding to it.

Remove the superincumbent masonry, in other words, and the chamber would actually open up of its own accord.

One ancient Arab account has it that the Queen's Chamber originally contained a limestone sarcophagus. Unlike that in the King's Chamber, however, this could never have rested on the Pyramid's north-south axis, since the chamber does not stretch that far westwards. Now, in any case, there is nothing in it beyond a niche in the left-hand wall, and two airshaft-openings somewhat similar to those in the King's Chamber.

The Niche is a somewhat puzzling feature. Neither a doorway nor an archway, it is simply a corbelled recess in the east wall, some forty-two inches deep and five feet across at the bottom. Mental bells start to ring, however, as soon as you count its sections.

From the base to the top, which is on the same level as the tops of the side-walls, there are five of them.

Its position, too, is odd. Instead of being placed squarely in the centre of the east wall, its axis lies some distance beyond that of the chamber itself.

Perhaps it is pure coincidence that this distance happens to be twenty-five inches – or five inches squared.

In the back of the Niche, a rough tunnel has been quarried. Explore it, and you will once again be able to examine the interior of the Pyramid's rough core-masonry. That was not the purpose of its nineteenth-century excavator, Colonel Howard-Vyse, however. To him, the Niche had all the characteristics of a doorway, and so beyond it must lie further passages or chambers. Not to mention treasure.

He was disappointed, of course. The Niche is not a door – nor even a false door.

This latter idea has become something of an obsession with Egyptologists of our own day. Many ancient Egyptian tombs had a *serdab*, or false door, on the outside, through which the deceased occupant could symbolically emerge to accept the ritual offerings laid before him by his family and descendants for the welfare of his soul.

The Great Pyramid's *serdab*, then, if ever it had one, should have

The east wall of the gabled Queen's Chamber displays a niche comprising five corbelled sections, and set curiously off-centre relative to the gable-ridge. Convinced that it was some kind of 'false doorway', Howard-Vyse cut a short tunnel into the back of it, only to draw a complete blank. Egyptologists, sharing the same conviction, generally identify it as a *serdab*, or ceremonial doorway whereby the deceased could emerge to accept the ritual offerings brought by his surviving family.

been sited on its eastern side, probably in the funerary temple which once stood adjacent to it. That, after all, was the logical position of the *serdab*. Since the land of the dead, or of the ancestors, lay in the west, the returning soul of the deceased must necessarily emerge from the eastern side of his monument.

But that, note, is not where the Niche is. Not only is it inside the Queen's Chamber. Its opening actually faces west.

Which makes it highly unlikely that the Niche was ever intended as a *serdab* at all.

Does the Niche, then, have some symbolic significance connected with the number five? And does it have some special measurement to reveal through its displacement towards the south wall of the chamber?

The two airshaft-openings pose further problems. You will see, they bear the legend 'Opened 1872'. Until that date the walls were entirely innocent of such openings. It was one Waynman Dixon who, noticing in that year a crack in the south wall at this point, inserted a piece of wire and discovered a cavity beyond it. A few minutes' work with a chisel revealed a neatly constructed airshaft – whose last five inches had simply been left uncut.

Is this, perhaps, how the Well-Shaft, too, was originally left? And can the number five be just another numerical coincidence?

Proceeding to the north wall, Dixon duly discovered the second airshaft-opening. Beyond the two openings – which, like those in the King's Chamber, lay on a level with the top of the entrance doorway – the shafts bored some seven feet horizontally into the masonry, and then sloped upwards towards the exterior at an angle of some forty degrees. With the chamber lying centrally in the Pyramid, it was clear that both must eventually emerge at the same level in the core-masonry.

To date, their upper openings have still not been definitely identified. Perhaps they, too, were left uncut to the extent of five inches. But a present-day hole in the ninetieth course of the north face may well be significant. Doubly significant, in fact.

The *King's Chamber* airshafts, you will recall, seem to identify numerically the course-level of the Pyramid's summit-platform. But the ninetieth course of masonry comes at the vertical half-way point between that same level and the base of the Pyramid. If, then, the Queen's Chamber airshafts emerge in the ninetieth course – as, geometrically, they ought to – the conclusion seems inevitable. They, too, were designed to pin-point the intended level of the base of the missing capstone, but in a different way.

For if you add together the levels of the two outlets, you necessarily obtain the height of the summit-platform, just as adding together the course-numbers of the two King's Chamber's airshaft outlets produces the platform's course-number.

What hidden significance, then, can this obviously vital level have in the Pyramid's symbolism – a level which is also identified, you will recall, by the distance from the entrance of the Pyramid to the end of the Dead-End Passage?

Meanwhile, the fact that the Queen's Chamber outlets have not so far been identified positively is not too surprising. Not only is the face of the core-masonry exceedingly dangerous to scale at the points in question. It also seems quite probable that the outlets – if their function is really to demonstrate a precise level – take the form of the narrowest of slits in the masonry, not unlike the cracks which originally betrayed their lower ends.

Perhaps, then, we shall have to await the advent of an abseiling expert with a chisel to settle the matter finally.

These features apart, the Queen's Chamber is remarkable only for its apparent roughness. Except near the walls, the floor is uneven, and a rough pilaster of undressed limestone has even been left proud on the west side of the entrance doorway. These features have suggested to Egyptologists that the Queen's Chamber, like the Great Subterranean Chamber, represents an abandoned tomb-chamber – that of 'Plan B', in fact, which was itself to be superseded by 'Plan C's' King's Chamber. But then we have already noted the dubiousness of the whole 'change-of-mind' theory.

Nevertheless there seems to be some evidence that a six-inch-thick floor of paving-slabs was originally intended to be laid in the chamber, not unlike those found in tomb-chambers elsewhere.

In which case, the resulting floor-level would have coincided with the base of the *twenty-fifth* course of masonry. And the ubiquitous five would thus come once again to the fore.

Is this level, too, then, of some special significance?

As well as the Niche and the floor-level, meanwhile, other features of the chamber, too, have clear connections with the number five. The level of the top of its north and south walls is exactly fifty Egyptian royal cubits above the base of the Pyramid itself, for example, while the upper ridge of the roof-gable coincides with the thirty-fifth course of masonry – which marks *one-fifth* of the height of the full-design Pyramid.

Can it be, then, that this whole chamber is intended to be associated with the number five?

There is also one strange, final feature that demands your attention. The walls of the Queen's Chamber are heavily encrusted with a white, crystalline deposit. In places you can see it literally growing, like a mould, out of the walls.

Listen to the guides, as they reverentially hold a candle close to it, and you will probably hear the word 'alabaster' mentioned in whispered tones. Do not spoil the illusion. Wait until they have gone.

Then moisten your finger-tip, rub it on the deposit and apply it to your tongue.

It is common salt.

Somehow those limestone blocks have been saturated – whether deliberately or not – with salt water. Only in the Queen's Chamber Passage, in the great gable over the topmost Construction Chamber, and here and there in the Grand Gallery are there similar blocks.

Why? What could be the reason for building certain parts only of the Pyramid in salt-impregnated rock? What possible symbolic meaning might salt have?

The either undressed or mutilated top end of the Granite Plug blocks the visitor's exit at the bottom end of the Ascending Passage, so making necessary a detour via Al-Mamun's Hole (left).

It is with this and a host of other unanswered questions buzzing around in your mind that you eventually leave the Queen's Chamber and, making your way back along the Queen's Chamber Passage, reach the foot of the Grand Gallery. With a last look up at this magnificent architectural enigma, you re-enter the confined tube of the Ascending Passage. Here you may well find a backward descent more comfortable than bending double down the slope.

And so you come once more to the now-battered top end of the Granite Plug, which blocks your further retreat towards the Descending Passage and the original entrance. Bowing to necessity, therefore, you clamber down into the cavernous chamber of Al-Mamun's Hole, and so make your way out, squinting, into the brilliant light of day.

Your tour of the interior is complete. The humdrum world lies before you. And perhaps, unknown even to you as yet, your experience of the Pyramid's chambers and passageways has already engendered within you new patterns of thought, new paradigms of consciousness. In some way, the experience has changed you, as it changes all who visit here.

The Pyramid's architect is still at work.

And in subsequent chapters, when you have had time to digest that experience, we shall explore together the implications of it all, and try to discover what it means.

PART II
FACT AND THEORY

'The probabilities of intention –
like every other question –
will be believed or disbelieved,
not so much on physical as on
metaphysical grounds, and
conditions of mind.'

Sir W. M. Flinders Petrie:
The Pyramids and Temples
of Gizeh, 1883

4
The Stone Enigma

Such, then, are the physical facts and features of the Great Pyramid of Giza, extraordinary and even improbable though a good many of them may seem. To the extent that they are embodied in solid stone, they are of course not amenable to revision or subject to the dictates of academic fashion or opinion. There can be no textual wrangles, no legal sleight of hand. Stone is stone is stone.

The Pyramid is undubitably there.

And so the human mind, confronted with the building's colossal conundrum, has always felt crushed, overawed, driven to seek some way, however unlikely, of coping with what it cannot directly comprehend.

Perhaps the reaction was inevitable. There, after all, it was. There it had always been, so far as anyone could tell. Like some ghostly, crystalline presence from another dimension, the gleaming white beacon that was the Great Pyramid of Giza had presided through countless aeons over the ancient land of Egypt, so that its presence no longer even caused any surprise. Down on the green delta the conquerors might come and go, the civilisations rise and fall, but up there on the windy rim of the western desert the Pyramid's colossal rhomboid continued to soar majestically heavenwards with supreme indifference.

Time itself, it was said, feared the pyramids. And certainly the Great Pyramid had already sailed serenely down untold centuries. No doubt it would continue on its untroubled voyage through time, until one day it brought its unknown cargo safely home to its equally unknown port.

Yet the reaction of those who saw it was still inevitable.

The Pyramid's incredible technology and enormous size would see to that. So would its sheer antiquity.

If the biblical Abraham ever visited ancient Egypt, as the texts suggest, then to him it was already an ancient monument. To the Egyptian priesthood of the time of Tutankhamun, its twenty-one acres of polished limestone casing not only marked the house of an ancient god, but may also have served as a seasonal calendar of brilliant solar reflections. The Greeks of the time of Alexander the Great were so overawed with it that they dubbed it the first of the Seven Wonders of their world.

And there it was, still communing with the gods and the sky and the sunlight, when the Romans appeared upon the scene – grandiloquently thumbing its nose, so to speak, at their own by no means inconsiderable feats of engineering.

It was at about this time, you will recall, that Jesus of Nazareth himself is supposed to have visited Egypt. That may or may not be so. But if he did, then the Great Pyramid's construction was already more remote in time to him than Jesus himself is to us.

Stripped by the later Arab mosque-builders of its resplendent outer casing, the Great Pyramid and its ninety or so lesser companions went on to moulder almost unnoticed among the sands on the desert's edge until, in the wake of the Renaissance, a new interest arose in the arts and sciences of the ancient world, and the mighty pile was 'rediscovered'. It was still there when the armies of the great Napoleon defeated the Mamelukes in its very shadow at the turn of the nineteenth century. Its core-masonry, now exposed to full view, revealed to his scholars and scientists something of the labour which had gone into erecting its two million or so blocks of solid limestone. Indeed, the young general

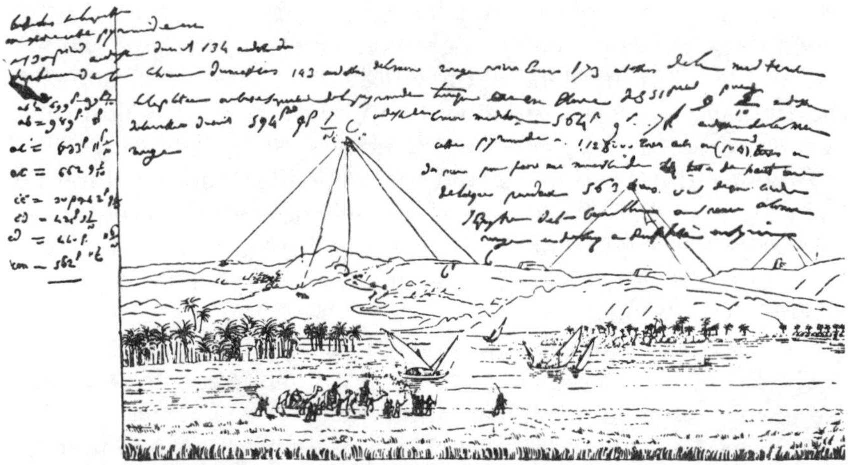

The great Napoleon Bonaparte, fascinated by the Great Pyramid, made detailed sketches and notes on the subject during his celebrated expedition in Egypt, as well as undergoing some kind of psychic experience in the building's King's Chamber.

was later to explore its passageways for himself and meditate on his future destiny in its mysterious King's Chamber.

And there, weathered, eroded, sand-blasted and tourist-trampled – yet still to all intents and purposes just as massive as ever – it still stands today, still posing the same, inevitable questions.

What is it? What was it for? What does it mean?

Faced with questions such as these, sooner or later somebody, equally inevitably, is going to try to answer them. And when nothing is known for certain about the real answers, the room for speculation is literally endless.

Any answer will do. Which no doubt is why, in the past, any answer has.

Take the *royal tomb* theory, for example.

Of all the suggested answers to the problem, this one is the best known and the most widespread. In most of the school history-books, it is reported – as so many other historical theories are reported – as if it were undoubted fact. Indeed, I have already referred to this theory.

What precisely does it propose?

Basically, that the Pyramid was built as the final resting-place of the fourth-dynasty pharaoh Khufu (or Cheops, as the Greeks were to call him), who allegedly ruled over Egypt nearly three thousand years before Christ. In building such a tomb, it is said, he was merely imitating his immediate ancestors, who had taken to building pyramids for themselves only a century or so previously. The great Step Pyramid of King Zoser at Sakkara, some eight miles to the south, is widely claimed to have been the first large stone structure ever raised by man on earth.

Yet Khufu's pyramid was to differ from its predecessors. Nearly all of them had merely been built over subterranean burial-chambers, with a sloping entrance passage emerging in the north face to point directly at the north celestial Pole. The same applied, also, to its immediate successors.

But Khufu's Great Pyramid was to contain no less than *nine* chambers, both underground and within the building's masonry. Of these, five were to be linked together by a complex system of shafts and passageways, while four were left totally sealed at the time of building.

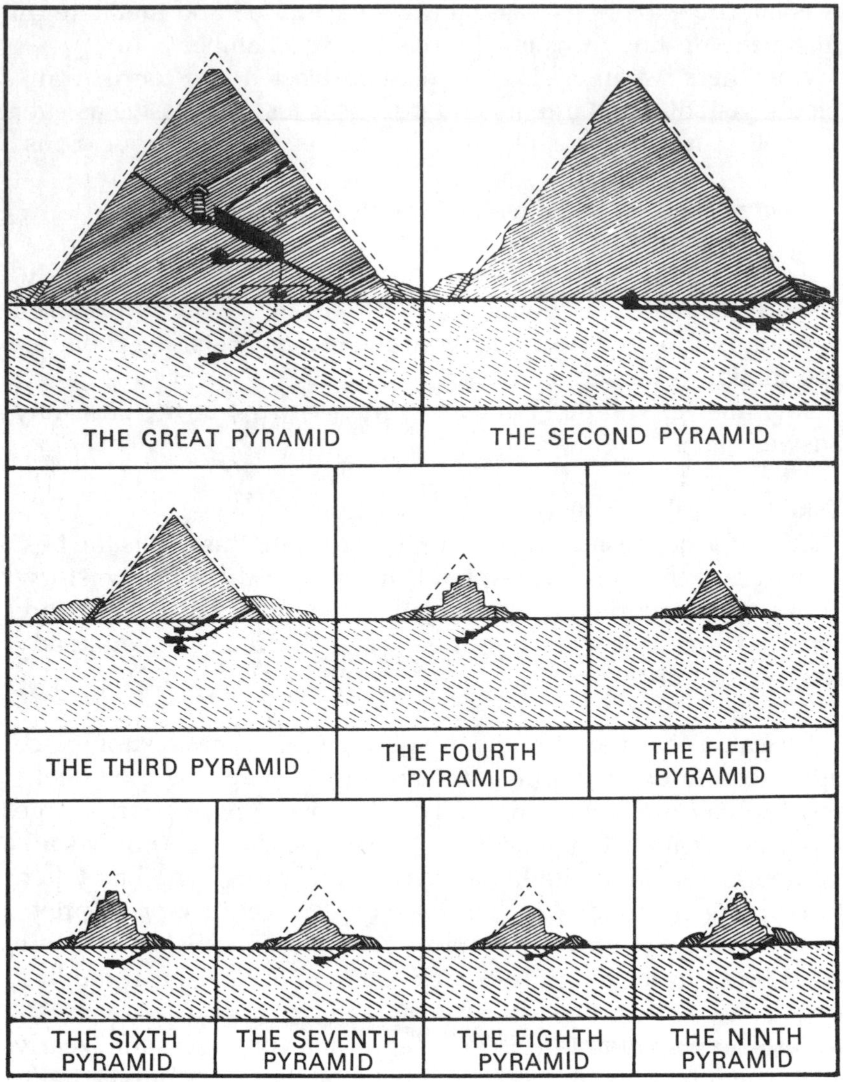

In the 1860s the Astronomer Royal for Scotland, Professor C. Piazzi Smyth, published diagrams of many of the Egyptian pyramids, including the nine surviving pyramids of Giza, despite the considerable piles of rubble with which all were surrounded. These diagrams reveal the central subterranean chamber and polar entrance passage typical of all nine pyramids – though in the Great Pyramid the chamber actually lies *beyond* the building's centre-line. Also apparent from the diagrams is the fact that the airshafts of the Queen's Chamber had not yet been discovered, thanks to the fact that they had actually been left uncut to the extent of five inches at their inner ends. Their discovery was eventually to come in 1872, thanks to the observant eyes of Waynman Dixon.

Baffling, you might think. Especially when the later pyramids are supposed to have been copies of Khufu's....

But the theorists have an answer to that one – an answer which I have already briefly outlined.

Originally, it seems, the plan was for the pharaoh's body to be buried in what is now known as the Great Subterranean Chamber (compare diagrams pp. 50-2). In this case the lesser Subterranean Chamber which, at six foot long, is just big enough to receive a body, would have served as some kind of ceremonial antechamber.

At about the time when construction work reached the level of the Pyramid's entrance, however, there was apparently a sudden change of plan. The roof of the smaller chamber was left unfinished, as was the floor of the larger one, and a new passage was cut upwards through the already laid lower courses of masonry, leading to a new chamber approached by a horizontal passage. This limestone chamber, now known as the Queen's Chamber, was so constructed that its great gable marked the exact east-west axis of the Pyramid. Astonishingly, perhaps, for an alleged tomb, it was also equipped with twin airshafts leading upwards through the masonry to the exterior. Even more astonishingly, the final five inches of stone at the bottom end of each shaft were never cut through the chamber's walls. Egyptologists generally attribute some kind of magical significance to these shafts, and leave it at that.

Now, at any rate, the building work could go on apace. Yet almost at once, it seems, the plan was changed again. A great, sloping, corbelled hallway was constructed – the present Grand Gallery – vaulting over the still-unfinished Queen's Chamber, and leading to a new complex of granite chambers at about a third of the height of the Pyramid. At the top end of the Gallery, a gigantic 'step' almost three feet high marked the entrance to a low passage leading, via an antechamber containing four stone portcullises, to the King's Chamber itself. The five further chambers above this, it is suggested, were merely an architectural device to protect the King's Chamber from the enormous weight of masonry overhead, and so these are called the Relieving, or Construction Chambers. And the King's Chamber's twin, open airshafts are once again said merely to have had some magical significance.

With the passage system now complete, then, the burial could commence. The god-king's mummy was placed in its oblong coffer of granite, then slid down the Descending Passage, up the new

Ascending Passage and Grand Gallery, and finally, via the Great Step and the Antechamber, into the King's Chamber itself. There the pharaoh was reverently laid to rest. Once the priests and dignitaries had left, workmen were called in to lower the portcullises and push three granite plugging blocks from their temporary storage site in the Grand Gallery down the Ascending Passage, until they jammed in its tapered lower end. Behind them, further limestone blocks were inserted, until the whole passage was packed with stone from top to bottom. In this way the king and his possessions would be safe for ever from the depradations of future grave-robbers.

But this didn't solve a further problem. How were the workmen themselves to get out? For this, an escape route had to be cut – the so-called Well-Shaft, which eventually comes out in the lower part of the original Descending Passage. It was at this point, then, that the workmen eventually emerged, carefully sealing their secret exit behind them.

As the great stone door over the entrance swung shut for the last time, the king's rest was at last assured for ever.

So, at least, the theory goes.

But there are snags. So many, in fact, as to be worth enumerating.

(1) Between the Pyramid's various chambers and passageways a clear system of geometrical relationships exists. The length of the great Subterranean Chamber, for example, equals the cubic diagonal of the King's Chamber plus the height of the Pyramid's entrance: its width equals the same distance minus the King's Chamber's height. Is it likely that the measurements of the Great Subterranean Chamber would have been based on those of the King's Chamber (and the obvious mathematical harmony of the King's Chamber makes it certain that it was this way around) if the King's Chamber was not planned until after the underground chambers had been abandoned?

(2) If the lower passageways and chambers were merely expensive errors, why were they not filled in with stone when the new, upper passageways of 'Plan B' were constructed? Even if we assume that they were left as a deliberate 'blind', why was a further, narrow passage – the so-called Dead-End Passage – cut *beyond* the Great Subterranean Chamber? And why was it the *roof* of the

Lesser Subterranean Chamber that was left unfinished, but the *floor* of the larger chamber?

(3) The new Ascending Passage, admittedly, was (as we saw earlier) *cut through* the Pyramid's masonry in the first instance, rather than constructed. But why was the masonry at this point clearly designed expressly for that purpose – with limestone of a much higher quality than that used in the rest of the core-masonry, and with joints of exceptional fineness? Other, that is, than because the upper passageways had been planned from the beginning?

(4) Why were the Queen's Chamber airshafts continued up through the masonry *long after* 'Plan C' had been put into operation, and construction of the lower end of the Grand Gallery had been started? Under the 'change-of-plan' theory, after all, the Queen's Chamber ceased to have any useful function as soon as this stage had been reached.

(5) How could the granite coffer have been taken up the Ascending Passage, when it is actually wider than the passage's tapered lower end?

(6) It may of course be that the coffer was built in from the beginning – in fact, the conclusion is inescapable. Could an *inner* sarcophagus, then, have been taken up through the Ascending Passage? Even this, as it turns out, would have been impossible, since the structural evidence suggests that the three granite plugging-blocks were not slid down the passage after the burial, but built in from the beginning. How, after all, can a plugging-block slide when its dimensions are virtually the same as those of the passage, and the clearance is consequently zero?

(7) Why did the extraordinary Grand Gallery – far bigger than was needed for storing the plugging-blocks – suddenly become necessary under the third and final plan, when nothing even remotely like it had been contemplated before in connection with the Subterranean or Queen's Chambers?

(8) Why is it that at least one of the portcullises in the Antechamber (the so-called Granite Leaf) was also clearly built in from the beginning, and could never have been lowered into the passage in any case, since its side-grooves stop short at roof height?

(9) Why was the King's Chamber, like the so-called Queen's Chamber, equipped with airshafts – devices which seem to have more to do with the living than with the dead?

(10) What is the logic of going to such extreme lengths of fortification in the upper passageways, when they could be by-passed merely by unsealing the bottom end of the Well-Shaft?

Such are some of the more obvious drawbacks to the 'change-of-mind' version of the *royal tomb* theory. And that is to leave out of account entirely the previously noted fact that the builders had already excavated a set of trial passages in the rock a hundred yards east of the Pyramid, incorporating all the features of the Pyramid's main passageways, with certain significant differences, *including the Well-Shaft* (see diagram, p. 17). Since it seems unlikely that these were constructed *after* the event (what, in this case, would have been the point of changing the design?), the conclusion is obvious: the Trial Passages were a kind of prototype.

Which would suggest that the whole system of passages and chambers, as displayed by the Trial Passages, was therefore envisaged *from the beginning*.

The accepted scenario for the burial, then, must obviously be abandoned. But is there some other possibility? Could the mummy have been dragged to its final resting place via the Well-Shaft?

This seems highly unlikely, as well as an unthinkably irreverent way of treating your dead god-king. In particular, it would have been virtually impossible to manoeuvre the rigid body around the sharp corners at the top end of the shaft.

Could the king's body too, have been built in from the beginning? This would, of course, have meant completing the upper two-thirds of the Pyramid after his death. Even so, it would seem to be at least one possible way of salvaging the 'royal tomb' theory.

Were it not for the fact that Herodotus, the earliest historian to describe the Pyramid, was assured quite categorically by the Egyptian priesthood of over four hundred years before Christ that Khufu was never buried in his Pyramid at all. Instead, it seems, he was interred on a secret, subterranean island surrounded by the waters of the Nile.

The body, in other words, was never there in the first place.

Which might explain why, when the upper passageways of the Pyramid were broken into by the Arabs some twelve hundred years after Herodotus, the body still wasn't there. But then the lack of a body cannot really be said to be so surprising. Fashionable it may now have become to assume that an empty sarcophagus means both that it once contained a body and that that body has been stolen. Yet we know for a fact that Egyptian sarcophagi were sometimes buried empty. Just such a coffer, made of alabaster, was discovered in 1954, for example, in the tomb of Sekhemket's unfinished pyramid at Sakkara. The sarcophagus of Queen Hetepheres (Khufu's own mother) at Giza was also found to be empty. Sekhemket's coffer had even been carefully sealed. Yet inside it, there was nothing.

Again, the common assumption is that pyramids were royal tombs. Yet in not one single instance, as we saw earlier, has a pyramid yielded up a body that can be positively identified as that of the pharaoh who built it. Some of the 'tomb-chambers', in fact, are too small to have received a body in the first place. Yet these facts are by no means as surprising as they may seem. Some pharaohs are known to have had at least two pyramids. Snofru, Khufu's own father, seems to have had no less than three. The eighteenth-dynasty Queen Tetisheri had not only two tombs, but a pyramid as well.

Even assuming, then, that in each case one monument was used for the actual body, the fact remains that two must have remained empty – their possible function being to act purely as a kind of cenotaph, or memorial monument.

Whatever the purposes of the Great Pyramid, then, it seems that royal burial was not one of them. To historians the Pyramid may have a tale to tell of a king who died, of a corpse placed in a tomb whose door was sealed with stone, of a god whose body subsequently disappeared from the tomb without trace. In this there seems to be an uncanny foreshadowing of the story of a later man, a certain Galilean, of whom the self-same tale is told. But as a factual account it unfortunately has very little to offer us.

And we need to find some alternative to what is called the *tombic theory*. Fortunately, there are plenty of suggestions on offer.

Take the *treasure-house theory,* for example.

In view of the massive construction of the great Egyptian pyramids, it is perhaps natural to assume that they were intended as some kind of strong-box, the ancient Egyptian equivalent of the Bank of England or Fort Knox. So natural, in fact, that much of the exploration of the Great Pyramid in particular has been prompted by this very idea. Caliph Al-Mamun's original forced entry into the Pyramid was at least partly motivated by the thought, though he was by no means the mere plunderer that he is sometimes made out to have been. In the event, his workmen found nothing beyond an empty, lidless sarcophagus in the King's Chamber. According to one account, there was also a similar, limestone sarcophagus in the Queen's Chamber, but of treasure, nothing.

Such was the workmen's disappointment that the Caliph, it is said, felt it advisable to stow a few trinkets of his own in the interior, so that his workmen might duly discover them and claim success for their labours.

Since the ninth century of our era others, too, have entered the Pyramid, treasure-bent. It is they whom we have to thank for a rough excavation under the coffer itself, a crude tunnel eastwards from the Niche in the Queen's Chamber, and the excavation of the outer end of the northern ventilator-shaft of the King's Chamber. It was a mania for finding secret chambers that inspired the Italian Caviglia, in the nineteenth century, to drive a tunnel westwards from the King's Chamber Passage, and to free the subterranean complex of the sand and rubble of centuries – not least that created by Al-Mamun's excavations. It was a similar mania that drove Colonel Howard-Vyse to blast his way up into the four topmost chambers above the King's Chamber, and to inflict the enormous gash still visible today on the south face of the Pyramid. As an extension of his quest, his assistant, Perring, went on to sink an exploratory shaft in the bottom of the pit in the Great Subterranean Chamber.

Yet none of these efforts uncovered the slightest hint of treasure.

Even today, under Dr Luis Alvarez of the University of California and others, the quest to find further chambers in or under the pyramids has continued, this time with the aid of such techniques as cosmic-ray detection and ultrasonics. Others, such as the retired Danish architect Hubert Paulsen or the Americans McCollum, Fraccaro and Robinson, have invoked mathematics to aid them in their search.

All of them are still intent on treasure. No longer, admittedly, are they concerned merely with the discovery of gold and jewels. Nowadays the treasure-seekers' thoughts are of richly adorned burial-chambers, priceless archaeological artefacts, new light on man's early history and thought. Gone are the days when such things would simply be plundered for personal gain – or even looted, like so much else, for the benefit of the major national museums. Yet still the hope of discovering such 'treasures' is a major driving force for researchers, with all that it entails of academic prestige, international celebrity and personal self-fulfilment.

Yet, for all that, it now seems that the Great Pyramid at least is empty of such caches. Unless, that is, there is a secret chamber deep in the rock-wall beyond the end of the Dead-End Passage, as certain of the measurements seem to suggest.*

The treasure-house theory, in short, has so far drawn a blank. And so, once again, we have to look elsewhere. This time, to the *storehouse or granary theory.*

The Hebrew Bible, you may recall, related how the early Israelites spent some four hundred and thirty years in Egypt, having originally migrated there to seek supplies in time of famine. By the end of this period, however, they had been turned into a nation of slaves, being employed chiefly in building granaries and storehouses for the reigning pharaoh.

Now the possible links between the Great Pyramid and the Bible have long proved a source of fascination for speculators of a religious turn of mind. In this particular case, for example, if the Israelites were employed to build storehouses, then might not the Great Pyramid and its companions be the direct fruit of their labours? What more splendid validation of the Bible's truth could be desired?

As it happens, the theory no more holds water than the pyramids themselves are likely to have held grain. For a start, the biblical 'store-cities' are recorded as having been Pithom and Raamses, both of which lay in the eastern delta, far from the celebrated west-bank necropolis. Then again, one of the Israelites' chief preoccupations seems to have been with the making of bricks, whereas the major pyramids, and in particular the Great Pyramid, were built of solid and uncompromising stone. And built, let it be said, long before the Israelites ever entered Egypt.

The chief objection to the theory rests on sheer practicalities. Over 99.9 per cent of the Great Pyramid's volume is taken up with solid stone. The percentage is even higher in the case of the other pyramids. Relatively speaking, their interior storage capacity is therefore negligible. Even in the Great Pyramid's case, the contents

* Compare Lemesurier; *The Great Pyramid Decoded* (Element, 1977) p. 130

of the entire complex of passages and chambers could be comfortably accommodated in a single, largish barn. The storehouse theory can therefore be totally ruled out.

However, this fact has not prevented numerous researchers from pursuing further the Pyramid's alleged biblical links. So extraordinary are the data, indeed, that a whole new science – known as 'Pyramidology' – has been developed around the idea, especially in Britain. Its insights are often so compelling and rewarding, and yet on the face of it so improbable, as to merit being looked into more closely in a separate chapter.

Meanwhile, even the storehouse idea was discarded only reluctantly. Especially in the 'biblical' camp, the idea long persisted that the volume of the King's Chamber, and in particular that of the coffer itself, was related to some kind of archetypal corn measure, while various other aspects of the design had been included by the Almighty Himself to furnish the basis of a universal system of weights and measures. This system, it need hardly be said, turned out to be none other than the traditional British one, brought to these islands, as it happens, by the lost tribes of Israel, whose descendants the British and Americans were alleged to be.

So powerful was this particular lobby to become, despite its apparently far-fetched claims, that it still has strong effects on our communal life even today. For it was partly thanks to the public fulminations of the theory's best-known protagonist, the then Astronomer Royal for Scotland, Professor C. Piazzi Smyth, that attempts to introduce the metric system into Britain were thwarted as long ago as 1869. The 'inch', it seems, was both divinely ordained and enshrined in the Great Pyramid of Giza. The fact that modern Britain has only recently been in the midst of renewed argument and controversy over metrication can thus be blamed very largely – extraordinary as it may seem – on the endeavours of 'biblical' interpreters of the Great Pyramid.

That anything so majestic as the Great Pyramid could have anything other than a royal or even divine purpose is an idea that still dies hard. Yet the perhaps unpalatable facts have to be faced, and the facts are that the Great Pyramid is as innocent of direct divine intervention as it is of royal burials and imperial treasure-hoards. Some more prosaic and down-to-earth explanation of the monument is therefore needed. And necessity, as usual, has proved to be the mother of invention.

5
The Mystery Deepens

With the demise of the *royal tomb*, *treasure-house* and *granary theories*, three of the more popular physical explanations of the Great Pyramid can clearly be ruled out of account. Yet, in a materially-orientated age, there has still been a marked reluctance among serious scholars to admit that so physical a structure could have anything other than a purely physical purpose.

Consequently the most extraordinarily erudite alternative theories have been proposed.

It has been observed, for example, that the originally polished limestone casing of the Pyramid must have cast huge solar reflections and shadows on the desert around it. There is some controversy over whether the outlines of the reflections could actually have been observed on the surface of the sand, or even, at times, in the dust-laden air – and, if so, where the observer would have had to stand to see them. But there can be little doubt that these outlines could easily have been traced simply by arranging for an army of officials to traverse the area in question, planting stakes in the sand at those points where they noticed a sudden increase or decrease in the intensity of reflected light from the Pyramid. The resulting patterns at noon on 2/3 December, 27/28 February and 20/21 June*, for example, would have been as in the diagrams overleaf.

With this continually changing configuration of shadows and reflections at noon, it has been argued that they could have been used as a kind of sundial regulating the agricultural and social calendar of ancient Egypt. The Egyptians, after all, are known to have called the Great Pyramid *Ta Khut* – the Light. And from this idea it is, of course, but a short step to argue that that must have

* For a consideration of the fascinating possibility that this particular configuration may in fact have been the original 'star' of the biblical Nativity traditions – with the three major Giza pyramids, inevitably perhaps, the three 'kings' of the story – see *The Great Pyramid Decoded*, pp. 260-4.

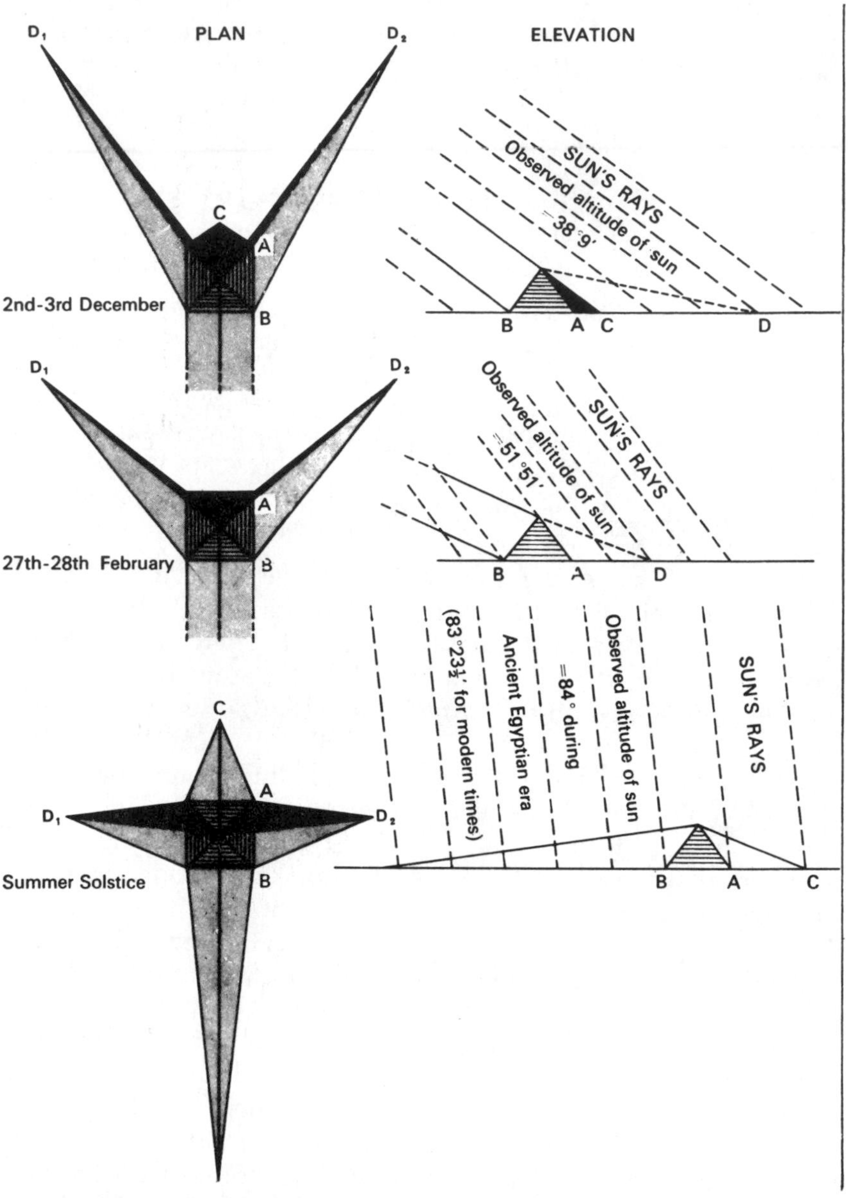

While it still retained its polished, white limestone casing, the Great Pyramid cast a constantly changing pattern of noon-shadows and reflections on the desert around it. In the summer half of the year, indeed, it cast only reflections: at midday it was, so to speak, a building without a shadow. These reflections could be measured, even if not directly observed, and the resulting configurations used as a seasonal calendar. The summer solstice reflection, in the unmistakable shape of a star, may additionally have had some special symbolic significance.

been the Pyramid's original purpose – were the *sundial theory* not such an obviously cart-before-horse proposition.

No farmer worth his salt, after all, needs to be told by officials when to plant and harvest his traditional crops. He is perfectly well aware of the movement of the sun, of the seasonal signs provided by the world of plants and animals. To suggest that the priestly bureaucracy were more aware of the onset of the various seasons than the peasants in the fields is little short of ridiculous, and reflects an attitude more typical of our own, city-orientated civilisation. Even the annual flooding of the Nile could have been quite easily anticipated, not merely by noting the brilliant, dawn rising of the Dog Star, Sirius – the traditional method of timing this event up to the time of Khufu – but also by careful observation of the water level and rate of flow further upstream, using special nilometers such as that still existing at Elephantine, near Aswan. The building of enormous stone monuments for this purpose was quite unnecessary. And from whom, it should perhaps be asked, would the priests have got their agricultural information in the first place?

Undaunted, however, physically orientated researchers have continued to think up other useful functions for the Great Pyramid.

For a start, there is the *theodolite theory*.

Originally proposed by an Australian engineer named Ballard, the theory suggests that the function of the major pyramids on the west bank of the Nile was to serve as a series of triangulation points. By using these, land surveys could quickly re-distribute the featureless, mud-covered lands of the Nile delta to their owners and tenants after each annual flooding, using only the simplest instruments and geometrical techniques.

The theory is admittedly an ingenious one. Certainly the pyramids *could* have been used in this way. But then so could the various trees, mounds and artificial eminences which were never covered by the floodwaters anyway. And if the pyramids were needed to perform this vital function, how was it that the delta had ever become divided up into permanent private plots in the first place, so that the pyramids were then needed to perpetuate the system?

Once again, then, we have here a typical cart-before-horse argument – and one which in any case pays too little attention to the evidence that the lands of the delta were in fact held in common under the pharaoh until long after the pyramid age was over.

To suggest, in other words, that the pyramids were built merely in order to lighten the annual administrative load of the pharaoh's officials is rather like suggesting that the skyscrapers of Manhattan, or the windmills and church-towers of East Anglia, were designed primarily as navigational aids for fishermen and inshore mariners. That, certainly, has nowadays become one of their functions. But one needs to be curiously out of touch and lacking in practical perspective to assume that it was ever their primary one.

Unable, then, to discover any physical theory for the Great Pyramid as we know it which could command general support, certain academic theorists have gone on to suggest a range of further possible uses for the Pyramid *before it was completed*. And, by and large, these have centred around the idea that it was designed for temporary use as an *astronomical observatory*.

The proposition is both effective and simple. During the Great Pyramid's construction, it has been suggested, work was temporarily halted at the fiftieth course of masonry – the level of the present King's Chamber floor – and the Grand Gallery was left open at its top, or southern end. This now provided the astronomers with a great vertical slit in the masonry, allowing them accurately to observe and record the passage of the stars and planets across the southern meridian of the night sky. Meanwhile, removing individual roofing-stones would also have served to plot the movements of individual northern stars, possibly with the aid of movable, calibrated rods suspended from horizontal bars fitted in the two grooves which run the length of either wall of the Gallery. Such removal was, of course, possible because of the distinctive, ratchet-like arrangement of the roofing-stones (compare diagram p. 199).

To permit all this to be done, however, it was essential that the Gallery should be accurately orientated. This was assured, first by cutting and building the Descending Passage in a direct line with the then Pole Star at its lower culmination, and subsequently by aligning the Ascending Passage and Grand Gallery in a similar way. This time, however, the alignment was achieved by observing the Pole Star's *reflection* in a pool of mercury or water at the passage intersection.

And so a superbly orientated astronomical observatory was constructed, having the added bonus of an immense platform on the roof for further observation work.

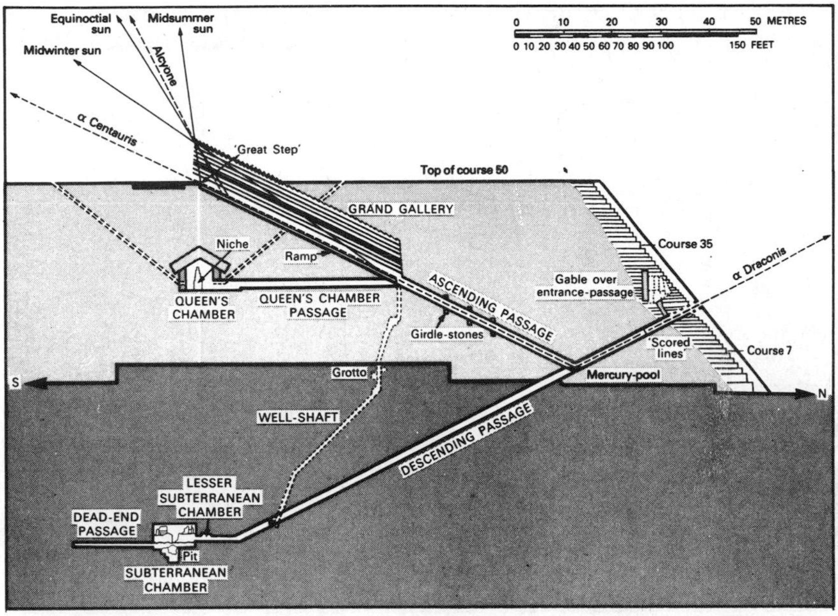

The 'astronomical observatory' theory, involving the use of the Grand Gallery as a kind of telescope.

As with so many of the Pyramid theories, then, the astronomical one is impressive in its ingenuity and in the extent to which it fits the architectural facts. The passage-system *is* aligned to true north with an almost incredible degree of accuracy. The masonry at the passage intersection *is* particularly finely put together, as it would have had to be to contain mercury or water. The Ascending Passage's angle of slope *was* originally 26°18′9.7″ – an exact reflection of that of the Descending Passage. And the open-ended Gallery *could* have been used in the way described.

And yet sheer common sense once again renders the theory highly unlikely. How, for a start, are the workmen expected to have cut the lower part of the Descending Passage in the dark, with their backs to the star on which they are supposed to have orientated it? Or are we to suppose that they had at their disposal some kind of mechanical digger with an advanced electronic sighting system, capable of locking onto a moving star for a few minutes each night and then preserving the heading with the aid of powered gyroscopes?

Who knows? Perhaps there is more to such ideas than at first meets the eye. But then perhaps simpler, alternative methods could

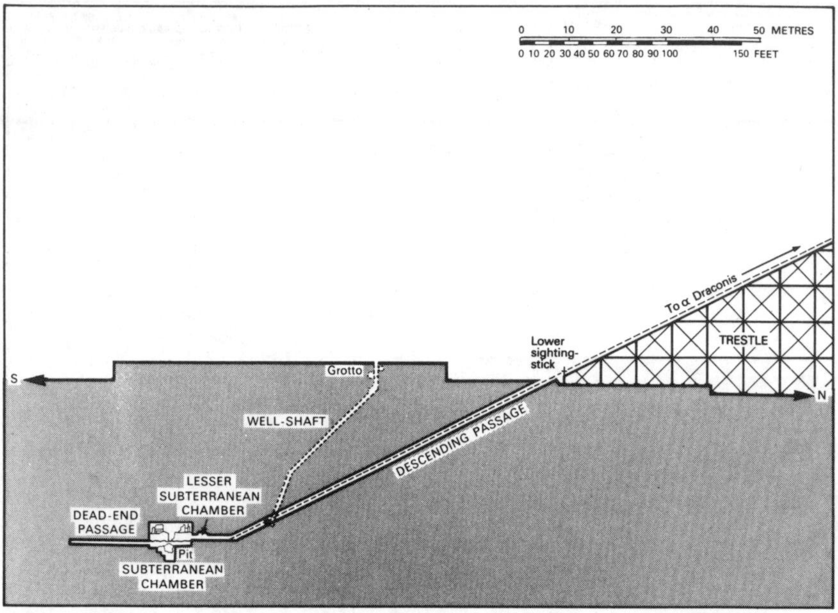

One view of how the lower part of the Descending Passage was first cut in exact alignment with the contemporary Pole Star before building work began on the Great Pyramid. The trestle or gantry would, it seems, have had to be 300 ft. high and 600 ft. long to produce the accuracy in fact achieved by the excavators. Quite how these would have been able to see the further sighting-stick, up to 350 yards away, with their backs turned has not been revealed. Once the passage was completed, it and the Well-Shaft could conceivably have formed a one-way system for removing the excavators' debris from the underground chambers, whilst at the same time ensuring a limited circulation of fresh air from the surface.

have been used. Sighting-sticks could have been set up at night, and the subterranean excavations then aligned to these, rather than directly to the Pole Star itself. Yet it has been estimated that to achieve the Descending Passage's accuracy of orientation it would actually have been necessary to erect a sloping trestle some 300 feet high and 600 feet long to support the two sighting-sticks. Moreover, then, once this had been done, the Descending Passage would no longer have been necessary for astronomical purposes, since the water- or mercury-bath could have been installed directly at the bottom end of the trestle, and work on the Ascending Passage could have been started without more ado.

There are other practical problems, too. One can have great fun imagining the bedraggled procession of astronomers with wet feet or sandals full of mercury squelching their way up the Ascending Passage into the Grand Gallery, the muffled imprecations in the darkness as they stumbled over the workmen's tools or stubbed their toes on piles of builders' rubble. Unless, of course, they somehow managed to enter the Grand Gallery from the upper end. . . .

Meanwhile it is difficult to see how the mercury-bath technique could in fact have been used for the construction of the Ascending Passage, when the Granite plugging-blocks at its lower end were so clearly built in from the beginning. It is also difficult to see why it was necessary to extend the building for a hundred yards east and west of the all-important passage-system, when a fraction of that thickness would have done just as well, leaving a simple, ramp-shaped structure.

Once again, then, a splendid idea has to be discarded because it is too impractical. It is all very well to propose uses for a building at various intermediate stages of its construction, but the result is likely to have far more to do with speculation than with hard fact.

The range of possible helpful suggestions, in fact, is almost endless.

At an early stage in its construction, for example, the Pyramid could have made an excellent parade-ground capable of holding the entire Egyptian army. Later on, it could have made an almost impregnable fortress in time of war, with its steep, slippery sides affording complete safety from any enemies below, and its narrow access-passage allowing only one intruder to emerge at a time. As the summit-platform of the growing edifice gradually shrank in size, it could still have been used by the priests for ritual purposes, or by the pharaoh himself as a saluting base. Spies, lookouts and cartographers could all have made use of its lofty eminence. The royal chefs could even have used it to fry the pharaoh's breakfast egg by the heat of the sun. Always assuming, of course, that the pharaoh got up at the crack of noon . . .

When it comes down to hard facts, however, nobody today knows how, when or why the Great Pyramid was built, let alone what uses it was put to during its construction. Even the most practical-sounding theories continually run up against apparently insuperable snags.

If, then, it was not intended as a tomb, nor as a treasure-house, nor as a granary, nor as a sundial, nor as a theodolite, nor as an observatory, what on earth *could* it have been designed for?

Perhaps the words 'on earth' need to be stressed. For, as the available physical answers steadily run out, the remaining possibilities start to become more and more 'out of this world'. Much to the scorn, I may add, of conventional researchers.

There are many, for example, who assert that the Pyramid was designed as a kind of *power-house* – a kind of transformer for stepping-down some unknown form of cosmic energy for terrestrial use via a world-wide system of 'power-points' and 'ley-lines'. But since the supposed energy involved is not readily detectable, the validity of the hypothesis itself must likewise remain unknown.

Others cite the various *pyramid power* experiments which seem to demonstrate that a dead body tends to be preserved if it is placed in the centre of an accurately orientated pyramid at a level a third of the way up from its base. Certainly it is true that the King's Chamber is around a third of the way up from the Great Pyramid's base, even though not at its centre. But since its coffer never seems to have contained a body in the first place, preservation of that body seems unlikely to have been the Pyramid's main purpose.

Undaunted, however, the experimenters have continued to insist that the pyramid shape serves to concentrate some kind of ambient cosmic energy, so enhancing all kinds of growth and fermentation, sharpening razor blades and aiding meditation. Certainly those who have braved the stench of urine sometimes claim to have undergone strange experiences while meditating in the coffer of the King's Chamber (a fact which adds two more, incidentally, to our list of possible uses for the Great Pyramid). Yet what the pyramid shape really seems to have concentrated has been the minds of the experimenters. There is, after all, no evidence that the Pyramid was ever intended for any of the purposes mentioned, and certainly there can be no question of it if the upper passageways actually remained sealed until the ninth century of our own era.

Improbable though it may seem, the Great Pyramid has also recently concentrated the mind of a low-temperature physicist who has managed to suggest a primarily *economic* role for the Great Pyramid and its companions. Rather like the American space programme (Kurt Mendelssohn has pointed out), the intense pyramid-building programme of the twenty-seventh century before Christ must have produced a massive socio-economic spin-off. Whatever its original purpose, it inevitably spawned a complex civil service, sophisticated systems of logistics, and a society more organised, perhaps, than the world had ever seen before. It was pyramid-building, in other words, that actually produced ancient Egyptian civilisation as we know it.

All of which, of course, is virtually undeniable, as Mendelssohn demonstrates. It also helps to explain why there were apparently more pyramids than pharaohs, since the massive labour-force needed to be kept in employment between jobs. Yet this view still fails to explain the project's original purpose. Whatever the cynics may claim, neither the American space programme nor, for that matter, the Vietnam war was devised as an economic pick-me-up, even though that tended to be their effect. And it seems equally unlikely that even Imhotep, designer of Zoser's archetypal Step Pyramid at Sakkara, was far-sighted enough to anticipate the full economic and political consequences of the programme he apparently first set in motion.

The socio-economic theory, in short, may go some way towards satisfying the experts' need for some convincing physical explanation. Yet it seems a trifle too devious to be likely, its logic just a little too rarefied to escape the suspicion that it is really no more down-to-earth an explanation of the project's real origin than a number of much more more way-out propositions. Among them, the theory that the Great Pyramid was built, or at least designed, by none other than the Atlanteans as a kind of *time-capsule*.

Clearly, this theory seems to pose even greater problems than any that we have considered so far. For a start, there is the vast question of whether Atlantis ever existed at all. Even assuming that it did, there is then the problem of chronology.

If, after all, we accept Plato's word for it that Atlantis finally disappeared beneath the waves in around 10,000 BC – a fact which would at least fit the geological evidence on past world sea-level changes – then we are hard put to it to explain how the survivors managed to produce a monument which, according to most Egyptologists, wasn't started until over seven thousand years later, during the reign of Khufu.

Of course, it is possible that the Egyptologists are wrong. Perhaps Khufu reigned much earlier than the accepted 2650 or so BC. The king-lists on which the modern data are founded are, after all, based in part on those provided by the ancient Egyptian priest-historian Manetho and by the Turin Papyrus. Manetho's datings have come down to us in a variety of editions, and can consequently be interpreted in a variety of different ways. It is possible to push back Khufu's dates over two thousand years on the basis of Eusebius's version of these figures alone.

Then again, why have Manetho's figures been taken as a basis by Egyptologists as far back as the First Dynasty, but not beyond? What of the preceding 5813-year dynasty of 'Manes'? What of the even earlier dynasties listed by Manetho, including a 5124-year line of 'demigods' and a 13,900-year era presided over by 'gods'? And what are we to make of the persistent claims by classical authors (including Plato, Berosus and Diodorus) that the history of Egypt, as recorded by the Egyptian priesthood, went back not merely tens of thousands, but some hundreds of thousands of years?

Quite apart from these large questions, we have other possibilities to consider as well. Virtually nothing, after all, is known for certain about the reign of Khufu. We can accept that he regarded the Great Pyramid as his cenotaph and symbolic monument. The remains of the ocean-going boats buried in the five great pits so far discovered around the foot of the Pyramid scientifically bear out a dating of some 2,600 BC. Yet neither of these facts necessarily dates the Pyramid itself to the same period. True, the rough markings discovered in the Pyramid's four topmost chambers include at least one painted cartouche containing the name 'Khufu', as we saw earlier. But there are other cartouches, too – among them the name 'Khnum-Khufu'. The fact has long been a source of embarassment to Egyptologists, implying, as it does, that the Pyramid was somehow dedicated to *two separate* pharaohs.

This version of Cheops's horizontal cartouche reads from left to right, 'Hrw – Hnum – HFW', and is to be found in very rough form in the Great Pyramid's Relieving, or Construction Chambers. One version of its meaning is: 'The Most High Khnum protects me'. On this basis, the name 'Khufu' itself would mean nothing more than 'He protects me' – a name which could thus apply perfectly aptly to the building itself, rather than to any particular human king.

Now it may be (as Zecharia Sitchin has argued) that these markings were in fact forged for reasons of archaeological prestige by one of Howard-Vyse's assistants at the time of the chambers' discovery in the 1830s. Certainly they contain sufficient stylistic and linguistic anomalies and anachronisms to cast serious doubt on their antiquity. Equally, it may be that they are genuine after all. Even in this latter case, however, a strange possibility arises – one, indeed, at which I hinted earlier.

Could it be that the Great Pyramid was originally constructed by a much earlier king called Khnum-Khufu, a name that was sometimes shortened by popular tradition simply to 'Khufu' (hence the 'unofficial' appearance of that name in the quarry-markings)? Could it be that the *historical* king (named in some lists as 'Suphis'), being determined to outdo the pyramid-building efforts of his immediate predecessors, decided to co-opt the already existing Great Pyramid as his own? All that was needed, after all, was a change of name to that of the earlier king, whereupon the monument already known to his generation as 'the pyramid of Khufu' would become his – an artefact of indescribable age which had only been waiting, as it were, for its 'rightful owner' to come along. Indeed, such was the ancient Egyptian reverence for word-magic that it would not be at all surprising if it were felt that the pharaoh had thereby taken up his ancient predecessor's very identity – thus, as it were, justifying the act twice over.

Khufu, in other words, would now have been seen to be a kind of reincarnation of that earlier monarch.

It is possible that such an act would have met with strong opposition from the priesthood. To them it might well have smacked of sacrilege. And indeed, such traditions as have come down to us relate that Khufu and his priesthood were at constant loggerheads, and that he was regarded as something of an irreligious upstart.

Khufu was not to know, of course, that the Pyramid contained a hidden upper passage-system, let alone sealed upper chambers containing inscriptions revealing that its builder's full name had apparently been, not Khufu, but Khnum-Khufu. And the architects of his eventual successors, being equally unaware of the existence of the upper passageways, would naturally not have copied these in their own great monuments, the Second and Third Pyramids of Giza – which would explain very neatly why each of these monuments contains only a *lower* passage-system to this day.

On this basis the history of Egyptian pyramid building would have to be radically revised. The Great Pyramid, it may be, stood alone in the desert as early as 10,000 BC. At that time, with the table of the Nile Delta at a much lower level, the sea would have stretched right up to the foot of the Giza plateau, thus permitting the year-round ferrying of its high-grade limestone casing-blocks from the quarries in the Moqattam Hills on the opposite side of the Nile, instead of only during the two-month High Nile season. At that time, too, Leo (and not Taurus) was the vernal, or reigning, sign of the Zodiac – which might explain why the perhaps contemporary Great Sphinx was carved in the form of a lion and not of a bull. During the same period, with world sea-levels rapidly rising after the last ice age, ancient civilisations were everywhere being drowned – and not least, if it ever existed, that of Atlantis. Perhaps, indeed, it was the survivors of the Atlantean cataclysm who were by then appearing in ever greater numbers on the shores of Europe and the Mediterranean as Cro-Magnon man; who first domesticated the animals which they painted in their sacred caves; who sowed the seeds of modern agriculture by domesticating both wheat in Eurasia and maize in Central America;* and who, perhaps, initiated the building of the Great Pyramid.

Thus, at any rate, the theory might go.

On this basis, the subsequent pyramids of the third millennium BC would then have to be seen as mere imitations. Zoser's Step Pyramid at Sakkara might represent the first attempt to erect a comparable structure by superimposing a series of *mastabas*, or burial mounds, one on top of the other. The very fact that this great pile was clearly constructed by instalments suggests that Imhotep, its architect, was not at first sure how large a structure he could safely attempt with the resources at his command. But eventually the monument was completed to its familiar, stepped design.

Yet why the steps? Why not a simple, smooth-sided pyramid?

One possibility which suggests itself is that the Great Pyramid on which it was modelled – already, it may be, over seven thousand years old at the time – had by now lost most of the upper part of its original limestone casing, so giving (above a still smooth-sided lower slope) the same, multi-stepped effect as it presents once more today. Alternatively it may simply be that Zoser's celebrated architect was unwilling to invite either invidious comparisons or

* Compare the detailed evidence on this question in *The Great Pyramid Decoded*.

structural disaster by making a direct attempt at a smooth-sided pyramid as such, with all the enormous cumulative skin-stresses which this would involve. Possibly, too, Imhotep felt constrained to reflect in his design not merely the fifty-two degree slope of the Great Pyramid, but also the stepped form of the traditional *mastaba* itself, which conservative opinion would no doubt have seen as essential to the design of any such funerary monument, with all its connotations of a 'stairway to the sky'.

It has to be said that the resulting building was not only extraordinarily impressive but also curiously modernistic in its overall effect.

More sophisticated attempts then followed. By a process of trial and error, gradual progress was made towards the true pyramid shape. A disaster at Meidum (graphically described by Mendelssohn in *The Riddle of the Pyramids*) prompted Snofru to modify the design of his Bent Pyramid, and then subsequently to construct his Northern Pyramid of Dahshur with a much-reduced angle of slope.

But then came the king known to us as Khufu. With a degree of daring that, as we have seen, probably amounted to sacrilege, he restored the Great Pyramid to its pristine glory, co-opted it as his own and, to prove it, arranged for at least five, and possibly more, of his own great 'solar boats' to be planted in ceremonial pits around its base.

And indeed, Khufu's own so-called Inventory Stela, rediscovered as recently as the 1850s confirms that the Great Pyramid and Sphinx were already standing long before his time. Not only that, but the former, which was already in urgent need of repair in his day, had apparently been dedicated not to Khufu, *but to the goddess Isis*.

So much at variance is this with accepted theory that the Egyptologists, unwilling to ditch their familiar historical framework, generally prefer to dismiss the Stela as a fake. (A late copy of a Fourth Dynasty original it may well be, but why anybody should wish to *fake* it has not been adequately explained.) Alternatively, perhaps it is the accepted theory that is fraudulent, and the Stela that should be believed.

A conclusion which would of course tend to favour Sitchin's 'forgery' explanation of the Construction Chamber hieroglyphs, rather than my own 'personation' version of the story. At the same time, however, it would have the effect of compounding to the *n*th degree Khufu's apparent sacrilege in rededicating the building to his own greater glory.

Either way, Khufu's son and successor Djedefre (or Redjedef) seems to have been somewhat dismayed by the whole business. As his own memorial monument, he attemped to erect a pyramid atop a 450 foot high rock at Abu Roash, some five miles to the north. Perhaps he felt that in this way he could withdraw somewhat from the ecclesiastical storm, while still outdoing his father in the matter of summit-altitude. Following Djedefre's premature death, however, his brother Khafre continued the former tradition – this time attempting a virtually straight copy of the Great Pyramid on slightly higher ground just to the south-west of it. Naturally, though, his architects copied only the lower passageways, not the upper part of the system, of which they were totally ignorant. For the same reason, their 'tomb-chamber' was not equipped with airshafts.

As for their angle of slope, this actually turned out to be slightly steeper than that of the Great Pyramid. In most other respects, however, it is clear even today that they were still not quite able to match up to the Great Pyramid's own exquisite standards of design and workmanship, magnificent though their attempt was in the event.

Khafre's pyramid is now called the Second Pyramid of Giza, but in its day it was referred to by the Egyptians as the 'Great' Pyramid (Khufu's, as we saw, was known as *Ta Khut* – the Light). Justifiably so, for if the theory that we have just expounded is correct, then it represents the summit of Egyptian pyramid building during the third millennium BC. Thereafter, its successors tended to become ever smaller and more shoddy in construction. Menkure's Third Pyramid, just to the south-west of his father's, is less than a tenth of the size of its predecessor, and was left with its casing-stones unfinished and proud. And, once again, its interior arrangement betrays total ignorance of the Great Pyramid's still-sealed upper passage-system.

In this way, then, the historical and archaeological facts could conceivably be reconciled with the *Atlantean time-capsule* theory and a construction date for the Great Pyramid of something like 10,000 BC, if Plato's reports in his *Timaeus* and *Critias*, and Edgar Cayce's trance revelations,* are to be regarded as at all reliable.

But once again, as with all the previous theories that we have discussed, we immediately encounter a snag. If the Great Pyramid is a time-capsule, where are its contents? Where are the documents and the artefacts? Where is the message?

Obviously, not in any of the Pyramid's known chambers. As we noted previously, these seem always to have been totally bare, apart from an empty, lidless sarcophagus – or possibly two. True, the lower passageways are known to have been open in classical times, even though the whereabouts of the entrance was subsequently forgotten. Possibly, indeed, they were always accessible to the Egyptian priesthood. But some at least of the Atlantean relics, if there were any, ought still to have remained hidden in the safety of the upper passageways until Caliph Al-Mamun's men first broke into the building in AD 820.

Now it may, of course, be that the existence of the Well-Shaft was known to the ancient priesthood even in the days of the Old Kingdom. It may consequently be that the contents of the upper chambers were removed by them or their successors for safe-keeping elsewhere. It may even be that the knowledge of this alternative means of access fell into unauthorised hands, and that the priceless cache was stolen. But it may equally be that it was never there in the first place.

In which case the message – the information stored in the time-capsule – must reside *in the design of the building itself*. The shapes and dimensions of its passageways and chambers, its various internal levels, the types of stone used, and especially the various numerical references apparently built into the design – all these may have been deliberately chosen to convey a message, much as the sleeping Edgar Cayce suggested. And the language chosen for that message would therefore have been primarily mathematical.

Certainly there would have been several advantages in using a simple number-code. For a start, it would not have been too obvi-

* Edgar Cayce, 1877-1945, known as 'the sleeping prophet', was an American small-town photographer whose extraordinary psychic gifts while in trance are fully described in the works referred to under his name in the bibliography at the end of this volume. The stenographic records of over 14,000 of his trance-revelations are still being analysed at the Association for Research and Enlightenment at Virginia Beach, Virginia.

Among Cayce's predictions was that an actual cache of Atlantean artefacts would be discovered 'between the Sphinx and the river' before the end of the present century. An analysis of his site description will be found in *The Great Pyramid Decoded*, pp. 206-18, while further, geometrical hints of a possible secret chamber beneath the Great Pyramid itself are to be found on pp. 130-1 of the same volume.

ous. Consequently the ignorant, not realising that it was there at all, would not be tempted to destroy the precious message. Indeed, only researchers with a fair degree of culture behind them would be likely to be able to decipher it, and in this way the information would not be wasted on an audience unequipped to make proper use of it.

Again, mathematics is a universal language. Using a mathematical code would thus be a neat way of circumventing the obvious difficulties of language and script which any other form of transmission through time might well involve.

Finally, the Pyramid's sheer bulk would tend to ensure that the message could never get lost.

To this extent, then, the *time-capsule* theory cannot so far be regarded as disproved. Any final assessment of it has to be based on a thorough assessment of the Pyramid's mathematics, and this I shall be attempting later on in this book.

Meanwhile, to the extent that we have considered the *time-capsule* theory at all, we have, of course, moved from an approach based purely on the physical to a more abstract one, especially if the 'mathematical code' idea is taken to be central to it. One by one we have had to abandon the more physical explanations, on the grounds either that they do not fit the facts or that they are too impractical and out of all proportion to the scale of operations involved in the building of such a vast monument.

One fact in particular stands out from all the mass of theories. Again and again, what the researchers and theorists have discovered in the Great Pyramid is their own preoccupations. It is, for example, Egyptologists such as Petrie – specialists, above all, in the Egyptian way of death – who have tended to conclude that the Pyramid was a tomb. It is plunderers such as Al-Mamun, avid for treasures, whether physical or merely intellectual, who have seen in it a treasure-house. It is the biblical zealots who have claimed biblical links with the pharaonic storehouses of the book of Exodus. It is British religious enthusiasts such as John Taylor and Professor C. Piazzi Smyth who have done most to propound for the Pyramid a role as the divine guardian of just such a system of weights and measures as is still preserved in the British Isles. It is astronomers such as R. A. Proctor who have proposed for the Pyramid an astronomical function, surveyors and engineers such as R. T. Ballard who have proposed for it a role in land surveying.

It is present-day geomancers and ley-line enthusiasts – encouraged by the works of Watkins and John Michell – whom we have to thank for the 'power-house' theory. It is 'pyramid-power' enthusiasts such as Bill Schul, Ed Pettit and Pat Flanaghan who have helped to spread it about that the Great Pyramid is really a combined mummification aid and meditation centre. And it is advocates of the legend of the lost Atlantis – among them the sleeping Edgar Cayce – who have seen in the Pyramid an Atlantean time-capsule.

To say nothing of oddball hydraulic engineers who see the Pyramid as an irrigation pump for the Nile Delta, or of amateur cosmologists who claim to find in the monument's design a whole host of mathematical and astronomical verities right up to and including the speed of light.

In almost every case, in other words, theorists on the Great Pyramid see in it whatever great themes and theories most exercise their minds. The building has become a kind of crystal ball, reflecting back to the gazer what he most wants to see in it.

Not that this is necessarily an entirely bad thing. If the design of the Great Pyramid helps thinkers to symbolise and objectivise the contents of their minds, the fact may be of benefit to all of us. Who knows, indeed, whether one at least of the architect's purposes was not to provide just such an aid for human vision and imagination?

The possibility might help to explain why specialists even in less obviously practical spheres than those just listed have long found in the Pyramid a much more esoteric structure – a structure whose meaning, they claim, concerns the very destiny of man's soul.

6
Mirror of the Soul?

There is nothing new about esoteric Pyramid theories. As long ago as the Middle Ages, groups of astrological devotees would assemble in the Great Pyramid, convinced that their presence there would in some strange, semi-magical way confer deep wisdom upon them. Indeed, it has long been held by many that the ancient Egyptians themselves subscribed to such beliefs. The Pyramid, it is said, was in those days nothing less than a *temple of initiation*, its function to bestow supernatural powers and magical knowledge on all those who willingly and with due preparation submitted themselves to its mysteries.

Nor is there any lack of circumstantial evidence to support the view. The ancient Egyptian *Book of the Dead* is full of apparent references to the Pyramid's initiatory role. Indeed, in its Saïte version, it even contains what seem to be direct references to the passages and chambers of the Great Pyramid itself, as though each of these were associated with some specific stage in the initiatory process. Among the apparent identifications sometimes proposed are the following (compare diagram p. 52):

Book of the Dead	*Great Pyramid*
Gate of the North	Entrance
Double-arched Gate of the Horizon	Double gable over entrance-passage
The Descent	Descending Passage
The Hidden Lintel	Roof-block formerly concealing entrance to Ascending Passage
The Door of Ascent	Entrance to Ascending Passage
The Hall of Truth in Darkness	Ascending Passage
The Hall of Truth in Light	Grand Gallery
The Double Hall of Truth	Ascending Passage & Grand Gallery

The Crossing of the Pure Roads of Life	Intersection of upper passageways
The Well of Life	Well-Shaft
The Orbit	Grooves in Grand Gallery's side-walls
The Throne of Radiance/ Judgement	Great Step
The Royal Arch of the Solstice	Entrance to King's Chamber Passage
The Passage of the Veil	King's Chamber Passage
The Chamber of the Triple Veil	Antechamber
The Chamber of the Open Tomb/Resurrection	King's Chamber
The Path of the Coming Forth of the Regenerated Soul	Queen's Chamber Passage
The Chamber of the Moon/ Regeneration/Rebirth	Queen's Chamber
The Chamber of the Shadow	Lesser Subterranean Chamber
The Chamber of Ordeal/Central Fire	Great Subterranean Chamber
The Gate of the West	Upper or Lower entrance to Well-Shaft, or recess in west wall of Subterranean Chamber
The Secret Places of the Hidden God	Construction Chambers

So convincing are the apparent resemblances, indeed, that one eminent Egyptologist, Sir Gaston Maspero, is recorded as having declared: 'The Pyramids and the *Book of the Dead* reproduce the same original, the one in words, the other in stone.'

There is a possible objection, however. The chapters of the *Book of the Dead* were originally found inscribed on burial papyri and sarcophagi. Consequently this collection of texts appears to have more to do with the progress of the soul through the underworld after death than with the initiation of living human beings.

On the other hand, we need to remember that the so-called *Book of the Dead*'s real title is 'The Book of the Coming Forth by Day' – which might, after all, suggest a *living* application. Then again, there is much evidence to suggest that the text did not *originate* on burial-papyri and on sarcophagi, but was copied onto them from an independent original – as Maspero's statement itself implies. And finally, we need to remember that the whole basis of the *Book of the Dead* – indeed, of a major part of the ancient Egyptians' religion – was the life, descent into hell, struggles, death and resurrection of the God Osiris.

It was by following in the god's footsteps that the would-be initiate hoped to share with him the ultimate mysteries of knowledge and power and eternal life – an attitude to the deity mirrored in our own time and civilisation by the liturgical calendar of Christianity. One function of the *Book of the Dead*, in fact, was to enumerate the stages of that way, and so to guide the postulant in his quest for initiateship. And if the Great Pyramid's layout, too, represented that same sequence of experiences, then it is by no means inconceivable that the Pyramid itself could have had a role in preparing candidates for initiation.

The Pyramid's interior, you could say, represented the deadly snakes-and-ladders game that every human soul, like Osiris himself, must eventually undergo. But that experience is not exclusively a post-mortem affair. The soul is also present during life. And it may be that the Pyramid, in consequence, was seen as portraying the overall route-map for the soul's total experience. A route-map which, if carefully, consciously and intensively followed, could help speed up the candidate's inner evolutionary progress and so lead to a total transformation of consciousness within a single lifetime.

It was in some such belief, then, that the ancient Egyptian postulants for the priesthood, after many years of prior training, are said to have undergone a variety of culminating lessons and trials prepared for them within the Great Pyramid's interior. The already-listed nomenclature from the *Book of the Dead* may give us some idea of what those lessons and trials were. In the darkness of the Great Subterranean Chamber, it may be, the candidate's courage was put to the test with the aid of a range of fearsome engines and devices. In the Queen's Chamber, perhaps, he underwent a preliminary graduation-ceremony and received further instruction. In the Grand Gallery he passed before a board of assessors. And finally, after mysterious preparatory ceremonies in the Antechamber, he was admitted into the King's Chamber itself. Here he was put into cataleptic trance and left for three days as though dead in the granite sarcophagus. Only after this 'ceremony of the little death' was he finally led back out into the light of day as a full, 'twice-born' initiate.

So, at least, the now-popular 'esoteric' traditions would have us believe. And among the graduates of the Pyramid's mystery-school – as a variety of sources assure us – were Moses, Plato, Heraclitus, Pythagoras, John the Baptist and Jesus of Nazareth.

The hypothesis, it has to be admitted, certainly has its attractive features. There is not one of the proposed initiates who could not have made it to Giza had he so wished. Several of them we know to have visited Egypt, not least Jesus himself. Yet even here there are a number of practical snags. The initation-process described involves the use of the upper passageways, *including the Ascending Passage*. Even assuming that the latter's title – 'Hall of Truth in Darkness' – means that this passage simply represented an aspect of experience destined to remain for ever unknown to the candidate (as it would have had to, being blocked with stone), we still have to explain how he and his priestly assessors ever gained access to the Grand Gallery. And in view of the presence of the immovable Granite Plug, the answer is inevitable. All concerned would have had to undertake an undignified scramble up the Well-Shaft – its existence having presumably already been re-discovered – as a result of which the subsequent ceremonies would doubtless have been performed by a dishevelled band of wild-looking men dressed, if at all, in filthy, and possibly torn, robes.

If there were ever initiations within the Pyramid, then, they are unlikely to have been the effete, exotic, stately affairs so often depicted in romantic words and pictures. The rites in question must have been experiences of the most down-to-earth, blood-and-guts kind.

Unless, of course, we take the view that these initiations really took place elsewhere, with only their sequence and nature governed by the archetypal layout of the Great Pyramid.

The practical difficulties, however, have posed no stronger barrier to the *temple of initiation* theory than to any other. Already a strong force within the ancient Masonic tradition, the hypothesis finally took wing with the advent of Mme H. P. Blavatsky and the Theosophical Movement towards the end of the nineteenth century. From this point on it was to become almost axiomatic among 'esoteric' enthusiasts that the Great Pyramid had an overriding initiatory function, and that its passages and chambers represented nothing less than a training programme for the human soul.

To this latter extent, at least, the theory also tends to meet with the approval of those who, for their part, regard the Great Pyramid as nothing less than *the Bible in stone*. Like the *Book of the Dead*, after all, the Bible is regarded by Christians as representing a kind of training programme whereby the human soul is fitted for eventual life in eternity. Not only does it define the objective; it also lays down the route to be followed, and describes the historical initiatory programme apparently undertaken by the so-called 'chosen people' themselves with a view to achieving that ultimate goal.

It would not be too surprising, in other words, if Bible, *Book of the Dead* and Great Pyramid alike contained a single message, not only in the broadest possible terms, but also – to some extent at least – in the matter of actual detail.

Look at the layout of the Pyramid's passages (p. 52) in this light, for example, and it may occur to you that the Ascending Passage could represent a spiritual upturn after an era of declining values, apparently represented by the first part of the Descending Passage. The sudden raising of the roof at the beginning of the Grand Gallery might represent an era during which some tremendous new injection of energy would lead those following the 'upper' path towards even higher levels of consciousness. Simultaneously, the Well-Shaft might represent the opening of a new path of redemption for their less evolved fellows on the 'lower' path. In the King's Chamber, with its lidless coffer, death itself would finally be overcome during an age destined to lead man to higher dimensions of existence entirely (i.e. the Construction Chambers). Meanwhile, in the Great Subterranean Chamber, Armageddon would have overtaken those still following the lowest path, who would be duly cast into the bottomless pit of everlasting damnation. And only the Queen's Chamber and its passage – apparently representing some kind of 'half-way house' – might prove difficult to interpret convincingly in terms of the accepted biblical view of history.

'History', indeed, is a key concept, as far as this approach is concerned. And basic to any historical viewpoint is chronology.

Now any system of chronology needs both a starting-point and a system for measuring time. If, then, the Pyramid's interior does represent a projected history of mankind, or rather a blueprint and prophecy – for the Pyramid antedates the Bible, and even the Hebrew race itself, by many centuries – then it, too, must have a clearly delineated starting-point and some kind of timescale.

In the event the Pyramidologists (as the biblical Pyramid enthusiasts soon came to be called) have had no difficulty in discovering either.

We have already noted (chapter 2) that the Great Pyramid's entrance passageway pointed directly at the then Pole Star (Alpha Draconis) during the third millennium BC. During our exploration of the underground parts of the passage-system, we also discovered a pair of carefully scored lines – one on either side wall of the Descending Passage, and at right-angles to its slope – some forty feet in from the entrance. We even considered the possibility that these lines could represent some kind of 'starter's grid' – the 'go'-mark so to speak, on the divine snakes-and-ladders board.

Now it was no less a figure than the already-mentioned Professor C. Piazzi Smyth, Astronomer Royal for Scotland, who was the first to realise the full chronological implications of the lines for the biblical theory. For if the elevation of the Descending Passage represented what, for want of a better term, might be called the plane of the Dragon Star, then it was clear that the scored lines could represent the intersection of that astronomical plane by another equally significant plane. Calculations soon confirmed the suspicion. It turned out that at one time – and at one time only – during the third millennium BC the plane denoted by the scored lines passed directly through Alcyone (chief star of the Pleiades, or Seven Sisters, in the constellation of the Bull) at the same time as the axis of the Descending Passage was locked directly onto the Dragon Star.

The scored lines, in other words, provided an exact astronomical 'fix' – and that 'fix', as it turned out, occurred precisely at noon of the vernal equinox, 21 March 2141 BC. Not that the date was to be undisputed. The possible margin of calculation error permitted a number of dates and times – always either noon or midnight – within a year or two of this. Yet all of them were to prove generally consistent with the orientation of the scored lines on the date mentioned – and on that date it was certainly noon or nothing.

At the same moment the sun was, in the very nature of things, directly over the Pyramid's meridian at the equator, as well as itself being in the constellation Taurus. And in chapter 1 we have already noted another phenomenon which can be observed in connection with the Pyramid on or about the date of the equinox – namely the celebrated 'éclair', or equinox-shadow.

Noon of 21 March 2141 BC, then – this, it was now clear to the Pyramidologists, was the starting date for the Pyramid's internal chronograph. And with this dating now suitably confirmed by apparently unimpeachable authority, it remained only to discover the symbolic timescale.

Curiously enough, this – for largely accidental reasons – proved just as easy to discover.

Already in chapters 2 and 3, we noticed some curious numerical coincidences when measuring various features of the passageways in common-or-garden British inches. The designed entrance, we discovered, like the *nineteenth* course of masonry to which it corresponded, would have been almost exactly 2 × 19 inches high. The north face of the Granite Leaf, in the Antechamber, is planed down by almost exactly one inch – except for the horseshoe-shaped 'Boss' and the rebates at either side. The axis of the Niche in the Queen's Chamber, permeated as that chamber is by the number five, is set almost exactly twenty-five – or 5^2 – inches to the south of the axis of the chamber itself. And the same chamber's airshafts were originally left uncut at the lower end to an extent which, measured in inches, once again produces the number five.

It was facts such as these that helped to convince the early British Pyramidologists of the apparently fantastic thesis that the Great Pyramid was originally constructed in what were, in effect, British inches. The British system of measures thus represented some kind of divine revelation bequeathed to the ancient peoples of the Middle East, and now preserved only by their true heirs, the Anglo-Saxon British. From this it was but a short step to linking the idea with the proposition, already current in certain religious circles, that the British were in fact the true descendants of the 'lost' Ten Tribes of Israel, the 'lost sheep' for whom Jesus of Nazareth's teachings were really intended, and whose foreordained destiny it thus was to lead the rest of the world to ultimate glory.

For sheer nationalistic arrogance this theory would be hard to beat. The opportunities it offers for racial smugness and spiritual complacency should serve as an awful warning to all those who are prone to jump to epoch-making conclusions whenever their own religious preconceptions are apparently confirmed by snippets of disconnected information from even the most unlikely sources – however right or wrong those preconceptions may be in themselves.

Perhaps it is as well, then, that not all Pyramidologists were to commit themselves to so shaky a view. For the whole idea is quite unnecessarily dramatic, and in no way essential to the pyramidological thesis as such.

Inch and foot, yard and mile are not, and never have been, the prerogative of the British alone. Together with the various Middle

Eastern cubits, the Greek plethrum and stadium, and the host of related units of area, arc, volume and weight, they merely represent one aspect of an ancient and possibly world-wide system of measures which is known to have existed in embryo as early as Sumerian times. Inch, foot and cubit, in particular, were already standard measures among the Romans of two thousand years ago. And consequently it would not be too surprising to find that the Egyptians, too, used similar measures. Egyptologists, indeed, confirm as much.

The question of exactly what measures were used in the Great Pyramid will, of course, be vital for our subsequent investigation of the 'code-message' theory, and the next chapter will therefore be devoted to it. Suffice it to reaffirm for the moment that the proposed 'pyramid inch' or 'primitive inch', as it is variously labelled by the Pyramidologists, is by no means as exclusively British – nor, consequently, as inherently ridiculous a concept – as the more extreme claims may at first sight make it seem.

And certainly its application produces some astonishing data.

The chronographical theories advanced by the Pyramidologists are perhaps best summed up and represented by Adam Rutherford's multi-volume *Pyramidology* of 1957 onwards. And basic to them is the idea that one pyramid or primitive inch (P″) – equal to 1.00106 British inches – along the sloping passage-floors represents the passing of one year. At first sight the idea may seem too naïve to be at all likely. And yet a simple test can be arranged. What happens, for example, if we measure back up the Descending Passage floor from the scored lines to the position of the designed entrance? On the basis of the existing surveys, the theoretical distance involved has been calculated trigonometrically by Rutherford to be 481.7457 P″. Working backwards from the dating for the scored lines (noon of 21 March 2141 BC), this 'dates' the entrance to the summer solstice of 2623 BC.

The mere fact that, starting from a spring equinox, we have managed to land fairly and squarely on a summer solstice certainly sounds suspiciously authentic. But when we realise that 2623 BC quite possibly falls *within the reign of the historical pharaoh Khufu himself*, fact and theory snap together with an alacrity that can at first sight seem distinctly disturbing – always assuming, of course, that we are talking about the right Khufu.

So supposing we apply the proposed timescale in a forward direction?

From the scored lines to a point on the Descending Passage floor directly below the 'sill' of the Ascending Passage is a distance of 688.0245 P″.* And so the era represented by the Ascending Passage begins 688.0245 years after 21 March 2141 BC. This gives its 'sill' a dating of 30 March 1453 BC on the Gregorian calendar. In other words (claims Rutherford), it foreshadows the Israelite Exodus from Egypt under Moses. And sure enough, immediately beyond the sill we find the Granite Plug, corresponding to the two blocks of granite on which Moses is alleged to have received the Ten Commandments on the summit of Mount Horeb.

The coincidence seems too good to be true. Certainly the granite of the plugging blocks is a red granite very similar to that of Horeb – even if there are three of them instead of the two required by the biblical story. Certainly, too, the Ascending Passage does seem to represent an 'upward' initiative, a turn in the 'right' direction.

And yet 1453 BC is a very early date for the biblical Exodus. For many years now it has been fashionable to date that event some two hundred years later, in the thirteenth century BC, under the pharaoh Meneptah. Nevertheless, the more archaeological evidence is unearthed, the further back the theoretical Exodus date has to be pushed. Not that there is any archaeological or documentary evidence that the Exodus itself ever took place at all – apart, that is, from the biblical account. Yet the well-known Meneptah Stela, set up in the fifth year of his reign, recounts how that pharaoh defeated the *Habiru* (apparently identical with the Hebrews) *in Canaan, or Palestine* – which effectively means that they must have left Egypt well before his accession, especially if we accept that the roundabout journey described took some forty years. Again, the Exodus account states that Moses' successor, Joshua, sacked

* This and other measurements quoted may seem extraordinarily exact for a crumbling, subsiding, stone edifice well over four thousand years old. But each measurement listed in this book represents an average of a large number of separate measurements, duly adjusted for subsidence and distortion in the light of engineers' reports, and checked trigonometrically against all the other passage-measurements within the precise geometrical figure that is their side elevation. The measurements here advanced (which are based throughout on those published by Adam Rutherford, *op. cit*) represent the best available estimate of those envisaged by the Pyramid's original designer. And since they in turn are based on, and fully consistent with, the data supplied by several generations of eminent surveyors, engineers, architects and astronomers – for the Pyramid is by now probably the most minutely and thoroughly surveyed building on earth – it is difficult to escape the conclusion that they are, for all intents and purposes, definitive.

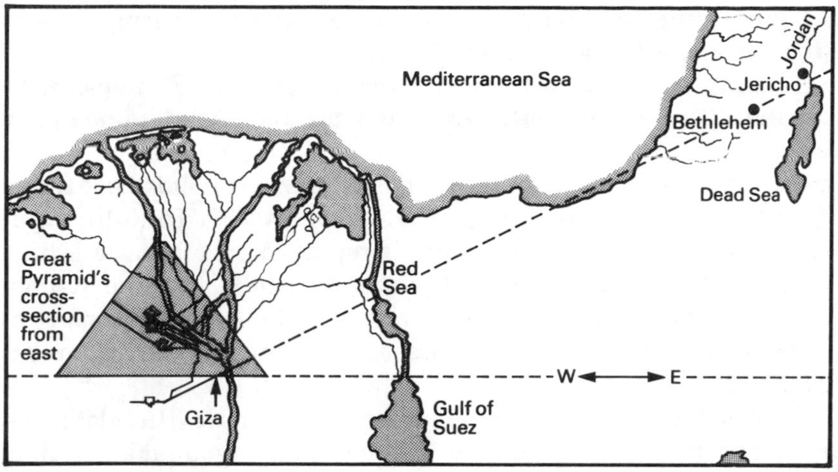

Superimposing the Great Pyramid's passage-angle on the map produces a rhumb-line bearing that marks a former ford across the one-time Yam Suph (or Reed Sea), passes directly through Bethlehem, and cuts the river Jordan in front of Jericho. The Pyramidologists detect in these facts direct links with the biblical stories of the Exodus and the Nativity. Compare *The Great Pyramid Decoded* pp. 238-260.

the Palestinian city of Jericho towards the end of the Exodus campaign. Yet it now seems certain from archaeological evidence that that event cannot have occurred later than 1400 BC. Which would, of course, fit the Pyramid's apparent Exodus dating of 1453 BC to perfection.

Moreover, there is a further curiosity. The biblical account is very precise about the date on which the Exodus migration began. The Israelites finally moved out in the early morning after the night of the first Passover – and the Jewish Passover festival has been celebrated at the same time every year ever since, in commemoration of the event. It falls invariably on the first full moon after the spring equinox.

And the first full moon after the spring equinox of 1453 BC fell fairly and squarely on 29 March. Any departure in the year 1453 BC, in other words, must have taken place on 30 March – just as the Pyramid apparently predicts.

Exodus or no Exodus, however, 30 March 1453 BC is certainly the correct 'dating' for the beginning of the Ascending Passage, if the Pyramidologists' chronographical theory as represented by Rutherford is to be believed. And so what is the 'dating' for the sudden 'raising of the roof' when, at its top end, the Ascending Passage finally leads into the Grand Gallery?

This time the floor distance involved is 1485.0068 P″. Remembering that there was never a 'year dot' (1 BC is followed immediately by AD 1 in our present system of year-numbering, first proposed by Dionysius Exiguus in the sixth century AD), 1485.0068 years after 30 March 1543 BC brings us to 1 April AD 33. To Rutherford, then, its significance is obvious. It represents nothing less than the date of the crucifixion of Jesus of Nazareth, and the sudden 'raising of the roof' at this point refers to the sudden human enlightenment, the release of divine power, which flowed from that event.

You may of course still be unconvinced either by the dating or by the proposed interpretation – though, once again, it is certainly possible to square the available documentary evidence with an AD 33 Crucifixion (compare, for example, the evidence set out in Rutherford's Book II).

So supposing we simply continue our measurements up the Grand Gallery to the point at its upper end where the floorline intersects the south wall? Here the distance involved turns out to be just 1881.2223 P″. Adding 1881.2223 years to 1 April AD 33, we come to 22 June 1914. And once again we have landed fairly and squarely on the summer solstice.

More to the point, however, this sudden 'coming back down to earth' of the Grand Gallery's roof marks the turning-point of a year which, with the onset of the First World War, was to mark in the most dramatic way the end of a former world order and the beginning of a new.

That new order – including, no doubt, our own tortured times – must therefore be represented in some way by the King's Chamber Passage and its Antechamber. And these in turn lead eventually to man's apparent attainment of immortality (i.e., the open tomb) in the King's Chamber and – who can say? – to five even higher dimensions of consciousness, perhaps, in the Construction Chambers above it. Until eventually, in the topmost chamber of all, man is eventually reunited in symbol with his Maker.

So much, then, for the destiny of the 'higher souls' – the biblical 'elect'. But what of the 'lower souls' from whom they parted company as far back as the time of the Exodus? What of the followers of the Descending Passage?

Their path, it seems, lies unremittingly downwards for 2675.006 P″ – i.e. until the year AD 1510. At this point in the mid-European Renaissance they finally enter the underworld of the Subterranean Complex. Moreover, we can continue to measure their progress through it by projecting each floor position onto its equivalent on the original slope. Between the mid-eighteenth and mid-nineteenth centuries, it seems, they are destined to pass through the apparent 'roof-fall' of the Lesser Subterranean Chamber – the world, in other words, will fall about their ears.

As, indeed, it did during this era of world-shaking revolutions.

At the beginning of the twentieth century, the souls in question duly tumble into the era of 'hell on earth' apparently symbolised by the fearful Great Subterranean Chamber. Once again, then, the critical era in question seems to be our own, and it can be successfully negotiated only by skirting the right-hand edge of the awful 'bottomless pit' which is the chamber's focus. At some stage during the present era, in other words, 'the bottom will fall out of the world' – and only a determined movement in the 'right' direction will save those facing the cataclysm from destruction.

There follows only a blind alley, a dead-end passage whose occupants, it seems, are heard of no more.

All of which leaves only the Well-Shaft and the Queen's Chamber complex to identify historically. The Well-Shaft seems to offer some kind of redemptive route – a bridge, you could say, between heaven and hell – centring on the events of the period immediately following AD 33. To Rutherford, then, it naturally represents the saving grace of Christ, the possibility of redemption for errant humanity – even, perhaps, Jesus' own alleged descent into hell. That redemption appears to be available to all those able and willing to reach the level of its bottom end – which lies just above the level of the Great Subterranean Chamber's roof – and this level in turn is attainable within that chamber only by climbing to its extreme western, or right-hand end – specifically, perhaps, via the symbolic recess in the top of its western wall.

The Queen's Chamber complex, however, is less easy to decipher. It, too, appears to be associated with the Nazarene initiative. Yet it seems to speak of some kind of 'inferior' path towards enlightenment, in that it lies *below* the glorious path represented by the Grand Gallery. This idea, of course, is not easy to square with the somewhat black-and-white claims of Christianity, and so Pyramidologists often tend to perform rather odd contortions of interpretation at this point. Rutherford, for example, posits an arbitrary dating of 1979 for the entrance to the Queen's Chamber – a date admittedly derived from his earlier conclusions elsewhere in the passageways – and then proceeds to work *backwards* along the Queen's Chamber Passage on a scale of one-hundredth of a 'royal cubit' per year. As a result, he finds that the beginning of the passage marks both the biblical date of Adam's fall in the Garden of Eden and Adam's symbolic identity with the 'Second Adam', Jesus Christ, in accordance with the teachings of St Paul. The figures, it has to be said, fit the case remarkably impressively. Yet such a procedure seems astonishing, to say the least, and it is difficult to see how the Pyramid's designer could have expected his monument to be read in such a roundabout way, let alone in close conjunction with a Bible that had not yet even been written.

Nevertheless, the Pyramidologists' difficulties at this point do help to focus the spotlight on one interesting feature of the design. All three of the horizontal passage-complexes start with some kind of 'step' – whether upwards or downwards, vertical or 'irregular' – while further 'steps' can also be identified within the two lower ones at least. At the same time it has been become clear of recent years that, if the interior features of these complexes are to fit known historical events at all convincingly in terms of the chronograph, then their timescales must be different from the simple 1 P″-per-year timescale applicable to the sloping passageways.

An obvious conclusion therefore started to suggest itself. The various steps represented changes of timescale.

Once this principle was recognised, there was an immediate rush to suggest appropriate new timescales, mostly on a highly arbitrary basis. A favourite one, the 'inch-month' theory, was advanced in the early years of our own century to explain the symbolism of the King's Chamber Complex. The beginning of the King's Chamber Passage clearly represented (it was argued) the start of the Great War (as it was then known). According to some Pyramidologists, indeed, it actually marked Britain's official entry into the war on 4 August. It seemed to follow, therefore, that the first low section of passageway must represent the period of that war – a period of four years and four months of 'severe judgement' actually having been predicted by one William Reeve on this basis as early as 1909. On the basis of the inch-month scale, the war's conclusion was therefore actually timed by the Pyramid at 11 November 1918.

As, indeed, proved to be the case.

Subsequent application of this particular theory, however, was to prove less convincing. The 'dating' for the Antechamber's Granite Leaf, on the same basis, is 10 August 1920; the beginning of the second section of low passageway 29 May 1928; entry into the King's Chamber 15/16 September 1936; and the south wall of that chamber 19/20 August 1953. It is difficult to see any special significance in these particular dates, especially when we recall that the whole symbolism of the King's Chamber and its open coffer seems to suggest that it represents man's final breakout from time and space. The last two dates mentioned, in other words, ought to mark the beginning and end of what Pyramidologists have identified as the final millennial age. If so, then that age has come and gone unnoticed.

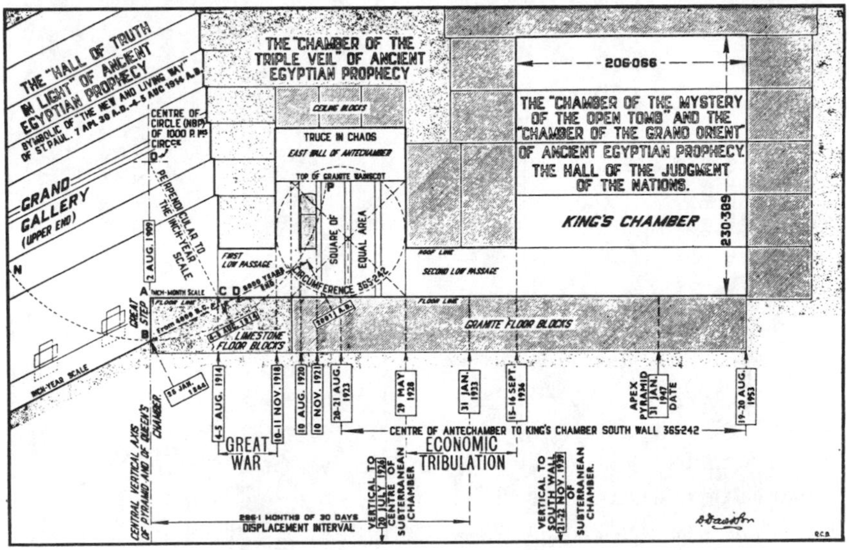

The agnostic structural engineer and mathematician David Davidson originally turned his attention to the Great Pyramid to expose the fallacies of Pyramidology. In the event, he himself was 'converted' by the facts. In subsequently interpreting the Great Pyramid in terms of the Bible, he employed a complicated mathematical system linked to the earth's rate of precession, and was even prepared to argue in terms of a non-existent passageway below the Descending Passage to prove his point (see previous diagram). Partly for these reasons, his symbolic datings differ slightly from those of the later Rutherford – who insisted that the entire chronology must be based on simple measurements along the centrelines of the passage floors. Davidson's acceptance – albeit reluctant – of the 'inch-month' theory was to produce some startling datings for the King's Chamber Complex (above), as well as winning him many followers in Britain.

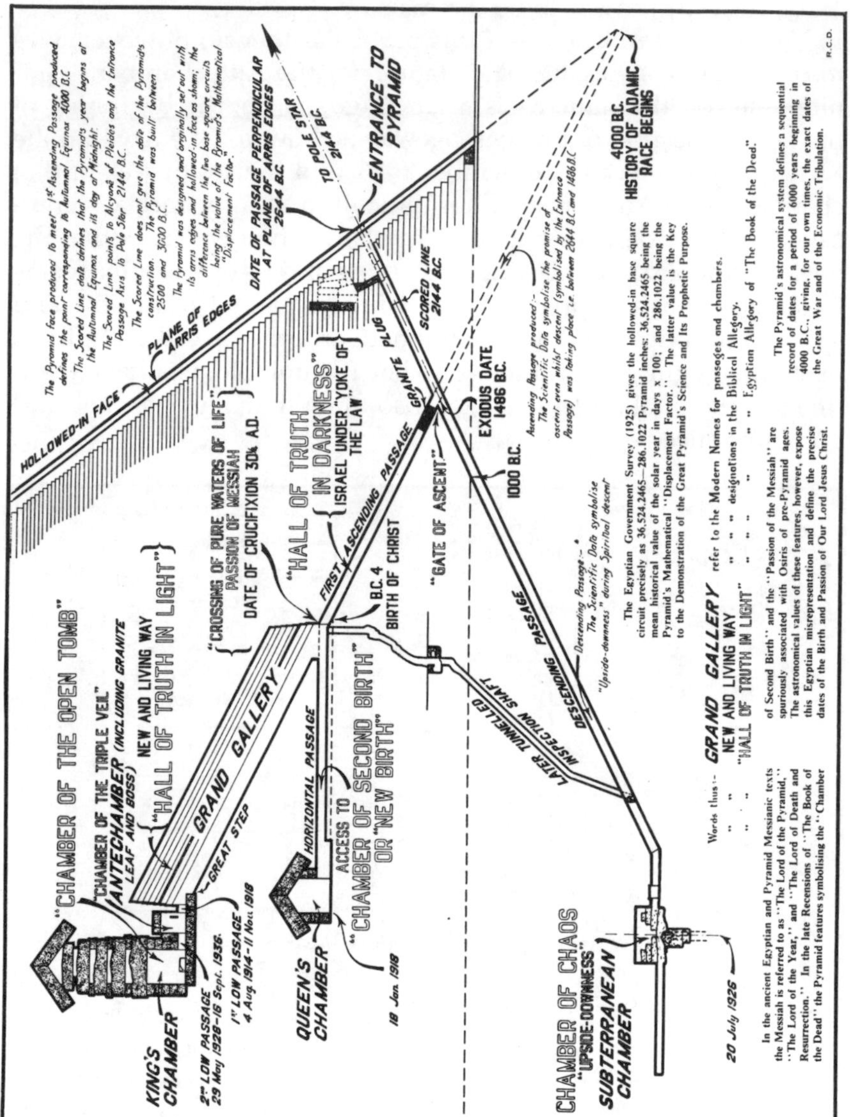

The result, inevitably perhaps, has been some hurried rethinking.

Some authorities, abandoning the inch-month scale and reverting to the former inch-year theory, have managed to put back the advent of the millennial age as far as the year AD 2183. Rutherford himself, having continued with the inch-year scale as far as the beginning of the Antechamber's granite floor (which he 'dates' at 1979), resolutely refuses to take his time-measurements any further, declaring that granite pertains symbolically to the spiritual, and is therefore timeless. Yet others have devised further, arbitrary timescales of their own, or have painstakingly measured their way all around the base of the walls of the King's Chamber, back out to the entrance and thence straight up the Pyramid's north face to the (non-existent) summit.

Yet while all these researchers recognised to some degree the possibility that a step might represent a change of timescale, it was many years before the obvious solution suggested itself – namely that each new timescale might be a simple function of the height of the step leading to the section in question.

Discovering the precise conversion formula to apply was inevitably a matter of trial and error. It had to be a formula such as would result in a reasonable fit between known history and reasonable expectation on the one hand, and the established features of the Pyramid's passageways on the other. Yet it also had to be a formula which, once discovered, could be applied perfectly objectively on the sole basis of the data available at the point in question. And these, it would appear, were simply the previous scale, the height of the step, whether it was an upward or a downward one, whether it was vertical or non-vertical, and whether it appeared at the beginning of the passage in question or in the body of it.

In my previous book on the subject, *The Great Pyramid Decoded*, I was at last able to suggest such a formula. And so the missing link in the system was, it seemed, finally supplied. At last it was possible to 'read' objectively the whole of the Pyramid's interior from the pyramidological point of view. Given only the reformulation of what appears to have been the designer's symbolic number-code, it was possible to fill in a great many details on the broad chronographical picture that the Pyramidologists had already sketched in outline. Certain specific phases during the Old Testament era now became apparent; the identity and date of birth of the crucial figure who died in AD 33, originally proposed by the Pyramidologists, could be confirmed and elucidated; the predicted fate of his followers and teachings could be discerned. Even more dramatically, the broad historical destiny of materialist civilisation could be traced from the time of the Renaissance until the latter part of the third millennium AD, with the period from AD 1914 to 2133 outlined in particular detail. And meanwhile, the even more surprising spiritual events still in store for man until at least the year AD 3989 could be revealed, as could his subsequent advance into timeless dimensions of as-yet unrealised possibilities . . .

Unfortunately, however, the results, far from confirming the Pyramidologists' confidently asserted and often rather fundamentalist religious views, started to cast worrying doubts on them. The picture which emerged turned out not, after all, to be the rather smug, élitist one which Christians have often accepted so uncritically. Indeed, the Pyramid turned out not to back up their more partisan religious views at all.

For what now started to suggest itself was that the Queen's Chamber complex – hitherto the source of some confusion to the Pyramidologists – really represented the path of Christianity itself, and – there could no longer be any doubt about it – this actually represented an inferior path, a deviation from the teachings of its founder. His *true* followers, it seems, were destined to be exterminated within a few years of his own death, only to return into incarnation during the culminating age which started in 1914 . . .

For human reincarnation, too, seemed to be symbolised by the design of the passage-system.

Moreover, there was to be not merely one 'Second Coming', but four of them; not merely one Millennium, but two. And all of them were clearly dated by the Pyramid's chronograph. The first Millennium represented the final, spiritual emergence of the true initiates – once dead, now returned – during what astrologers have come to call the Age of Aquarius. The dates of the second Millennium, an era of emergence for those continually incarnating along the Queen's Chamber path, seemed to correspond to the much later zodiacal Age of Sagittarius, during which the rest of mankind could finally reap the fruit of some thousands of years of learning within the physical environment.

True, the idea of a 'first resurrection' (of those 'dead in Christ') and a 'second resurrection' (of those who 'are alive and remain') is certainly present in the teachings of St Paul. But it never seems to have been suspected by official Christianity that they might take such a surprising form.

Yet all this, it still needs to be pointed out, arises as a direct result of feeding 'known' values into the Great Pyramid in the first place. Start by attaching biblical concepts to various features of the passage-system, and it is almost inevitable that your conclusions will emerge in biblical form – even if they differ markedly in detail from the conclusions which Christians generally draw from the Bible. Continue to feed in biblical data (notably the obscure prophecies of Daniel, which are notoriously easy to fit to almost any desired chronological scheme of things) and you are liable to reach even more 'biblical' conclusions – perhaps finishing up by using the Pyramid simply to 'prove' the Bible.

Which, it need hardly be said, can never have been the intention of the Pyramid's designer, who (I repeat) lived long before the Bible – or indeed the Jewish race itself – was ever thought of.

Useful it may be to decode the Pyramid in terms of established, familiar values – in this case the spiritual concepts popularised the world over by Christianity. I myself attempted to do precisely this in my earlier book. Such concepts, after all, do represent a convenient shorthand for talking about human consciousness and its development through the ages – if, indeed, that is truly the subject of the Great Pyramid's presumed message at all.

Yet even this technique of interpretation can never have been the intention of the Pyramid's designer. If his building has a message, then it was presumably designed to be able to proclaim it entirely without help or interference from external belief-systems. It is capable, in other words, of speaking for itself, quite competent to stand on its own massive feet.

Less convenient it may be to start your investigation from first principles, eschewing all ready-made systems and reading the Pyramid purely in its own terms, strictly for what it actually says. Yet that, if finally we are to solve the mystery of whether or not the Pyramid really contains a message – and, if so, what it is – is precisely what we have to do.

Basic to our whole enquiry must be the facts – the solid facts that have been standing there now for four thousand years at least, waiting amid the sand.

7
Measure for Measure

If we are to attempt any decoding of the Great Pyramid, whether pyramidological or otherwise, it is vital first to establish what units of measure* were used by its architect, so that we can then apply them to his building.

On the face of it, the task should not be too difficult. Examine a British house built in 1900, for example, and you are likely to deduce from it that the woodwork at least was originally measured in multiples and simple fractions of British feet and inches. Measure a modern French house, and you may well find that the corresponding measurements fall more naturally into metres and centimetres. Such are the inevitable results of the systems of measurement inherited and used by their respective builders and architects.

There is, of course, no original woodwork to measure in the Great Pyramid. But such were its builders' craftsmanship and mania for accuracy that the stone itself was often cut and honed with even greater care and accuracy than is involved nowadays in the construction of wooden joists and door-frames.

It should thus be a simple matter to discover what basic measures the builders used. The entrance-passage, for example, is 41.26 British inches, or 104.79 centimetres, wide. This, as it happens, is equivalent to two ancient Egyptian royal cubits, as we know from surviving measuring-sticks. The King's Chamber is 412.57 British inches (1047.92 cm) long and 206.28 British inches (523.96 cm) wide. These measurements, similarly, work out at twenty and ten royal cubits respectively. The Queen's Chamber, which has the same width as the King's Chamber, consequently also displays a measurement of ten royal cubits, while its length, at 226.91 British inches (576.36 cm), comes out at eleven royal cubits. The niche in the chamber's east wall, meanwhile, turns out to be two royal cubits deep, three royal cubits wide at the bottom and one royal

* Readers of a non-mathematical disposition may prefer to spare themselves the details in this chapter and turn instead directly to chapter 8.

cubit wide at the top. In addition, the King's Chamber Passage is exactly two royal cubits wide and high, while the length of the granite section of flooring in the Antechamber is five royal cubits.

Consequently, the further fact that the diagonal of the King's Chamber's north and south walls itself comes out at fifteen royal cubits, or that the chamber's cubic diagonal comes out at twenty-five, can be regarded as sheer bonus.

The Pyramid's builders, it is quite obvious, worked in traditional Egyptian royal cubits.

And so, inevitably, non-pyramidological researchers generally assume that the whole building must have been designed on the same basis. Its length of base-side, in particular, must similarly have been planned to measure a round number of royal cubits. Even the most up-to-date and sophisticated analyses, in consequence, generally assume a base-side of exactly 440 royal cubits.

Yet this distance is, on average, some seven inches too long for the Pyramid as built, if Cole's official government survey of 1925 is regarded as authoritative – and over five feet, or three royal cubits, too short, if Rutherford's 1957 figures for the projected full design are accepted.

What we know of the builders' standards of accuracy makes it quite clear that such discrepancies cannot be explained merely on the basis of constructional error. All four base-lengths of the existing building fall within four inches of their average, for example, while even the longest side falls some three inches short of the hypothetical 440 royal cubits. We must therefore conclude that this distance cannot after all have been intended as the Pyramid's original length of base-side.

Again, by no means all of the Pyramid's other measurements come out in exact multiples or convenient fractions of the royal cubit. This applies, in particular, to the lengths of the various passages and to their displacement eastwards from the Pyramid's centre-line. As well as the traditional Egyptian system of measures, in other words, a further set of considerations seems to have been at work. But what?

On this question at least the earliest Pyramidologists were in no doubt.

It was none other than the great Sir Isaac Newton who first proposed that, in addition to the 'profane', or royal cubit, the Great Pyramid also enshrined a somewhat longer, 'sacred' cubit of between 24.8 and 25.02 British inches. This he concluded on the basis of the first scientific survey of the Pyramid by one John Greaves, Professor of Astronomy at Oxford, whose *Pyramidographia* was published in 1646. It was Newton's belief, indeed, that the so-called sacred cubit (also used, it appears, in King Solomon's temple) would turn out to have some direct relationship to the dimensions of the earth – a question which was then of much importance to him in his efforts to produce a comprehensive theory of gravitation.

As we now know, Newton's theory of gravitation subsequently proceeded to its triumphant conclusion. But the question of the Pyramid's units of measure was to continue to exercise the minds of scholars for a further two centuries or so before any further progress was made towards its solution. The chief problem was the difficulty of taking accurate exterior measurements. Because of the vast accumulation of sand and rubble around the Pyramid's base, it was only towards the end of the nineteenth century that the building's true dimensions could be established for the first time with any real degree of accuracy.

Which makes it all the more remarkable that a former editor of the London *Observer*, one John Taylor, should have 'intuited' their real significance as early as 1859. On the basis of Napoleon's celebrated survey of Egypt, together with more recent figures supplied by Caviglia, Howard-Vyse, Perring and others, Taylor was the first to suggest that the Pyramid had actually been designed to incorporate the mathematical value π. The Pyramid's height, he suggested, stood in the same relationship to the perimeter of its base as a circle's radius to its circumference.

At once, Taylor recalled the widespread tradition among classical writers, that the dimensions of the Great Pyramid were in some way related to those of the earth itself – the same tradition that had earlier filtered through to Newton. In view of this, might the height, he wondered, have been intended to represent the radius of the earth, the base-perimeter its circumference at the equator?

The published base-measurements for the Pyramid, Taylor observed, had an interesting tendency to grow with time. The reason for this was simple. As more and more sand and rubble was gradually cleared from around the building's base, more and more of its lower courses started to become visible, and consequently the distance around its base constantly increased. The most recent figures suggested to Taylor that the base-perimeter actually measured some 36,600 British inches.

It was at this point that he was suddenly struck by a new thought. 36,600 was remarkably close to one hundred times the number of days in the solar year. Could it be that the Pyramid's designer had actually intended this correlation, using a unit of measure very close to the British inch?

By the same token, if the length of each base-side was now divided by Newton's proposed 'sacred cubit', a figure of 366 or so likewise resulted. Could this correlation, too, have possibly been intentional?

At this juncture, support for Taylor's ideas suddenly came from a totally unexpected quarter.

The search for an earth-commensurate system of measures had been in the forefront of scientific thought ever since the time of Galileo and Newton, and at the time of the French Revolution had thrown up the familiar metric system which has come down to us today. By the 1850s there was even pressure to adopt the system in Britain.

At once, however, the proposal encountered objections. One of its chief opponents was the celebrated astronomer Sir John Herschel, who pointed out that the French metre, quite apart from being incorrectly calculated, was an unscientific basis for measurement. Since the earth is not a true sphere, the metre – at one ten-millionth part of the surface distance from pole to equator – was impossible to calculate geometrically with any exactitude.

Instead, proposed Herschel, a more scientific basis for a worldwide system of measures would be the earth's polar axis. This, by contrast, was a known and fixed distance. On the basis of a contemporary Ordnance Survey, it worked out at some 500,500,000 British inches. Therefore lengthen the existing British inch by one thousandth part, Herschel argued, and you would have the ideal earth-commensurate measure. This you could of course subsequently group into convenient 'yards' of fifty inches, or 'cubits' of twenty-five.

An inch, then, of 1.001 British inches; a cubit of 25.025 British inches. The proposed measures fitted the pyramidal conclusions of Newton and Taylor almost to perfection.

But had such measures really been used by the designer of the Great Pyramid?

Taylor was in no doubt. The Pyramid was nothing less than a repository of advanced geometrical and astronomical knowledge. And since the accepted outlook of his time admitted neither of

Atlantis nor of extra-terrestrial aliens, he had to fall back on the only possible explanation left to him.

The Pyramid had been designed by none other than the Deity Himself as a revelation of His wisdom and, in particular, of His true intentions as regards a world-wide system of weights and measures.

Among religious enthusiasts – and especially among that vocal minority who, as we have seen, regarded the British as the descendants of the Ten Lost Tribes of Israel and thus as the true Chosen People – Taylor's religious thesis was avidly and appreciatively devoured. In non-religious scientific circles, however, it merely served to discredit all the valuable insights which had led up to it. To a scientist, after all, who regarded the Deity with just as much scepticism as he viewed the likelihood of advanced prehistoric civilisations or visitors from other worlds, only one conclusion was possible.

The facts simply could not be as Taylor had represented them. He was deluded. Mistaken.

It was at this point that Professor Charles Piazzi Smyth, Astronomer Royal for Scotland, entered the arena.

Smyth, admittedly, was something of a partisan. Himself trained as an astronomer by Herschel, and also much impressed by Taylor's arguments, he decided that the only way to convince his sceptical scientific colleagues of their validity would be to travel to Egypt and take measurements for himself.

But these were to be no ordinary measurements. Smyth equipped himself with a whole range of instruments designed specifically with the Great Pyramid in mind. A measuring-bar with built-in thermometers to correct for any expansion and contraction caused by temperature variation; a custom-built clinometer for measuring the slopes of the passageways with unprecedented accuracy; a set of measuring-rods designed by an expert optician; a clinkstone measuring-standard accurate to a hundredth of an inch. For photographing the Pyramid and its neighbourhood a special miniature camera was obtained, and Smyth himself helped to develop new techniques of magnesium-flare photography and stereoscopy which he was subsequently to use in the Pyramid's interior. Add to these a whole range of surveying instruments, plus Smyth's own astronomical instruments and skills, and there seemed to be a good chance that the debate over the real facts would at last be settled once and for all.

In many respects, indeed, it was. The present slope of the Descending Passage, slightly distorted by earth-movements and subsidence under the Pyramid's centre, checked out at 26°27′ – some

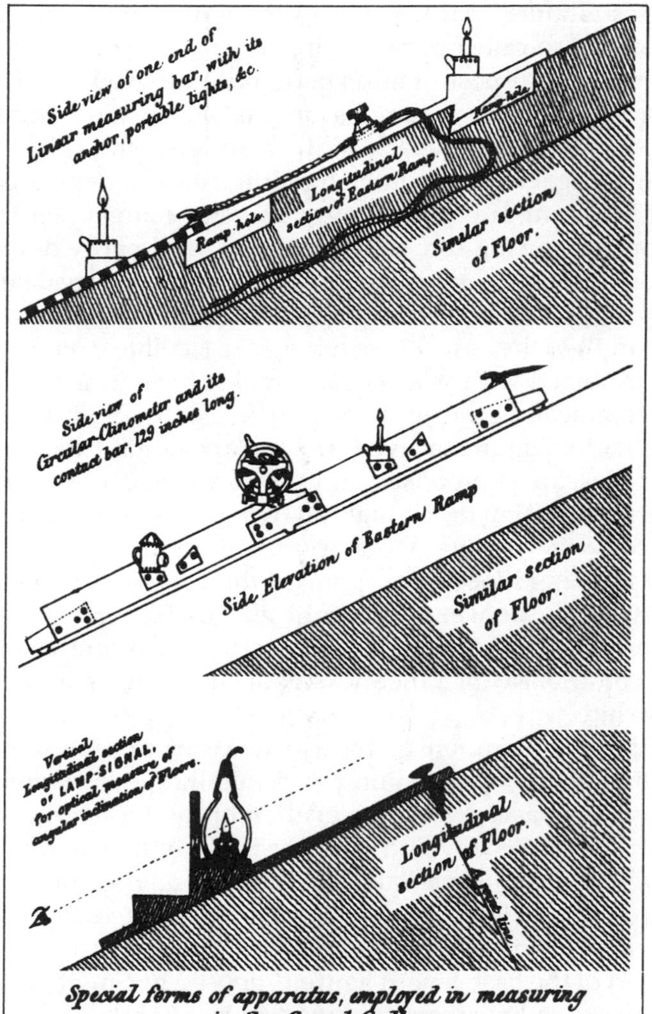

Special forms of apparatus, employed in measuring in the Grand Gallery.

Not content with existing astronomical and surveying instruments and techniques, Piazzi Smyth was to devise a number of new techniques and pieces of special apparatus specifically for use in the Great Pyramid. These included new methods of stereoscopy and magnesium flare photography, as well as the equipment illustrated above.

nine seconds of arc steeper than its apparent original value. The Pyramid's exact geographical co-ordinates were obtained from astronomical observations on its summit. The ancient building's orientation to true north was found to be more exact than that of any other known building on earth. And the boss on the Antechamber's Granite Leaf was found to be off-centre – by just one of Herschel's so-called primitive inches.

But the main purpose of the expedition – the checking of Taylor's claims regarding the Pyramid's original height and perimeter – proved a harder nut to crack. With both apex and original stone casing missing, estimates of the building's height depended on an exact assessment of its base-length and slope-angle. On the basis partly of the existing core-masonry slope, and partly of measurements by Herschel of such pieces of casing-stone as had survived, the slope-angle was determined as being some 51°51′14.3″.

The length of the base, however, was difficult to compute. Being still encumbered with piles of sand and rubble, it had to be measured piecemeal. In the event, therefore, Smyth preferred to average the earlier figures arrived at by Napoleon's expedition and Howard-Vyse, and proposed a figure of 736.81 feet per side.

Nevertheless, Smyth felt that the two results amply bore out his earlier convictions. The necessary result of the slope-angle was that the building indeed incorporated the value π (or 3.14159+) in the relationship between its height and its base-perimeter. And the latter was close enough to the ideal 36,524 primitive inches to all, but confirm Taylor's theories about the arcane measures used by its architect.

Yet final confirmation of the existence of primitive inch and sacred cubit still depended on a new, definitive measurement of the Pyramid's base. A fresh excavation of the four corner-sockets was therefore needed, and this Piazzi Smyth was unable, for reasons of time, to undertake. He had already spent some four months of 1864 in Egypt, and so the task was reluctantly delegated to two passing British engineers. Their eventual results fell somewhat short of the base-length figure proposed by Smyth. But these, in turn, were to be superseded in 1869 by slightly higher figures arrived at by an Ordnance Survey expedition.

Thanks to the still unhelpful site conditions, in other words, the true figure for the Pyramid's base-length was still a virtual unknown. Consequently it could be treated as a more or less fluid quantity. Smyth could claim that Taylor's thesis had been fully vindicated, and that the hand of the Deity therefore lay behind it all. The scientific establishment could claim with almost equal conviction that it had not, and that Smyth was no more than a raving pyramidiot.

Matters were not improved when a Scot by the name of Robert Menzies came up in 1865 with the theory that the Great Pyramid's passages and chambers represented nothing less than a prophetic blueprint for mankind – the equivalent in stone of the Bible itself, based on a timescale of one primitive inch per year. Smyth, naturally, was as delighted as his opponents were sure that their worst suspicions had been confirmed. Smyth's own calculations, based on the Scored Lines in the Descending Passage (see p. 30), actually bore out Menzies' apparently way-out thesis. In his successive writings, therefore, Smyth duly developed the whole theme, and was subsequently to be imitated by a whole rash of lesser writers.

Yet there were still some underlying weaknesses in the argument, and Smyth's critics were prone to pick on them with great glee. If the building was really based on the primitive inch and the sacred cubit, why were those measures not more in evidence? How could it be claimed that the building's base-measurements represented the solar year, when the latest estimates of them actually fell short of the required figure?

To resolve these doubts, one of Piazzi Smyth's supporters, an engineer by the name of William Petrie, decided that a new expedition must be mounted. For all of twenty years he worked to design even more sophisticated instruments than Smyth's, eventually involving his young son in the project too. But as time went by it became increasingly clear that the ageing engineer would never make it.

Imbued by now with all his father's enthusiasm, the son naturally felt frustrated. Since the age of thirteen he had become increasingly wrapped up in the quest for unearthing ancient measures. For years he had tramped the countryside, measuring churches and ancient monuments. Before long, he had produced his own superbly professional survey of Stonehenge – and a book to match.

So it was that, by the age of twenty-six, the son (now a fully qualified surveyor) had laid the foundations for a career in what was, in effect, a new science. For his name was Flinders Petrie, and the new science of which he was to become one of the founding fathers was archaeology itself.

And it was at this point that he decided to go it alone.

Arriving in Egypt at the beginning of 1881, the young Petrie was determined to undertake an accurate survey of the Giza complex, and to establish once and for all the precise dimensions of every aspect of the Great Pyramid. In this way he hoped to be able either to confirm or to refute Piazzi Smyth's theories, and so finally to clinch the long-running argument.

Petrie's mania for accuracy was almost obsessive. During his many months in Egypt, he would spend whole days at each triangulation-point, using a theodolite capable of measuring to a single second of arc. With calipers, tapes, chains, rods and plumb-lines he would measure each feature again and again, until he was sure that he had its true dimensions. And, like Smyth, he employed a whole battery of thermometers to compensate for errors of expansion and contraction in his instruments.

The results were, of course, far more accurate than any that had ever been achieved before. Most of Petrie's measurements of the exteriors of the various pyramids were correct to within a fraction of an inch. Inside the Great Pyramid itself, clad only in his pink underwear to combat the heat and frighten away the tourists, he was often able to measure to better than a hundredth of an inch – sometimes to as little as a thousandth. The levels, slopes and dimensions of the main chambers and passageways were finally established to within extremely fine tolerances – and these tolerances Petrie himself was able to state with absolute conviction in each case.

His results were finally published in his *The Pyramids and Temples of Gizeh* of 1883, and their conclusions for the Taylor/Piazzi Smyth hypothesis were shattering.

While the π-proportion, the royal cubit, and an intricate system of internal mathematics based on round numbers of square royal cubits were certainly inherent in the Pyramid's design, of the so-called primitive inch and sacred cubit there was no trace. Neither in the Pyramid's base-dimensions, nor in the form of individual occurrences of such measurements, was there the slightest evidence that they had ever been present in the architect's design.

The precise stage at which Petrie reached these conclusions is, of course, unknown. It seems unlikely, on the face of it, that he had already made up his mind before he began work, since he seems originally to have shared his father's pyramidological enthusiasm. Yet there seems to be more than a suspicion that he mentally wrote off the Taylor/Piazzi Smyth hypothesis at an unwarrantably early stage in his investigations. Only in this way can we explain the extraordinary upshot of the affair.

For Petrie seems to have remained blissfully unaware to the end of his days that his published figures actually vindicated the hypothesis up to the hilt.

His measurement for the mean base-side of the Pyramid as built, for example, was 9068.8″±.5. He was also fully cognisant of the concavity in each face of the core-masonry, which he assessed at

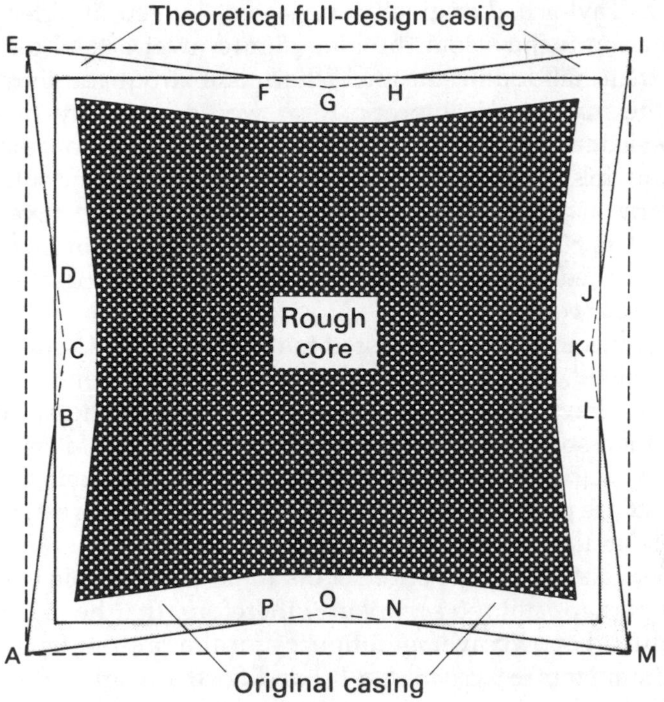

The original Great Pyramid had a concave core and straight casing-edges. Logically, however, the casing-edges ought to follow the shape of the core. Extending them out towards the four corner-sockets, the resulting shape (here greatly exaggerated) would be as in A(BD)E(FH)I(JL)M(NP). This would have the effect of lengthening the square base-perimeter by eight times the depth of the concavity in each face – a total of 286.4″, or 286.1 P″. AEIM, in other words, would now measure 36524.2 P″, where the base-circuit of the original building measures only 36238.1 P″. Moreover AE, like the other three sides, would now measure 365.242 sacred cubits, ABDE 365.256 sacred cubits, and ACE 365.259 sacred cubits – figures which correspond to the lengths in days of the earth's mean solar tropical, sidereal and anomalistic years respectively. These measurements naturally represent a considerable refinement and updating of Petrie's published data. Compare text and Appendix A.

'about 37″' (the word 'about' suggests a none-too-precise measurement in this particular case). Assuming, then, that the casing was at some stage intended to reflect the contours of the core-masonry, it is possible, on the basis of Petrie's own data, to calculate the figure for the designed square base-circuit. This comes out at 36571.2″±2* – which, expressed in terms of Smyth's proposed primitive inch, gives a final figure of 36534.7 P″±2.

The figure, it has to be conceded, is remarkably close to a hundred times the number of days in the mean solar tropical year, much as Taylor had originally suggested. Indeed, it differs by less than eleven inches from the ideal figure, over a total distance of more than half-a-mile. In any other context but the Pyramid, in fact, the mathematical proposition would probably have been acknowledged as having been proved beyond all reasonable doubt.

Meanwhile, more recent estimates of the exact depth of the concavity, facilitated by further clearing of the site, have given a figure of 35.8″. This figure, if accurate, is totally consistent with a final designed square base-circuit of 36524 P″ – the ideal figure for a solar-year correlation.

Yet Petrie adamantly persisted in denying that any such correlation obtained. Not that he disputed that a larger ground-plan might originally have existed. Indeed, on the basis of the still-existing foundation-sockets, he even estimated the length of its south side as some 9140″. Divided by the proposed sacred cubit of 25.025″, this distance produces a figure of 365.235 – once again extraordinarily close to the ideal solar-year figure.

Yet of this fact, too, Petrie seems to have been oblivious.

It is perhaps not too surprising, therefore, that he also failed to notice that his own averaged figures for the present length of the Antechamber (116.3″, or 116.2 P″) and for the height of the axis of the thirty-fifth course of masonry above the Pyramid's base (1162.4″, or 1161.2 P″) were, likewise, highly significant. For 116.2 is equal to 365.2 divided by π, and 1162 is ten times that figure. Both distances, in other words, seem originally to have been deliberate references to the diameter of a circle whose circumference was 365.2 P″ (or ten times that distance) – another apparent reference to the solar tropical year, only slightly masked by the building's subsequent subsidence and distortion (compare upper diagram p. 60).

* $(4 \times 9068.8 \pm .5) + (8 \times 37) = 36571.2 \pm 2$

Petrie seems to have been no more perspicacious, either, where the proposed sacred cubit was concerned. Having variously assessed the builders' royal cubit as ranging from 20.765" (Entrance Passage) to 20.61" (Queen's Chamber), he seems to have expected the sacred cubit, if it existed at all in isolation, to check out with considerably greater accuracy than this.

Here, much hinged on exact measurements of the Queen's Chamber and its niche (compare diagram p. 196). As Petrie himself observed, 'The curiously eccentric Niche on the east wall seems as if intended to mark some distance.' But what distance? Petrie obtained a variety of measurements. The eccentricity of the front of its base, relative to the sides of the chamber, came out at 25.1". Relative to the ridge of the roof, the figure was 25.08" – compared with the theoretical sacred cubit of 25.025 P". One would have thought that, with a royal cubit varying by 0.15", a sacred cubit varying by only half that amount represented a notable hit by the Pyramidologists.

But not so.

The distance, concluded Petrie, was 'nearer to the theoretical quantity, though . . . too large for the theory'.

In view of the above, it is not very surprising to find that Petrie was, in the event, equally disparaging about the presence of the primitive inch itself in the Pyramid. Not only was he totally unable to deduce its existence from the measurements already quoted above. He was also unable to discover a single case of its use in isolation.

The Pyramidologists claimed, of course, that the primitive inch was prominent in the design of the Antechamber's Granite Leaf. The 'Boss' on its north side, it was claimed, was offset to the right of the chamber's centre-line by one such inch, as well as being one primitive inch thick. So much importance was attached to this conviction, indeed, that one of Piazzi Smyth's followers, it is said, was one day caught busily filing the Boss down to the thickness required by the theory. So, at least, legend has it. On the other hand, not only does the legend fail to name either culprit or discoverer, or to date the event in question, but the Boss itself shows no sign whatever of ever having been filed down. The operation would in any case have been totally pointless, since the Granite Leaf's Boss and side-rebates were originally formed simply by planing down the rest of the north side of the Leaf, thus leaving all three features proud. Consequently the rebates (which, then as now, were embedded firmly in either side-wall) originally had the same thickness as the Boss itself – and their thickness is, of course, quite impossible to tamper with, without dismantling the chamber's masonry.

What, then, were Petrie's figures for these vital features?

For the thickness of the side-rebates he quotes a vague 'about an inch'. For the thickness of the Boss itself he gives a variety of measurements ranging from 0.94″ to 1.1″. This gives a mean value of 1.02″, to compare with the theoretical value of 1.001″ for the proposed primitive inch.

Almost exact, one would have thought.

Yet, once again, Petrie professed himself dissatisfied. It seems as if somehow – whether through a natural spirit of filial rebellion, or a simple desire to debunk established assumptions – he had made up his mind in advance of the evidence. Neither sacred cubit, primitive inch, nor solar-year correlation had any part to play in the design of the Great Pyramid. Not, at least, on the evidence as he interpreted it. And the 'biblical chronograph' theory, consequently, was highly improbable, even though – as he himself put it – 'the facts agree within a wide margin of uncertainty'.

But then, as Petrie admitted, 'the probabilities of intention – like every other question – will be believed or disbelieved, not so much on physical as on metaphysical grounds, and conditions of mind'.

It was, after all, not merely a question of the actual evidence. There was also the sheer improbability that the design of the Pyramid should have incorporated two separate and unrelated systems of measurement. The suggestion was too fanciful by far for the prevalent Western 'condition of mind' to accept.

Oddly enough, however, it subsequently turned out that the idea was not nearly as fanciful as it might at first have seemed. Primarily because the two systems *are not,* as it happens, separate and unrelated at all. Indeed, they are intimately bound up together in terms, once again, of our old friend the solar year.

We have it on the authority of a number of classical sources that the standard Egyptian unit of area was the so-called *aroura,* of ten thousand square royal cubits. That it is to say, it was the area of a square whose side measured one hundred royal cubits. But of course it is not necessary for an area of land to be square for us to measure its area. It could equally well take the form of an oblong, a parallelogram or a circle, for example.

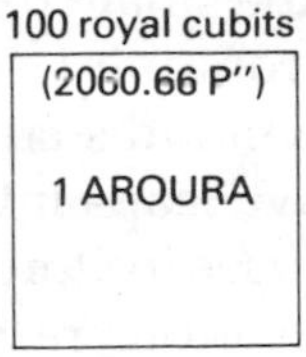

In the case of a rectangle, we could thus choose any length convenient to us and, by adjusting the length of the adjacent side, still produce an area of one *aroura*.

To take (for the sake of argument) our initial measurement from the Great Pyramid itself, the intended height of the axis of the prominent thirty-fifth course of masonry above the Pyramid's base appears to be 1163.8″. The best modern estimate of the true value of the Pyramid's inch, meanwhile, is 1.00106″, and so in terms of this the same distance amounts to 1162.6 P″.

With this measurement as one side of our proposed *aroura* rectangle, we now have only to divide the figure into ten thousand square royal cubits to obtain the inevitable length of the side adjacent to it. The Great Pyramid itself seems to establish the value of the royal cubit as 20.6284″, which works out on the above basis at 20.6066 P″. We have to divide our figure of 1162.6 P″, in other words, into an *aroura* of ten thousand square royal cubits, i.e., 2060.66 × 2060.66 P″, or 4,246,319.6 P″².

If you have a calculator handy, try it. The result may well surprise you.

For the answer comes out at 3652.4 P″ – exactly ten times the number of days in the mean solar tropical year.

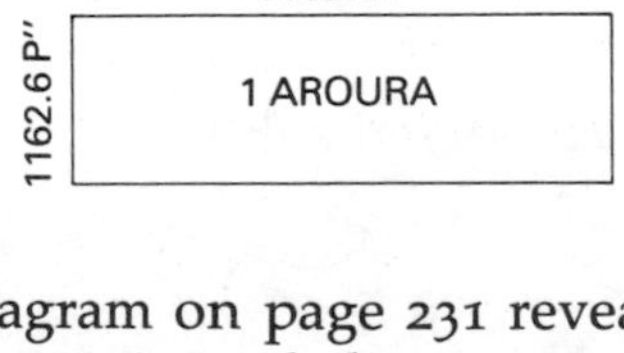

From this, as the diagram on page 231 reveals, it seems that the Great Pyramid's design is intended to portray not only the quantity 3652.4, but also two *aroura*-parallelograms in each of its full-design cross-sections, since the area of a parallelogram is, of course, equal to its base times its height.

And since, incidentally, the axis of the thirty-fifth course comes exactly one-fifth of the way up from the Pyramid's base to its designed apex (at 5813 P″), the small, remaining inset-triangle ABC at the centre of each side's concavity represents an exact one-fifth scale-model of the Great Pyramid's cross-section. Once again, in other words, the number five leaps into prominence.

But there are further surprises in store. For if we now experimentally divide the shorter side of our rectangle into the longer one, we find that they stand in an extraordinary relationship to each other – for dividing 3652.4 by 1162.6 produces, as we saw earlier, the answer 3.1416, or the irrational number π. If we were to construct a circle of diameter 1162.6 P″, in other words, its circumference would measure 3652.4 P″ or, once again, a figure equivalent to ten times the number of days in the mean solar tropical year.

What, then, is the area of such a 'year-circle'? Astonishingly enough, it is exactly one quarter-*aroura* – a measurement which itself is known to have been widely used in ancient Egypt.

1 QUARTER-AROURA

Moreover, that circle is reproduced almost exactly in the area enclosed by the sarsen-ring of trilithons *at Stonehenge*, whose official inner diameter is 97 feet, or 1162.8 P″. . .

Royal cubit and primitive inch, then, turn out after all to be intimately bound together in terms not only of the geometry of square and circle, but also of our planet's orbital astronomy. In consequence, the relationship between sacred and royal cubit is equally a fixed and stable one, expressible mathematically in the form

$$1 \text{ royal cubit} = \frac{365.242}{250\sqrt{\pi}} \text{ sacred cubits.}$$

In no sense, then, are the traditional Egyptian system of measures and the system envisaged by the Taylor/Piazzi Smyth hypothesis either separate or unrelated, as was at first supposed. Indeed, the very logic of their interrelationships suggests that *both* systems must originally have derived from the concept of the 'year-circle', with the square *aroura* itself a later development based on the *aroura*-rectangle. And since the royal cubit could not in any case have arisen until *after* the side of the square *aroura* had been

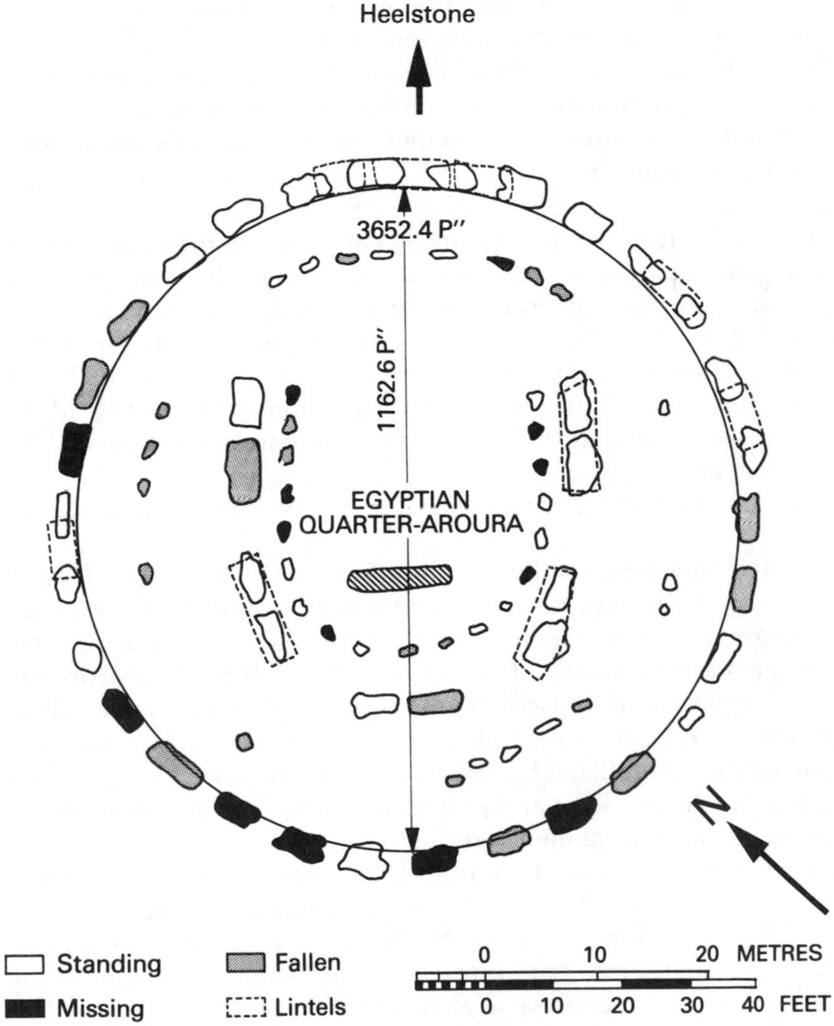

As the official groundplan of Stonehenge demonstrates, the circle enclosed by the outer sarsen-ring of trilithons is virtually identical to the ancient Egyptian year-circle, or quarter-*aroura*.

subdivided into a hundred parts, it becomes obvious that the system based on primitive inch and sacred cubit was in fact the *original* system, and that the royal cubit was very much an afterthought historically.

A fact which adds weight to the idea that the Great Pyramid may be even older than we think . . .

Meanwhile, with the Great Pyramid's basic measures thus firmly linked not only to the known length of the solar tropical year, but also to the quantity π (whose value can of course be carried to a theoretically infinite degree of exactitude), it now becomes possible to undertake even further refinement of the Pyramid's theoretical, designed dimensions.

All this, however, is for the most part unknown to the general public, no less than to the learned scientists of the establishment who still presume, even today, to discount both primitive inch and sacred cubit – not to mention their application on a 'chronographical' basis to the Great Pyramid's interior. One would almost think that Petrie's conclusions of 1883 had been the last word on the subject, and that no significant work had been done on the building since.

In fact, of course, such a conclusion would be very far from the truth.

Such a view ignores the patient efforts of the brothers Edgar to expand on Petrie's data, and to update the 'biblical prophecy' idea in the early years of this century. It overlooks entirely the detailed mathematical analysis and interpretation of Petrie's figures undertaken by David Davidson in the 1920s, with all its resounding effects among British Pyramid enthusiasts particularly. And it totally ignores the official Egyptian Government survey undertaken in 1925 by the surveyor and engineer J. H. Cole to establish finally the Pyramid's true dimensions.

Cole's figures for the Pyramid's base-measurements are quoted by a number of readily available sources, not least L. C. Stecchini in Peter Tompkins's *Secrets of the Great Pyramid*. Converting his metric measurements into primitive inches for purposes of comparison, we obtain a total figure of 36239.19 P″ ±5 for the base-perimeter of the Pyramid as built. Allowing for the known concavity in each face of 35.76 P″, and extrapolating for the full-design Pyramid, this gives a designed square base-perimeter of 36525.27 P″±5.

Cole's figures, in other words, provide as conclusive a piece of evidence as could be desired to establish once and for all the validity of the solar-year hypothesis originally proposed by Taylor and subsequently taken up and extended by Piazzi Smyth. And since primitive inch and sacred cubit are themselves direct functions of the hypothesis (for the above figure would of course give an average side-length of 365.2527 sacred cubits ±.05) their potential validity too is likewise established, with only specific examples of their individual use needed to substantiate the whole pyramidological theory of measures.

At least two such examples actually seem, as we saw earlier, to have been provided unwittingly by Petrie himself. Later investigation was to reveal further examples. The floor-line distance between the Grand Gallery's north wall and the north wall of the Well-Shaft entrance turned out to be just 25 primitive inches, as did the distance from the east end of the Granite Leaf (where it is embedded in the wall) to the centre of the so-called Boss. So, too, did the distance from the thirty-fifth-course axis to the top and bottom of the same course. In all three cases, in other words, the sacred cubit was revealed in actual use.

Meanwhile the British Pyramidologist Adam Rutherford, during a long life devoted to collating and refining all the available data and to expounding the Pyramid's presumed religious message, was to score a notable double success. The first was to discover that the Pyramid's Antechamber actually reveals in its very design the true relationship between all the various measures involved. Not only does it contain individual examples of primitive inch and sacred cubit; not only does it also provide a specific case of the royal cubit (distance from north wall to surface of Boss); its granite east wall (ABCD on lower diagram p. 60) forms a square whose area, at 25 square royal cubits, is identical to that of the largest circle that can be inserted within the chamber's longitudinal cross-section – and which, not unexpectedly perhaps, itself has a circumference of 365.242 P″. The Antechamber, in other words, contains the very key to the Pyramid's whole system of measures.

Meanwhile Rutherford's second, and perhaps greatest, achievement was to collate, compare and check trigonometrically the results of all the earlier surveys. From these he was able to devise a complete set of theoretical measurements for the Great Pyramid as designed, duly allowing for subsidence and distortion in the building over the centuries, and expressed in terms of a primitive inch of 1.00106 British inches, a sacred cubit of 25.0265 British inches, a mean solar tropical year of 365.24235 days* and a value for π of 3.14159+. It is these data – which are undoubtedly the most accurate available to date – that form the basis of the present book. They may, indeed, be regarded as virtually definitive.

Book I of Rutherford's *Pyramidology* first appeared in 1957. Curiously enough, it was in the same year that, under the auspices of International Geophysical Year, the earth's mean polar radius was finally computed on the basis of observations of orbiting space-satellites to measure 3949.89 miles – which works out notionally at 250,265,030.3 British inches.

On this basis, it became possible to determine, once and for all, just what one ten-millionth part of that distance really was, and what Herschel's proposed earth-commensurate unit would consequently have measured.

The answer was, of course, 25.0265 British inches.

The Pyramid's sacred cubit, to four places of decimals!

*This, it should be stressed, is the value adopted by the Pyramid's architect according to Rutherford. However, the figure is known to be variable, being currently assessed at 365.242191 mean solar days.

PART III
CHRONICLE OF CONSCIOUSNESS

'The Pyramids and the *Book of the Dead* reproduce the same original, the one in words, the other in stone.'

Sir Gaston Maspero,
former Director General
of Antiquities, Cairo

8
Cracking the Code

And so, with the Great Pyramid's dimensions and underlying system of measures finally known, the Pyramidologists at last had all the necessary figures at hand for arguing their case – the time-honoured claim that the design of the passage-system represented a historical blueprint for humanity's spiritual and social evolution.

But then it has to be said that those figures were really something of a bonus for them anyway. It was, after all, a basic part of their underlying conviction that humanity already had such a blueprint in the Bible, and since the Bible was, in their view, either God-given or at the very least divinely inspired, it followed that its blueprint was the only possible one.

There was an inevitable consequence. The Pyramidologists proceeded, almost to a man, to argue from the Bible to the Pyramid rather than vice versa – however much they endeavoured in their writings to give the contrary impression.

Their objective, or so it appears, was not so much to convince *themselves* – since for the most part they were already fully convinced – as to advance irrefutable arguments for their prior convictions in an attempt to sway the army of materialistic unbelievers who had been pulling the carpet from underneath institutional Christianity ever since the time of Darwin.

And so they were only too prone to resort in their pyramidological researches to what one can only describe as 'mathematical sampling'. There was little general attempt, in other words, to posit a comprehensive and definitive code for interpreting the Great Pyramid's system of passages and chambers. Instead, numbers and measurements were plucked out of the masonry virtually at random wherever they fitted the biblical thesis, and carefully – though no doubt unconsciously – ignored wherever they did not.

Thus, the Edgars were not above adding the odd inch here and subtracting it there (perfectly openly, it has to be admitted) wherever it suited their exegetical purposes. Davidson – who never actually visited the Pyramid – was quite happy to use the geometry of non-existent passageways to prove his biblical thesis (see diagram p. 128). The more scrupulous Rutherford was perhaps an exception, in that he, like Davidson, was originally an agnostic, and so started out with no special religious axe to grind. But even he, while mathematically much stricter (indeed a real purist in this regard), was eventually to perform the most extraordinary interpretative gynmastics (see page 126 above) in order to establish a link between Christian creation-dogma and salvation-theology on the one hand and the features of the Queen's Chamber Passage on the other, rather than simply reading those features as they came, in the sequence presented by the masonry.

Yet it seems clear that if the Pyramid's designer really intended his monument to be 'read' at all, then he would have done so on the basis of a totally consistent code. Every feature and its measurements would have been deliberately chosen, every application of a number or a distance significant and consistent in its meaning.

Which suggests, of course, that the only truly satisfactory way to proceed is to start by listing what you conceive to have been the designer's intended code in its totality, and then to 'read' each feature in turn in the light of it.

This, consequently, was precisely the method used in my earlier book of 1977, which was designed to test the pyramidological thesis that the Pyramid contained a historical blueprint for humanity's spiritual and social evolution in the first place – and to spell out that blueprint if it turned out to exist.

The word 'historical' should be noted. There was no attempt to explore the Pyramid's alleged role as a temple of initiation, or to 'read' the Pyramid in terms of the post-mortem destiny of the soul, since neither approach had any place in the typical pyramidological scheme of things. The accent was firmly on the history and prospects of the human race and the consequences for the planet as a whole.

Step number one, then, was to reconstruct the designer's presumed code. In my efforts to do so, I took full account of existing symbolic and numerological traditions, both biblical and otherwise, duly testing each feature against the witness of the stones on the one hand and the known facts of history on the other. Types of stone, levels of masonry, directions, slopes, shapes, geometrical measurements, arithmetical quantities and factors, and even the four basic mathematical functions of addition, subtraction, multiplication and division – all were allotted a symbolic meaning which, after due testing and adjustment, was eventually refined and fixed.

Moreover, because the proposition to be tested was the familiar pyramidological one, I expressed each code-meaning in terms of the familiar interpretative vocabulary used by the Pyramidologists, which was of course basically biblical – i.e. Judaeo-Christian – in character.

While it is true, as I pointed out earlier, that such a vocabulary provides a familiar shorthand and frame of reference for discussing the topics involved, I nevertheless feel, in retrospect, that this was a mistake, even though I felt it to be the best approach at the time. By which I do not mean that the conclusions themselves were necessarily 'wrong', but that the terminology in which they were expressed was inappropriately limiting.

It is not just that the designer can never have intended his monument to be interpreted in Judaeo-Christian terms in the first place (since no such terms existed in his day). There is also the point that it is unwise to use 'religious' language to the non-religious, since they do not understand it – and equally unwise to use it to the religious, precisely because they think they *do* understand it. Anything deemed to be 'said' by the Pyramid, in other words, is liable to be overlaid, if not actually swamped, by the 'religious' reader's own prior spiritual assumptions.

But then it had possibly been asking for trouble to consult numerological and symbolic sources outside the Pyramid in any case. The Pyramid, as I pointed out earlier, is presumably perfectly capable of being decoded *in terms of itself* – perfectly capable of standing on its own interpretative feet. It is altogether beyond the bounds of credibility to suppose that the designer expected its decoding to be dependent on the survival of such fragile witnesses as any given body of numerological lore, let alone on that of an as yet non-existent Bible.

Which is as clear a hint as any that a clear restatement of the proposed code is called for, innocent of all contamination by prior assumptions, free of traditional 'religious' overtones, and derived exclusively from the building itself and its physical environment – whether biological, geophysical, astronomical or whatever.

My reconstruction of the code on this basis is set out in full in Appendix B. It is incumbent on me, however, to offer some insight into how it was arrived at. I therefore offer the following notes on a number of its more basic features, without in every case setting out the full mathematical facts underlying my conclusions, since these are already to be found listed in *The Great Pyramid Decoded*.

The full-design Pyramid

The frequent references to the quantity *pi* (π) in the building's geometry make it clear that, as designed, it stands in some way for the circle. Moreover, the fact that these references are displayed in *three*, rather than merely two, dimensions immediately suggests a reference to a sphere. The numerous occurrences of figures such as 365.242 then make it clear that the sphere – or rather spheroid – in question is undubitably *Planet Earth itself*, in total harmony with its cosmic environment. Speed of rotation, orbital frequency, size and eccentricity of orbit, polar radius and precessional frequency – all are portrayed in the full-design Pyramid as a single, interrelated whole (see pp. 230-31).

The passages and chambers

It follows, then, that the Pyramid's passageways are *the path of whoever is passing through earthly experience*. They are, in other words, *our* path, whether as individuals or as a race. The fact that the Pyramid is ostensibly designed as a tomb further suggests that we who are those symbolic pilgrims are in some way to be regarded as *the dead*.

286.1 primitive inches (P″)

This notion of 'deadness' is in turn reflected in the fact that the passage-axis lies not on the Pyramid's centre-line, but 286.1 P″ (some twenty-four feet) to the east, or left of it – the direction 'left' (in Latin, *sinister*) having very ancient threatening connotations. Yet this distance is also the exact amount by which the perimeter of the Pyramid as built falls short of that of the full design, so destroying a good many of the latter's mathematical correlations with the rest of the cosmos. Our planet's apparent lack of harmony with the rest of the universe is thus seen to be a direct function of our own 'deadness', or lack of centredness. Since, however, the Pyramid's centre-line can be regained both in the Great Subterranean Chamber and in the culminating King's Chamber – with its open tomb and all that this clearly signifies of resurrection and renewed life – the most obvious meaning of the distance 286.1 P″ is *loss or regaining of balance and harmony, and/or the shift of conscious-*

ness which produces it.

As for the nature of that shift, it may be useful to think of the Pyramid as symbolising not only the terrestrial globe, but the sphere – or rather the two hemispheres – of the human brain. The leftward displacement of the passageways, in other words, could be seen as reflecting the growing tendency of all advanced civilisations (over the last two or three thousand years, at least) to over-emphasise the brain's left hemisphere – with its tendency towards linguistic analysis, sequential thinking and consequent fact-orientated materialism – at the expense of its more holistically, intuitively and emotionally inclined right counterpart. In this case the regaining of the centre-line would represent humanity's discovery – or rediscovery – of psychic balance, wholeness and integration.

The idea of brain-hemisphere specialisation, admittedly, is a comparatively recent one. Yet there is no real reason to suppose that the Pyramid's designer cannot have been aware of it. Indeed, the very construction of the Great Pyramid itself must – like that of its causeway before it – have produced more than enough cases of lateralised brain-damage in the workforce to make the point potentially quite clear, even if the effects of common-or-garden war injuries had not already done so.

For head injuries are, as it happens, among the most frequent medical results of major civil engineering projects, as today's almost universal wearing of 'hard hats' in the construction industry testifies.

Left, right

Seen in the above light, these two directions can thus be taken to represent the *loss and regaining of psychic balance and wholeness* respectively, possibly with especial reference to over-emphasis of the rational and analytical at the expense of a more holistic and all-inclusive attitude to experience.

Forwards (southwards), backwards (northwards)

Presumably *progress and regression through time* – since it is, in the nature of things, only in time that any losing or gaining of inner balance can be achieved.

1 (P″)

Apparently *one year,* at least in the sloping parts of the passage-system (see chapter 6).

Steps

Again, apparently *changes of scale* based (where the step is vertical) on the height of the step in question and the base-unit of the previous scale (see *The Great Pyramid Decoded* for detailed formulae). The one mid-passage step (in the Queen's Chamber Passage) seems, in the light of the rest of the eventual read-out, to indicate a change of scale applying to *the whole of the passage in question:* its position in the passage seems to be determined by symbolic considerations unconnected with the actual timing of that scale-change. Again, on the basis of subsequent inspection, the scale on granite floors appears to be one hundredth of a royal cubit per year.

The scored lines

Start counting from here: the 'go' square on the Pyramid's snakes-and-ladders board.

Up/down

Progress towards, or falling away from, balance and integration (see *Levels* below).

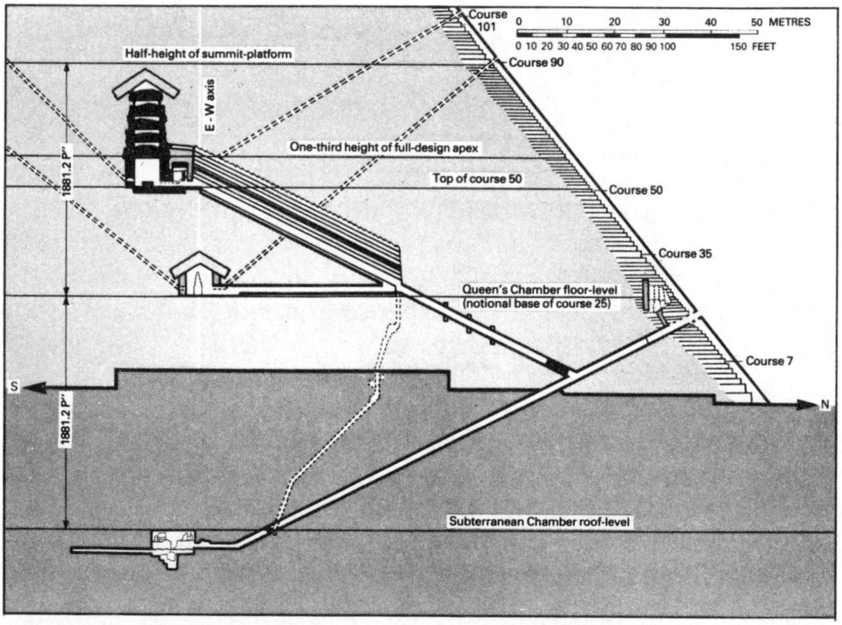

Levels of possible symbolic significance in the Great Pyramid.

Levels

Evidently *levels of achievement in the quest for wholeness and integration* (see diagram). The Great Subterranean Chamber roof-level seems to represent a *level of imbalance beyond which redemption is next to impossible.* The Queen's Chamber floor-level – clearly the pivot of the whole system – begs to be identified as a *level of dawning or at least potential reintegration.* And the half-height of the summit-platform – the vertical mid-point of the Pyramid as built – seems to stand for the *level of emergence or transcendence.*

The level corresponding to one-third of the height of the finished Pyramid, meanwhile – which of course marks the actual centre of gravity of the whole edifice as designed – suggests itself as the *level of perfect balance and integration,* while the top of the fiftieth course of masonry clearly has some special significance in connection with its course-number (see *5, 10 and Factorisation* below).

1881.2 P″

In the light of *Levels* (above) and the diagram, this distance would seem to represent some kind of *quantum-leap of consciousness.*

Limestone, granite

Since virtually the whole earth-symbolising Pyramid is built of local limestone, the latter's meaning begs to be identified as *materially orientated or physical*: the expensively imported granite, on the other hand, is found only in the Granite Plug and the King's Chamber Complex, and therefore seems to have a meaning that in some sense both stands apart from and goes beyond the purely physical. Defining such a meaning is not a task which normal words are, of course, designed to perform. Even the obvious word 'spirit' has in practice acquired an aura of 'thingness', and thus of ersatz materialism about it. I therefore suggest *supraphysical or hyperconsciousness.* (The apparent grammatical indeterminacy is, it seems, perfectly in order, since the various code-features seem to partake more of the nature of Chinese ideograms than of English parts of speech.)

Square/rectangle, circle

As for *limestone* and *granite,* since the only circular references are within the King's Chamber Complex (see lower diagram page 60), and all the main passages which lead to it are rectangular in cross-section.

Major chambers

As simple inspection of the diagram suggests – and especially in view of the proposed chronographical interpretation – *ages of culmination.*

Minor chambers

In the light of their positions in the passage-system, *stages preparatory to culmination.*

Airshafts

Since the dead need no air, apparently *pathways of life,* possibly connected with some kind of emergence.

Portcullises

Evidently *interventions on the part of hyperconsciousness,* since they occur only in the granite King's Chamber Complex.

35.76 P″

This measurement always occurs further on in the *limestone* passageways than the measurement *286.1 P″*, and is likewise a direct function of the built Pyramid's reduced dimensions (see diagram page 141): consequently some such meaning as *physical result* suggests itself.

8

Since 35.76 is exactly one-eighth of 286.1, *8* would seem to have an associated meaning: possibly *result or manifestation.*

6

With the unfinished Pyramid and the 'non-final' King's Chamber (there are, after all, five more chambers above it) both having eight corners and six sides (including the base), *6* seems to mean *imperfect or incomplete,* or even *preparatory.* *8 × 6,* in other words, stands for *manifestation of incompleteness* (see *multiplication* below).

5

The number of sides and corners of both the finished Pyramid as a whole and the capstone which is needed to complete it. Hence, *perfection, completeness.* Possibly – in view of the well-known solar symbolism attached by the Egyptians to their capstones – even *illumination* or *enlightenment.*

7

The number of surfaces of both 'final' chambers – i.e. the Queen's Chamber and the gabled, topmost 'Construction Chamber' in the King's Chamber Complex. Not, however, a function of the finished Pyramid's exterior. Hence *inner or psychic culmination or perfection,* or the circumstances capable of producing it.

10

While this number is characteristic of the King's and Queen's Chambers, it seems to have direct scalar links. Hence *age,* possibly *of culmination.*

4

As for *square/rectangle.*

Pi (π)

As for *circle.*

19

Death (compare chapter 2 above).

29.84 P"/37.995 P"

Both measurements are, like the number *19,* direct functions of the death-symbolising Descending Passage's interaction with the external, earth-symbolising masonry (see diagram p. 183). Hence *physical death.*

41.21 P" (two royal cubits)

The width of all the (rectangular) main passageways: thus, presumably *mortality, physicality, earthly experience.*

33.5 P"

Subsequent inspection reveals that this measurement normally occurs only in conjunction with features of the passageways indicative of sudden change or progress towards integration: hence, *transformation or transformer.*

Factorisation

Apparently a legitimate procedure for establishing the meaning of larger numbers and measurements by reference to smaller, known quantities (see +, −, ×, ÷ below). Rather akin to the dictionary's defining of 'difficult' words in terms of 'easy' ones.

+, −, ×, ÷
Plus and minus seem to have their usual meaning. × can usually be rendered by its familiar equivalent *of* (occasionally *times*). ÷ seems to indicate *by, through* (i.e. the idea of an *agent*).

Tolerances
The standard procedure seems to be to *round down* fractions, rather than round them up. In other words it is the number of *whole inches* that counts. The main exception to this policy seems to be the distance 37.995 P″, which is altogether too close to 38 P″ (i.e. 2 × 19) to admit of any other interpretation in the circumstances of its first appearance in the passage-masonry (see diagram page 183).

Once given the basic quantities listed above, it then becomes possible to elaborate a whole range of further code-meanings. Some of them are virtually self-evident purely from an inspection of the passage layout. Others – such as *1, 2, 11* and *13* – only become apparent as it were by default, once the rest of the readout has been established. What clarifies the various code-meanings more than anything else, however, is the simple technique of factorisation, as explained above.

Thus, further light is thrown on the meaning of the number *10* by the fact that it is equivalent to *2 × 5*. Once the distance *1881.2 P″* is rounded down (as the code permits) to 1881, it turns out to equal *9 × 19 × 11*. And *286.1 P″*, rounded down to 286, comes out at *2 × 11 × 13*.

There are few features of the Pyramid, in fact, on which this particular procedure fails to throw considerable light – a point which tends to add weight to the view that its designer did indeed have in mind a symbolic code such as I have suggested.

Which might, of course, account for the fact that the perimeter of the present summit-platform is 286.1 P″ *too short* for the final capstone, whose base-perimeter is clearly designed to measure 2288.8 P″. The capstone – the symbol of the building's (and thus our planet's) ultimate perfection – can thus be installed only when the Pyramid has been extended to its full dimensions.

In place of the characteristic human *loss of balance and harmony*

(−286.1 P″) reflected in the current state of Planet Earth, in other words, a new world-order (reflected in the capstone) is destined to arise whose basis is the *regaining of inner integration*, and whose nature is the very *manifestation* of it ($2288.8 = 8 \times 286.1$).

On the face of it, a tall order. It is difficult to imagine quite how such an obviously Utopian state of affairs could possibly be achieved. And perhaps that is precisely why the designer, his code established, apparently goes on to spell out his route-map in the Pyramid's interior.

9
Blueprint for Destiny

Base your code on 'religious' language, and some kind of 'religious' readout necessarily results. Determine in advance that your interpretation is going to be a pyramidological one – i.e. one which interprets the features of the Pyramid's passage-system in terms of a historical blueprint for humanity – and that is the kind of interpretation that you are likely to get.

My earlier readout in *The Great Pyramid Decoded* was, for reasons that I have already explained, just such a readout. In particular, its language was undeniably religious. Thus, to one initial preconception a whole lot of others were liable to be added just as soon as my readers clapped eyes on it.

But things do not necessarily have to be that way. Given the much more rigorous and non-committal code-reconstruction outlined in the last chapter, and set out in full in Appendix B, it is perfectly possible to summarise the main features even of my earlier readout in terms that determinedly refuse to beg the familiar questions.

And the historical 'fit' which results is quite good enough to suggest that the pyramidological approach is far from inappropriate.

It goes without saying, however, that it is for the reader alone to decide whether mere appropriateness is enough to qualify any given conclusion as the 'right' answer, let alone the final and definitive one.

Even in such comparatively neutral terms, the initial scenario depicted by the Pyramid's internal symbolism is a depressing one. Humanity, it seems, is set on a downhill path, mortally imbalanced in favour of language and the intellect, beset by a materialistic form of consciousness that threatens to tear the familiar world apart and consign it to the trash-heap of cosmic history. Moreover – according to the Pyramid's chronograph at least – that has been the situation since at least 2141 BC. Possibly, indeed, it has been the case ever since 2623 BC and even earlier.

Such are the conclusions forced upon us by an analysis of the symbolic features of the entrance and of the first part of the De-

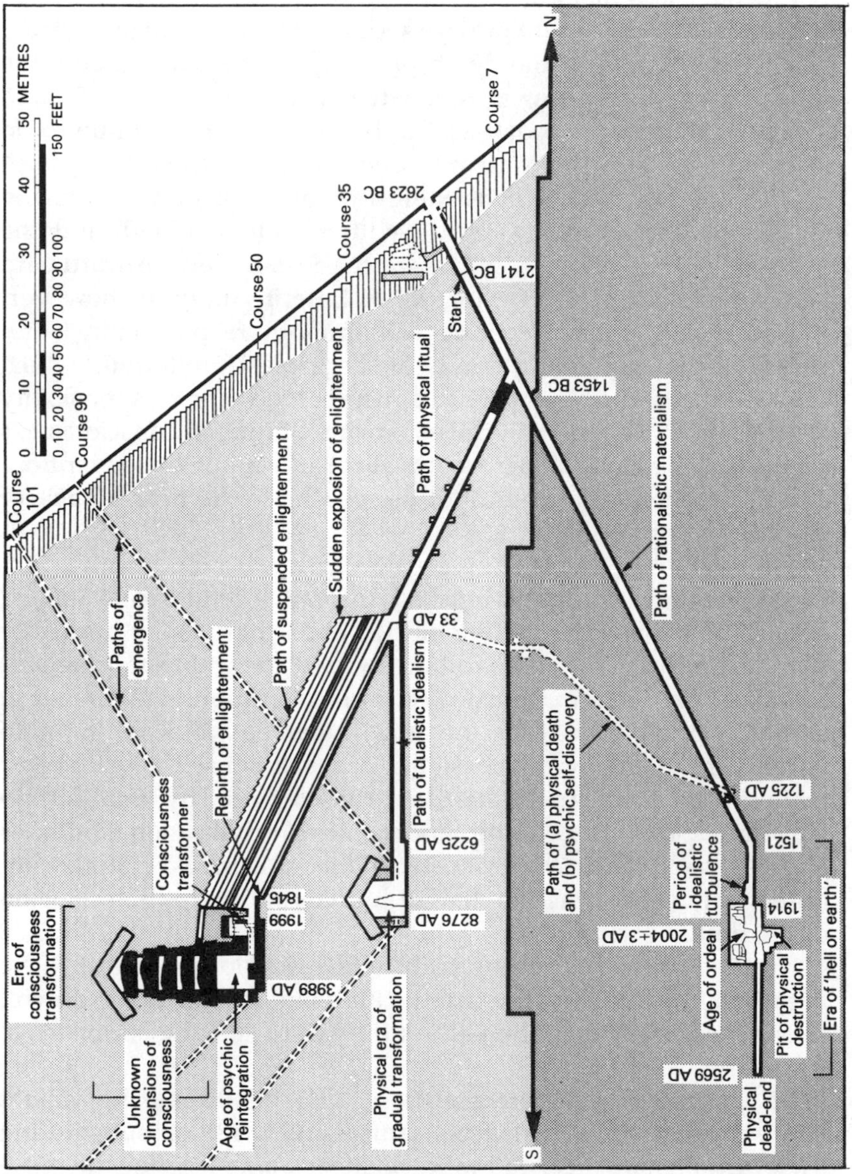

At-a-glance summary-chart of the Pyramid's prophetic blueprint for humanity.

scending Passage. (Compare the diagrams on page 183 and overleaf).

To this extent, then, the view of the Pyramid's designer is in tune with that of other ancient traditions – and notably the Hindu one, which sees mankind as having undergone some kind of 'fall from grace' at some point prior to 3000 BC. To that event (associated by the tradition with the death of the god Krishna) it traces the dawning of a dark age, or Kali Yuga, which is said still to hold sway over humanity today and to be destined to continue to do so for at least a further four hundred thousand years.

The Pyramid, however, is more optimistic, if only marginally so. In the spring of 1453 BC – so the 'Hidden Lintel' and the beginning of the Ascending Passage suggest – a new, upward path is destined to open up for mankind. Entering upon it, however, is conditional upon accepting a mammoth responsibility – represented by the 'taking down' of the triple Granite Plug which blocks the entrance to the new, upward slope. That responsibility involves nothing less than the expansion of human consciousness far beyond the limits of mere materialism and linguistic convention, and the eventual opening up of the psyche to the near-miracle of its full inner potential.

Unsurprisingly, the offer is rejected. Instead of symbolically 'taking down' the three great granite blocks, even that part of humanity that does respond chooses to burrow past them through the surrounding *limestone* masonry. The human response to the stern demands of what I have termed the 'hyperconscious' is simply to circumvent them. For the possibility of real inner self-development mere *physical* acts are substituted. Truth is replaced by ritual, knowledge by dogma. And in the process human civilisation continues to slide even further into its morass of rationalism and materialism, obsessively cultivating one half of human nature to the exclusion of the other.

For the lower, descending path, which would, in symbol, have been finally blocked by the Granite Plug had it been 'taken down', remains open. And so the path of humanity actually bifurcates at this point.

On the one hand there are those who, while making valiant efforts to rediscover their true nature, still insist on substituting irrelevant physical acts and rationalistic explanations for the nitty-gritty of acquiring real self-knowledge. On the other hand there are those souls – conceivably more honest – who simply see the physical and the rational as the only reality, and act accordingly.

But what historical developments could possibly correspond to this strange prediction of a time of human endeavour and schism during the fifteenth century BC? What human race or group was actually to embark on a new path of self-discovery at this time – a path characterised by ritual acts rather than true self-searching, by clever ideas rather than gut realities, by a willingness to change anything and everything as long as it was not actually themselves?

Curiously enough, there were several.

In India, for example, this was the period when the celebrated *Vedas* were being written down for the first time. Ostensibly concerned with the ritual propitiation of a whole pantheon of nature-gods – though in fact equally concerned with the universal task of inner self-realisation – this vast collection of texts, which lies at the very basis of the Hindu scriptures, seems to betray a subliminal awareness in its authors that man had, in a sense, sacrificed nature – both inner and outer – to his way of life. To redress the balance, therefore, he must now in turn sacrifice his way of life to nature.

The thought is logical enough in its way. The proposed price, however, was clearly too great. Logic, after all, would seem to demand some kind of total sacrifice, yet the early *Vedas* appear – on a superficial level, at least – to lay more stress on a whole range of ritual sacrifices which are to be performed instead. In myriad ways and forms, food and drink and even livestock must be offered on the fire. The whole Hindu way of life, indeed, was to be turned into a kind of sacred rite, its every aspect subjected to minutely prescribed ritual restraints. And so, for the total reform of consciousness which was really at stake, a plethora of symbolic acts was substituted in practice, by the masses at least. The fundamental reality of man's growing inner imbalance and his lack of attunement to the universe around him was altered, consequently, scarcely one iota.

But this attitude to reality is precisely the one apparently predicted for the period in question by the Great Pyramid. And even during the Vedic period itself, an awareness seems to have grown up that it was a far from satisfactory one. Increasingly it came to be seen that the ancient gods were no more than ritual masks imposed upon a single, underlying reality. Increasingly, too, the realisation arose that man himself was also a direct function of that reality. As the later Upanishadic commentaries on the *Vedas* were to put it, reality was one: it was only man's ignorance that divided it. And if the knowledge of that reality was to be regained, the living-out of that reality re-achieved, then man must commit himself to a new quest for inner wholeness.

In India, then, the Vedic period was characterised not merely by ritualism, but also by a growing movement towards a form of monotheism. In this, the terms and concepts used were, very naturally, mainly religious in character. The oneness of reality became reflected in the doctrine of the One God. But we should not let this blind us to the fact that it was human consciousness itself that was really the point at issue.

Such developments were not confined to India. In contemporary Egypt, a discontented subject-race of Semitic extraction seems to have come up with a set of almost exactly parallel ideas at about the same time. Led by an Egyptian-trained activist of a prophetic cast of thought – one Mosheh, or Moses – the Middle-Eastern tribes now known to us as the Israelites were likewise smitten with a sudden urge to reject the resplendent Egyptian pantheon in favour of a single deity. In ascribing to this deity a name which apparently meant 'I am', they too seem to have acknowledged that the ultimate reality was in no way separate from the root of their own being. Yet they too responded to the challenge of this new mode of awareness by merely setting up a kind of ritual code-book, known to them as the *Torah* or Law, and corresponding to the first five books of the familiar Bible.

Like the Vedic code, this was a manual of conduct which imposed ritual restraints on almost every aspect of life. At best, therefore, it represented a set of half-measures, as the later Jesus of Nazareth was himself to point out. Yet the Israelites were quick to observe that the more wholeheartedly they entered into the spirit of the thing the more things seemed to flow their way. There were clear advantages to be gained, in other words, even from such half-hearted attempts to re-attune to the will of the universe.

Yet it was not easy to carry through this would-be revolution of consciousness within the conservative atmosphere of ancient Egypt. Still obsessed as it was with its ancient hierarchies of gods, Egypt, under the dead hand of its priestly bureaucracy, was agonisingly slow to respond to change. It would be some eighty years before the heretic-king Akhenaten would feel able to institute his own monotheistic, solar religion of love. And by then it would be too late. The tide of psychic evolution would have passed Egypt by. The reaction would be both violent and final.

To Moses and his Israelites, therefore, a wholesale exodus from Egypt seemed the only answer. The final revolution of consciousness must be carried through in the ancestral fastnesses of Canaan. And so the long trek duly started.

Various dates have been proposed for this event. Traditionally, the Exodus is put somewhere in the latter half of the thirteenth century BC. Yet a date as late as this is difficult to square either with the existing documentary or archaeological evidence. Excavations at Jericho have made it quite clear, as we have seen, that the completion of the Exodus – if it took place as described in the Hebrew scriptures at all – cannot have occurred later than 1400 BC. This dating would accord very satisfactorily with the apparent prediction of the Great Pyramid. Rutherford, indeed – putting on his hat as an expert Bible chronologist – seems to make a cast-iron case for an Exodus beginning in the year 1453 BC. In which case, since the date of the Exodus is firmly linked by the text with the date of the first full moon after the spring equinox, the actual date of departure can be easily determined. The Exodus began on the morning of 30 March 1453 BC – the exact date apparently pinpointed by the Great Pyramid's architect.

Coincidence it may be. Sheer inspiration may have been at work. Yet in view of Moses' known Egyptian training, inside knowledge of the Great Pyramid and its message cannot be entirely ruled out. Especially when we consider that the semi-legendary crossings of both 'Red' Sea and Jordan apparently took place (as I have demonstrated in *The Great Pyramid Decoded*) exactly on the 'sunrise-line', marked out in advance by the Great Pyramid's own passage-angle (compare the diagram on p. 123). Not to mention the fact that there is an odd similarity between the handing down of the stone Tables of the Law on Mount Horeb and the symbolic necessity within the Great Pyramid of 'taking down' the three massive blocks of the Granite Plug before entering the Ascending Passage . . .

In due course, then, the Israelites, bearing with them those same sacred stones, went on to set up a new, ritually ordered society in their new Promised Land.

Just as, some two or three hundred years earlier, a similarly sunrise-orientated group from the Welsh Presely Mountains had already migrated a similar straight-line distance to their new cultural centre on Salisbury Plain, bearing with them the sacred bluestones that were to form the nucleus of Stonehenge . . .

Of the beliefs and way of life of the people of that earlier, northern culture we know next to nothing. They were to leave us no written records such as have come down to us from the ancient Hindus, the Egyptians and the Hebrews. But it is perhaps a fairly safe assumption that their reaction, too, to the realisation of their society's growing out-of-tuneness with the natural universe – and with the true inner nature of man himself – was to take refuge in ritual acts, in the propitiation of some imagined god 'out there'. Anything, once again, rather than the total revolution of consciousness which – whether they were fully aware of it or not – the restoration of man's long-lost wholeness actually demanded.

And in this they, too, would have been acting in total accord with the apparent predictions of the Great Pyramid.

I have gone into some detail on the question of the possible links between the Pyramid's message and actual events during the fifteenth century BC, and not without good reason. Pyramidology's would-be 'historical' interpretation, after all, needs to be assessed carefully.

In the event, the fit seems to be a remarkably close one – even if (almost inevitably in view of the period) it is very much a function of religious, rather than overtly psychological events. How far, then, can the same be said of what appear to be the Pyramid's subsequent predictions?

After the events of 1453 BC the Ascending Passage seems to have little to tell us (apart from possible indications of critical periods during the early eighth, sixth and fourth centuries before Christ) until the year 2 BC. At this point, however, the passage's floorline cuts the Queen's Chamber floorline – which we have already identified as the 'plane of dawning reintegration'. Moreover, 33.5 P″ later (on 1 April AD 33, to be precise) it enters the Grand Gallery. At the same moment the roof-height suddenly increases by 286.1 P″.

In the light of the proposed code, the implications are inescapable. The advent of some kind of transformer (and/or transformation) has succeeded in turning even the Ascending Passage's path of limited progress into an avenue of dawning psychic reintegration and wholeness. This figure (or initiative) seems to be symbolised specifically by a particularly noticeable triangle in the geometry of the passageway's side-elevation – a triangle which seems, astonish-

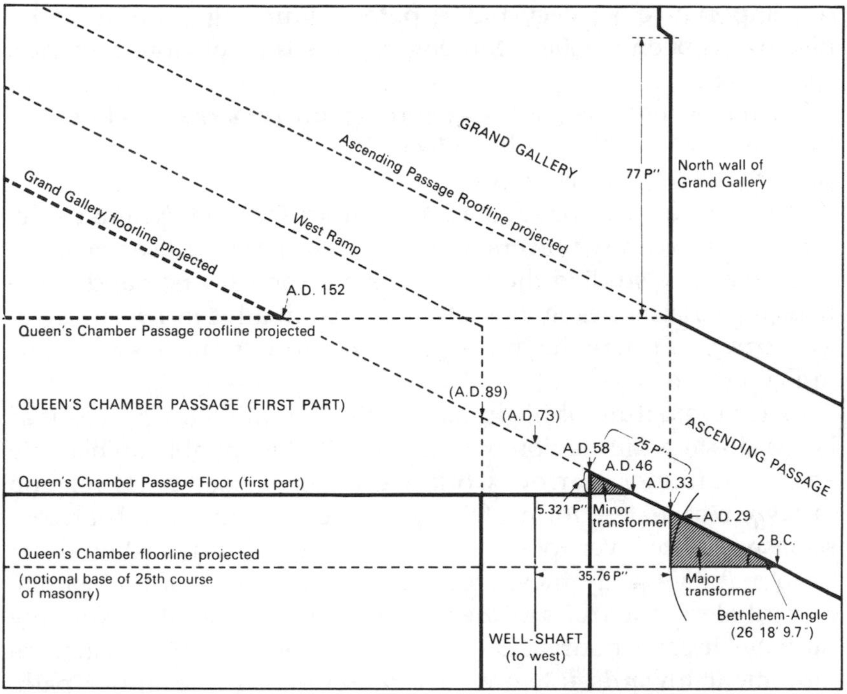

The crux of the matter. The intersection of the Pyramid's upper passageways depicts in intricate and interlocking detail mankind's arrival at the crossroads of consciousness at the very beginning of our era.

ingly enough, to be directly described in the text of the familiar New Testament (compare *The Great Pyramid Decoded*, page 55).

The floorline continues for a further 25 P" before breaking off at the entrance to the Queen's Chamber Passage. Its last few inches mark out the hypotenuse of a second triangle which seems to symbolise a lesser transformer, or transforming initiative, between AD 46 and 58. The entrance to the Well-Shaft then opens up to the right, apparently indicating a period of death and destruction centred around the year AD 73 – though one whose effects are (as we shall see) likely to be of great potential benefit to those still following the downward path. And meanwhile the Grand Gallery, with its provision for a sliding floor half-way up its walls, and its roof of forty (or possibly 39) blocks, seems to speak of the 'suspended results of illumination' (or the 'suspended achievement of perfection') and of the transformation of humanity. . . .

With the entry into the Grand Gallery, clearly, some event of first importance has occurred. A potential turning-point in world-history has been reached. Moreover, there is an obvious historical correlation.

For the dates 2 BC to AD 33 correspond remarkably closely to those of Jesus of Nazareth. Indeed, Rutherford argues extremely cogently that the fit is *exact**.

In which case we have to assume either that the Pyramid's designer had uncanny powers of foresight or that Jesus' secret sponsors may have studied the Pyramid's message at first hand (compare my earlier investigation of the Jesus-initiative in *The Armageddon Script*). Certainly he in his turn is reported to have spent time in Egypt.

As for the nature of his initiative, the Pyramid clearly sees it as laying down a foundation of perfection that is capable of 'blasting apart' the former, narrow world-view of ritualised mass religion in favour of a new form of integrated consciousness. That consciousness, however, poses such a threat to the established order as to make virtually inevitable the physical death of its bearers. Nevertheless, the fruits of their achievement do not die. Not only do they directly nourish those as yet untouched by the general movement towards integration represented by the upper path; they themselves are only 'suspended'. In due course, in other words, the seeds which those fruits contain will sprout and bear fruit on their own account . . .

In all of which we may trace the story of the life and death of the early Nazarenes – as of their contemporaries, the early Christians – and the dire events that were to surround the Jewish revolt and genocidal Roman backlash which was to culminate in the sacking of Jerusalem in AD 70 and the Jewish mass-suicide at Masada in AD 73. And even the revisionistic activities of the apostle Paul – apparently the direct basis of the 'lower' path represented by the Queen's Chamber and its passage – seem to be foreshadowed in the Pyramid's masonry.

On the face of it, the proposition is preposterous. The whole

* The received tradition that Jesus was born in 4 BC is based on the idea that Herod the Great died in that year. Yet all the ancient historians actually deny this: the tradition seems to rest on a single, dubious translation of Josephus. As for the apparent paradox of Christ being born 'two years before Christ', the point needs to be re-emphasised that the present system of year-numbering – which started, by the way, not with the year nought but with the year one – was not proposed until the sixth century of our own era.

thing, surely, has to be coincidence?

Coincidence or not, however, we can only continue to 'read' the Pyramid's masonry in the light of the proposed code.

The next specific 'dating' within the passageways marks out the year AD 1223. It is the year when the original Descending Passage, as it bores down through the rock beneath the Pyramid, cuts the plane of the Great Subterranean Chamber roof – the level, as we interpreted it earlier, of 'death', darkness, despair and total lack of inner balance. At this point, in other words, the pigeons of linguistically orientated materialism start to come home to roost. Humanity's inner split reaches the point of psychosis. The state of undeclared civil war between man's physically based reason and intellect on the one hand and his long-suppressed emotions and intuitions on the other is liable to break out into the open, with the latter surfacing, if at all, mainly in warped and twisted forms, if not in actual conflict.

Quite how far this development can be linked with the typical religious psychoses of the Middle Ages is a matter for debate. Nevertheless, the passage now descends a further 286.1 P″ (on its eastern side at least) before reaching rock-bottom. And at this point the even more constricted Subterranean Chamber Passage starts its horizontal journey towards the south, the events it portrays apparently being a direct result of the total lack of balance and wholeness already symbolised by this part of the passage-system.

The junction between the two passageways actually suggests some kind of 'sliding fit'. Yet the dates represented by the intersections of the various roof- and floorlines are not much in doubt. The new era of imbalance and linguistic materialism finally gets into its stride between AD 1440 and 1521.

Once again, then, we need to establish what was actually happening world-wide between 1223 and 1521 – and in particular what was especially crucial about the last eighty years of the period. How far were language and materialism, human conflict and the war between reason and deeper intuition its characteristic trademarks?

The answer has to be 'very considerably'.

In contemporary China, for example, this period marked the beginning of the early modern period of Chinese history. It saw the development of political parties, the invention of paper money and of printing with movable type, the production of encylopaedias, the institution of civil service examinations and a heyday in the arts and sciences. At the same time it saw the invention of rockets, flame-throwers, bombs, grenades and early forms of musket and cannon – all of which would be used in connection with the bloody invasion of the Mongols under Genghis Khan in the thirteenth century.

Truly an age both of war and of benevolent materialism, with the latter in particular closely underwritten by language and linguistic techniques.

A similar situation prevailed in Japan. Here again the civilised arts flourished in the midst of a bloodbath of dynastic wars which were to give rise to the celebrated class of *samurai*, or feudal knights.

In India, too, this was a period of endemic warfare, made all the more ferocious and uncomprehending by the addition of a religious dimension. The Indian wars between Muslims and Hindus were mirrored in the West by the so-called Crusades – equally fanatical wars between Muslims and knightly Christians over the suzerainty of Palestine.

Yet in Europe particularly the experience was not all loss. The returning Crusaders brought home with them not only a rash of fresh ideas and outlooks, but the knowledge of a whole range of new techniques – not least those involved in the making of paper, the magnetic compass, the sternpost rudder, the foot-operated loom and the spinning-wheel. As a result, the foundations were laid for a dramatic improvement in Western material well-being over the next couple of centuries.

As the Muslim Saracens faded from the picture, however, the Christian Church turned its attention to imagined enemies nearer home. There were anti-heretical crusades and massacres; the Dominican Order and the Court of the Holy Inquisition were set up to preserve the purity of the Faith (which meant, in effect, the integrity of its linguistic formulae and dogmas). And the politicians, not to be outdone, embarked on a whole series of dynastic and territorial wars, notably in the case of the Hundred Years' War between France and England.

And then came the Renaissance.

Perhaps the most characteristic aspect of this extraordinary rebirth of learning and culture was the return to written sources. As a result, contemporary humanity suddenly rediscovered the scholarship and scholastic methods of classical times. Linguistic rationalism soon ruled supreme. In no time a similar approach was being applied to the scriptures themselves. The result was the religious revolution that we now know as the Reformation, and the birth of a form of Christianity which, in 1521, finally dubbed itself 'Protestantism'. What fuelled the spread of such typically Renaissance ideas more than anything else was the re-invention in Germany of the oriental technique of printing with movable type. This occurred in 1440.

From 1440 to 1521, then – these are exactly the dates pinpointed by the Great Pyramid's chronograph as the crucial dates for the culminating phase of humanity's general descent into language-based materialism. And just in case it should be objected that this was a purely European development, it should be remembered that it was from this time that Europe started to export its culture and habits of thought world-wide, to the point where they are nowadays almost universally taken to be synonymous with the very idea of civilisation. From this point on, European concerns were to become world concerns, European crises world crises – indeed, in our own times, European wars world wars.

The results are detailed with awful precision in the Subterranean inset itself. The new, constricted passage – only 35.76 P″ wide – leads first to a small antechamber characterised by an apparent 'roof-fall' carefully sculpted into the limestone rock beneath the Pyramid, and opening to the right. A time, it would seem, of idealistic physical turbulence and disorder between 1767 and 1848.

And so, indeed, it was to prove to be – for this period encompasses the American War of Independence, the French Revolution, the Napoleonic Wars and the 1848 'Year of Revolutions', when country after European country overthrew its rulers in the name of freedom and social justice. Not only that – it was also the period, in the arts, of idealistic Romanticism. And even in the religious sphere it was the time when the various European Bible Societies took upon themselves the truly idealistic task of evangelising the entire world as a prelude to the dawning of the Kingdom.

The Subterranean Passage continues, until, at a point corresponding to the summer of 1914, the floorline breaks off, to plunge headlong into the chaotic nightmare of the Great Subterranean Chamber, the ancient Egyptian Chamber of Ordeal.

The beginning of Hell on Earth – that, at least, is how the Pyramid seems to portray this period. Certainly it marks the end of everything that has gone before. As, indeed, it very largely was. Not merely in the matter of the First World War, which put an end to almost all the ancient European dynasties and changed the former political map of Europe for ever. As a further result of that war, for example, a whole generation of European fathers was virtually wiped out, so upsetting the masculine aspect of the handing-on of society's traditional wisdom and habits of thought. At the same time the war itself had cast serious doubt upon the whole system of ethics and values of the societies and social classes which had brought it to pass. Henceforth, in consequence, not even the most everyday assumptions would be above suspicion. Meanwhile, advances in military and medical technology had also had the most profound of unforeseen effects – not the least of which, on the medical front at least, was the fuelling of a massive world population explosion.

Yet other changes were also afoot. Reversals of values were also occurring elsewhere. Not only were there revolutions in China (1911) and Russia (1917); science, too, was undergoing a revolution at the hands of the young Einstein, while in the mind of Adolf Hitler were already germinating the seeds of the pseudo-occult dreams of German world domination which were to plunge the world into a second holocaust before even half the century was through.

But the Pyramid hints at other, quite separate developments at this time. For the summer of 1914 is indicated in the *upper* passageways, too – at the top end of the Grand Gallery. By this time, it seems, the 'suspended results' of the former illumination are ready to come back into physical play. Human transformation is once more in the air. Indeed, the symbolism of the Great Step, 35.76 P″ high, suggests that it has been in the air ever since 1845.

So, with the year 1933, a great concentration of transformative influences starts to make itself felt as humanity enters the King's Chamber Passage. At the same moment there are signs of the presence of a strange 'anti-transformer' between 1933 and 1944 – a possible reference, it has been suggested, to Hitler himself, with his distorted version of the ancient messianic vision of world-integration (compare diagram page 202). And the rest of the King's Chamber Complex has necessarily to refer to our own times and our immediate future destiny.

Sudden hyperconscious influences behind the scenes from late 1985 onwards; the foundation of a new world-order based exclusively on supraphysical considerations from early 1999; direct intervention on the part of hyperconscious forces in October 2039 (after clear advance warning in late 2034), and again in 2134, 2264 and 2394. . . . Such are the events apparently foreshadowed by the onset of the Antechamber's granite ceiling and floor, and by its four portcullises. Whether or not, with the religious, we choose to interpret these events in messianic and millenarian terms, extraordinary developments are certainly afoot.

Meanwhile, in the Great Subterranean Chamber, humanity has been staggering from crisis to crisis, with major setbacks during the years immediately after 1971, and further, if slightly lesser, ones after 1977. The oil crisis of the seventies and the trade recession of the early eighties spring immediately to mind. Then comes the Big Crunch – the virtual collapse of materialist civilisation and its rationalistic assumptions shortly after 2004 (2007 currently seems to be the most likely date), as humanity tumbles headlong into the Great Subterranean Chamber's 'bottomless pit'.

The awful experience, it seems, is not without its positive side. As a result of it there is a new search for worthwhile values, a lurch in the direction of wholeness and reintegration. More than enough progress is made in this respect, in fact, to restore mankind's long-lost inner balance. Indeed, there is a distinct risk of *over*balancing in the direction of the deeper aspects of the psyche – aspects which 'civilised' man has neglected for so long that he has largely forgotten how to handle them. So he is particularly liable at this stage to fall prey to hot-headed emotionalism and misleading forms of pseudo-spirituality. Yet even these are signs that a quantum-leap of consciousness is in the air – a real inner revolution capable of saving 'lower path' humanity from a fate worse than death.

For, by climbing to the far western end of the Chamber – which lies well beyond the Pyramid's centre-line – humanity can, in symbol, regain the level of its roof and so gain entry into the rough, and thus 'undated' lower end of the Well Shaft. This (thanks to the great consciousness-transforming initiative of the beginning of our era) has been awaiting such an eventuality, only just above that critical level, for the past two thousand years. Emerging from its top end, those who choose to take advantage of it can – even at this late stage – rejoin the upper path which the mass of their symbolic ancestors rejected as long ago as the fifteenth century BC . . .

And if not? Well, even physically orientated humanity is destined to climb out of the pit eventually. By the late 2050s, civilisation is recovering. By the 2080s it has reached more resplendent levels than ever before. Yet its path becomes ever more narrow and constricted. The so-called Dead End Passage is 29.8412 P″ wide *and* high. Death, it seems, is the order of the day, and nothing more is heard of this path after the year 2569.

On the topmost path, meanwhile, 'hyperconscious' humanity has been going from strength to strength. The final road to reintegration begins in 2499, the King's Chamber's culminating era of supraphysicality and living wholeness in 2989. And, by 3989, emergence into other dimensions of experience entirely, while the planet itself is restored to its primordial wholeness . . .

At the same time the followers of the Queen's Chamber complex's rather lower path continue to pursue their more physically orientated destiny – the natural continuation of the Ascending Passage's path of fixed religious and social ritual – until they, too, achieve a measure of emergence and completeness with at least some basis in hyperconsciousness between 2279 and 3279, or – and this seems more likely – between AD 7276 and 8276.

With this the Pyramid's apparent historical blueprint, if not actually humanity itself, comes to an end.

10
Touchstone of the Psyche

Such, then, in its barest outline, is my own revised version of the 'historical' type of readout favoured by the Pyramidologists. It is an account whose accuracy in terms of past events may well seem impressive – though the reader is of course entitled to exercise a degree of scepticism, especially in respect of its would-be predictions for the future.

The point nevertheless has to be admitted that, if the Pyramid's designer *had* intended to leave the message that I have outlined (and specifically as detailed in my earlier book), and had chosen to express it in terms of the code proposed, then the almost inevitable result would be the Great Pyramid as we have it today.

So it seems that there may after all be something in the Pyramidologists' thesis – even if that something is not necessarily what they themselves have long supposed it to be. The Pyramid's design could indeed have some relevance to the destiny of humanity, even if interpreting that design as 'the Bible in stone' stretches belief altogether too far.

Yet while such a readout does seem to portray the historical route whereby humanity is destined to achieve inner harmony and thus planetary reintegration, it fails signally – or so it seems – to offer much in the way of actual practical advice, other than in describing the likely results of the various approaches depicted.

At this point, consequently, we are thrown back on the equally venerable tradition that the Great Pyramid's internal passageways were designed as a *system of initiation* – whether for the living in search of enlightenment, or for the dead in quest of immortality and union with the divine.*

That is not to say that the adoption of an 'initiatory' hypothesis immediately invalidates the 'historical' one. If the architect was

* There is, of course, no inherent contradiction between the two as far as the Pyramid is concerned. As we saw earlier, its symbolism makes no bones about describing the living themselves as in some sense synonymous with the dead.

able to predict the likely shape of human history, after all, then he presumably had to get his ideas from somewhere. While clairvoyance cannot be entirely ruled out, it seems much more likely that he based his conclusions on observations of known phenomena. And since it seems improbable that he could have had sufficiently detailed records of much earlier historical cycles to use as a basis (if indeed such cycles there ever were), it begins to seem much more on the cards that he based his 'historical' blueprint – surprising as it may at first seem – on *observation of the typical development of the individual*.

Psyche, in other words, is psyche. Whether individual or collective, it tends to follow a more or less fixed pattern of development – as indeed observation tends to confirm. For it is by no means difficult (as I have demonstrated in my book *The Cosmic Eye*) to trace within the history of human society itself, as within current events, precisely those stages of development – and in precisely the same order – that are undergone by each individual human being. Even the archetypal symbolisms and the dream-life of the individual are reflected with extraordinary exactness in the typical cultural manifestations of the human race *en masse*.

This would not account, of course, for what seems to be the 'historical' blueprint's extraordinary accuracy of dating. Possibly we should have to bring in an astrological element to account for this – though not necessarily in the sense of regarding celestial events as actually *causing* whatever happens on Earth. Universal synchronicity, in other words, might have a role to play. Yet the overall shape of collective human destiny still seems capable of being derived from a study of *individual* experience. In which case it would in no way be surprising to find that we can interpret the Pyramid's interior not merely as a collective blueprint, but as an individual one too.

This would, of course, help to explain the whole tradition that it was designed as a temple of initiation – a centre, in other words, where individuals could undergo in advance the formative experiences of life and so, by creative use of their imagination, speed up their own inner development to the point where they achieved a level of consciousness well in advance of that of their uninitiated contemporaries.

But if the Pyramid's passageways – or at least an analogue of them elsewhere in the vicinity – *were* used in this way, then we may well hope to discover within them not merely a descriptive route-map, but a good deal of practical advice as well. If so, the fact would be entirely apposite. For it is through the intimate and personal choices of individuals, and not through the mere mechanics of the collectivised decision-making processes which reflect them, that the shape of society is ultimately forged.

Reading the Pyramid as a 'house of initiation', in other words, could provide us with a source of invaluable inner guidance – guidance, moreover, of precisely the kind needed to help us discover our own inner wholeness and so contribute to the eventual healing of the strife-torn planet on which we live.

But on what basis can we read the Pyramid's interior in an individual sense? Can the code as reconstructed be applied more or less as it stands?

Unsurprisingly, perhaps, the answer seems to be 'Yes'. Only in the matter of dating does there need to be any reformulation.

The 'historical' readout, after all, covers thousands of years. The individual has only a few decades to play with. Simple observation, too, suggests that the inner developmental processes which take only a few years to mature within the individual take many millennia to come to fruition in the larger context of humanity as a whole.

Thus, while the scale-changes indicated by the various steps within the passageways still need to be taken into account, some kind of general scale-conversion will be needed.

How is this to be achieved?

Given that the entire passage-system is now to be seen as representing an individual life, two points can immediately be identified – its beginning and its end. Its beginning is presumably represented by the entrance, and its end by its furthest point. However, it is quite evident from the passage-diagram on p. 165 that we have no less than *three* 'furthest points' to choose from. Which of them, then, is to be regarded as the datum for our terminal measurement?

Looking at the datings proposed in the last chapter, it is clear that, as far as the historical chronograph is concerned, the Queen's Chamber offers the latest 'raw' dating. A simple glance at the passage-diagram, however, suggests that this is not the natural end-point of the passage-system. And indeed there is sufficient ambiguity about the Queen's Chamber datings themselves (see *The Great Pyramid Decoded*, p. 182) to confirm this impression. In the case of the other two passageways, however, there is absolutely no chronographical ambiguity. In which case the definitive 'end-point' has to be the south wall of the King's Chamber. This, indeed, seems appropriate when we consider that it is the obvious symbolic goal of the whole passage-system.

Physical life begins, then, at the entrance. It terminates at the south wall of the King's Chamber. So far, so good. But if we are to get any clear advice about what happens in between we are now going to need to put some figures on it.

It needs no genius, of course, to associate birth with point zero. Death, however, is a more tricky matter. What *is* the typical human life-span? Is there, indeed, such a thing?

Possibly there is not. The human life-span has certainly varied over the centuries with environmental conditions, just as it still varies across the world today. To that extent, we may regard the intended timescale in a fairly flexible light – which in turn would suggest that we should not be justified in assigning too much mathematical precision to any personal 'datings' we may glean from the passage measurements. Such figures as we arrive at should thus be regarded as average, or notional ages only.

On the other hand there is a long tradition that, as the Authorised Version of the ninetieth Psalm has it, 'the days of our years are threescore years and ten'. Moreover, it seems certain that the notion of a seventy-year lifespan was already an ancient tradition at the time this particular text was written (its authorship being traditionally ascribed to Moses himself). A fact which might mean that the 'seventy-year' tradition actually dates from at least as far back as the Israelite captivity *in Egypt*.

So that it is not entirely beyond the bounds of possibility that the idea was actually of Egyptian origin, and thus, perhaps, familiar to the Great Pyramid's ancient designer himself.

Be that as it may, the tradition does seem to offer us a reasonable working hypothesis – namely that the south wall of the King's Chamber represents the attainment of the notional age of seventy.

Comparing the 'individual' figures with the historical chronograph, we thus have to set a lifespan of seventy years against a 'planetary' chronograph of 6611 years (always remembering that there was never a year nought). This gives a ratio of one personal year to 94.44286 'world years', or roughly a quarter of an inch per day on the initial, sloping scale.

A possible alternative ought to be considered, however. Ninety four and a half primitive inches or so could be seen as a rather odd distance to represent a year of personal time, given that it

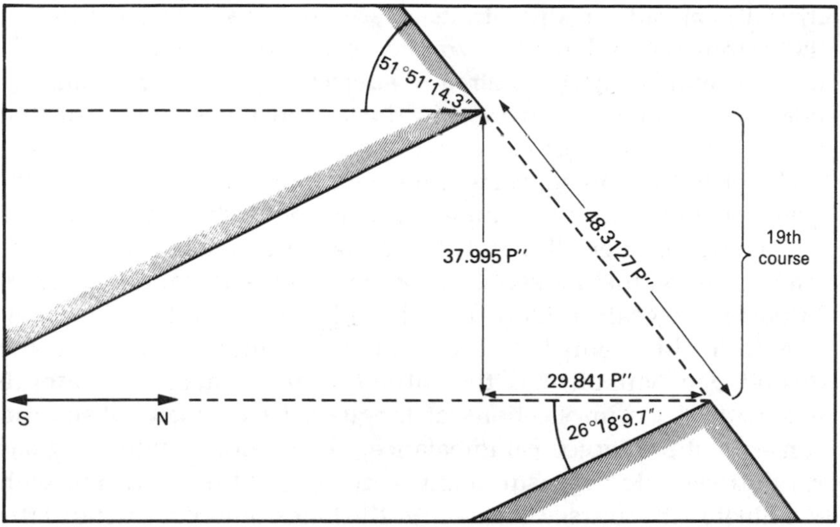

Symbolic features of the Entrance.

does not correspond to any ancient Egyptian measure, whether known or conjectured. The possibility cannot be excluded, therefore, that a *known* measure was intended – in which case the most likely distance seems to be 82.42636 P″, or four royal cubits. Applying this scale within the passageways would give a 'terminal' age of just over eighty, with each day equivalent to around a fifth of an inch in the sloping parts of the system. This, curiously enough, also ties in rather well with the biblical tradition, which goes on to consider the alternative possibility in the words: '. . . and if by reason of strength they be fourscore years . . .'.

Certainly the alternative scale seems reasonable enough for us not to rule it out of account entirely, and I therefore propose to quote between brackets the figures based on it in the course of the 'personal' readout which follows.

A readout which – it needs to be said in advance – has to stand or fall on its own terms (compare the code listed in Appendix B with the data set in Appendix F of *The Great Pyramid Decoded*), and owes nothing to received wisdom on the subject, whether conventional or otherwise. A readout, moreover, whose validity readers will ultimately need to assess for themselves in the light of their own experience.

On the face of it, the newborn child no sooner leaves the womb than it is already in dire straits. If we are to take the features of the entrance literally, the Pyramid seems to suggest not merely that the human infant is already subject to physical mortality (a not unreasonable assumption in the circumstances) but also that it is already fatally lopsided in favour of language and the intellect.

Closer inspection suggests, however, that to draw such conclusions is to jump the gun somewhat. The 'go'-mark in the Pyramid's passageways, after all, is not the entrance but the 'scored lines'. And these, on the 'personal' chronograph, mark a notional age of just over five years and one month (or five years and ten months). It is from this point, in other words, and not before, that the death-laden symbolism of the entrance starts to make its presence felt, with all its implications of language-based materialism and consequent psychological imbalance. The vertical height of 37.995 P″, the associated measurement of 29.841 P″, the overt link with the nineteenth course of masonry, the limestone construction, the

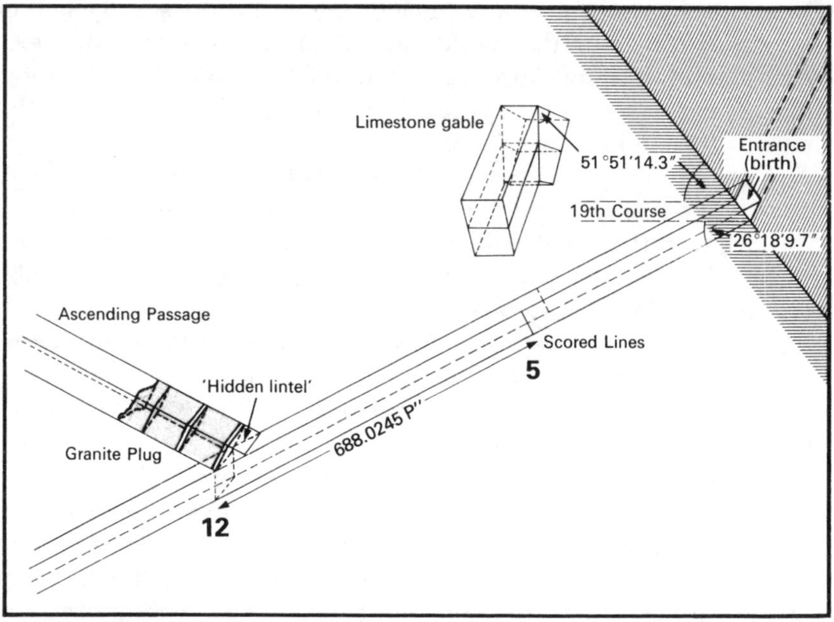

The message begins. Following a decline into language-orientated materialism from the age of five, a possible new path of extended consciousness opens up at the age of twelve. This diagram of the Descending Passage shows the double gable over the Scored Lines and the beginning of the Ascending Passage. Large figures refer to symbolic ages.

rectangular cross-section of the passage, the displacement of its centre-line 286.1 P″ to the east, or left, of the Pyramid's axis, the downward slope – all these factors point inescapably in the same direction.

At first sight, such pessimism in respect of a five-year-old may seem unwarranted. Yet it is an established fact that by the age of six most normal children have already acquired an almost total command of their mother-tongue's basic grammar and syntax, even if there is still much to learn in the matter of vocabulary and the finer shades of meaning.

By this point, in other words, the overall framework has already been laid for the child's subsequent understanding of the world. Henceforth he or she will see it exclusively in terms of the received linguistic categories of the mother-tongue. All other modes of perception are closed. Just as language itself is now experienced (consciously or unconsciously) exclusively in the image of the mother-tongue – i.e., in the case of English, as a playground of independent, yet interacting nouns and verbs conditioned by various types of qualifier – so the whole of reality itself is now divided up, functionalised and subjected to qualification along similar lines. And so the foundation is laid for the whole edifice of social conditioning which will ensure that the child is a faithful reflection of society's own assumptions and prejudices.

Henceforth, then, the child is potentially as 'dead' as the adults around it, and for the time being – so at least the Pyramid suggests – there is next to nothing that can be done about it.

Only at around the age of twelve (14) does a glimmer of light start to appear. For at this point – represented in the Pyramid by the beginning of the Ascending Passage – a path of potential integration starts to become available. It is theoretically possible at this stage (so the symbolism of the Granite Plug suggests) for the burgeoning adolescent to take on board all those aspects of consciousness which have hitherto been proscribed in the interest of social conformity. Moreover, doing so would effectively block the continuing personal decline into ever-increasing materialism based on linguistically orientated thinking.

Such a development, however, would run directly counter to the whole ethos of existing society. For obvious reasons, therefore, society cannot permit it. (The Pyramid's designer says as much by arranging for the Granite Plug to be immovably jammed into the

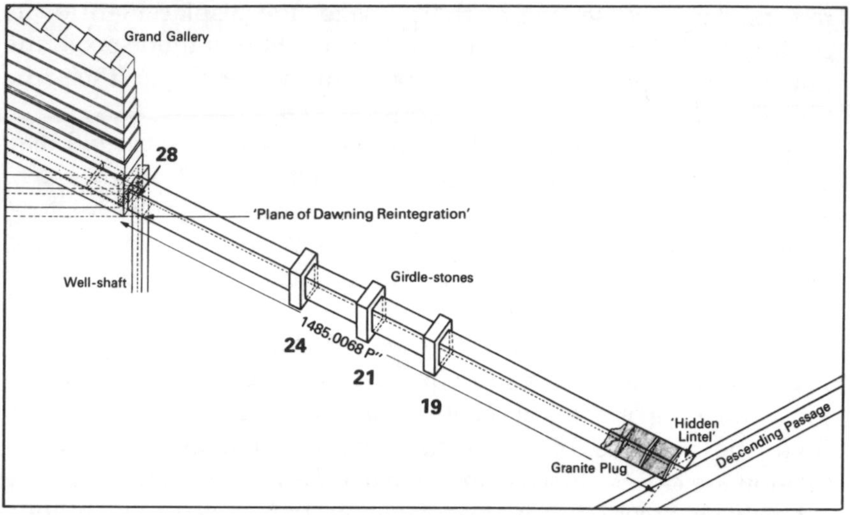

The Ascending Passage depicts the individual's struggle to achieve inner integration through mere ritual acts, starting from the age of twelve. Much against the odds, it seems, it may actually lead to a sudden burst of true illumination during the twenty-eighth year. Large figures refer to ages.

tapered lower end of the Ascending Passage.) So, with the whole weight of social convention stacked against him or her, the best the idealistic adolescent is likely to be able to do is to 'go through the motions' of entering the Ascending Passage.

As symbolised by the necessity of *burrowing around* the Granite Plug through the softer, limestone masonry, this amounts to the adoption of any one of a number of physical, linguistically orientated rigmaroles by way of a symbolic substitute for the real inner revolution which the circumstances actually demand. Conventionally, this might take the form of self-commitment to one of the world's religious orthodoxies. Alternatively, it might be reflected in the joining of some kind of idealistic youth-movement, or even in the adoption of a frankly anti-social stance. Either development, it seems, is a mere apology for what ought to be involved.

Yet even this half-hearted form of commitment to the neglected aspects of consciousness is not without its rewards.

For the path in question *does lead upwards*. There are signs (in the three great encircling Girdle Stones) of particularly encouraging developments at the ages of nineteen (22) and twenty-four (27), despite the intervention of a more difficult time at age twenty-one

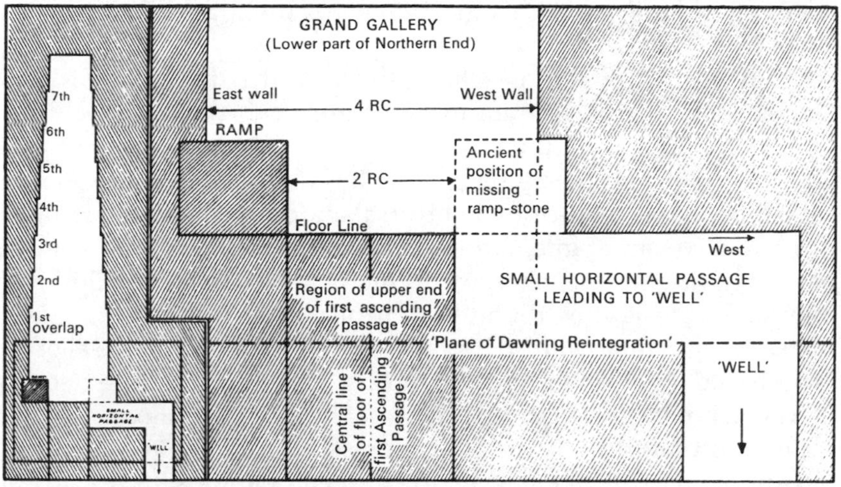

Cross-section of the lower end of the Grand Gallery looking southwards. Note the step and low tunnel leading to the top of the Well-Shaft.

(24-5). And by the twenty-eighth (32nd) year, thanks to a good deal of sheer hard work, a level is actually reached at which real integration can begin to dawn.

Provided the inner work is persisted with – symbolically for a further 33.5 P″ – a quite extraordinary personal transformation is then likely to follow within the year. Suddenly there is a virtual quantum-leap of inner integration, an unprecedented degree of balance and psychological wholeness. For a while even the individual's physical path becomes one of astonishing progress and perfection.

Yet this development – represented by the sudden rise of the roof-level and the subsequent 25 P″ of ascending floor at the lower end of the Grand Gallery – is too good to last. For fairly obvious reasons, it is by no means easy to maintain a truly integrated form of consciousness in the midst of conventional society, still less to live practically in accordance with it. There are conflicting interests, competing avenues of self-development. This juncture, in short, is in many ways a time of crisis.

The fact is reflected in the design of the passage-system at this point. To the right, the yawning pit of the Well-Shaft – its axis 35.76 P″ beyond the Grand Gallery's north wall – opens at the end of a low, limestone tunnel 20.6066 P″ high, which is entered via a *downward* step of the same height and so seems, paradoxically enough, to indicate both a move towards integration *and* physical death.

That death, indeed, is actually *based on* the discovery of inner wholeness, as the diagram makes quite clear: the one is a direct function of applying the other.

Straight ahead, meanwhile, there lies (in the limestone Queen's Chamber Passage) the possibility of abandoning the uphill struggle towards true inner integration in favour of resting on one's laurels and entering a long phase of formal stasis. Yet taking this path involves cutting the ground from beneath one's own feet, at least in so far as the upward path represented by the Grand Gallery is concerned – for entering the Queen's Chamber Passage necessitates removing a lengthy section of the Grand Gallery floor, so cutting off all further upward progress.

And so what is one to do? Accept the apparent self-destruction – the martyrdom, as it would seem – involved in a full-blooded right-turn in the direction of true integration at this point? Attempt to continue the upward struggle along the existing lines of received religion and/or idealistic forms of endeavour, despite an inevitably mounting sense of their irrelevance in the light of the direct personal illumination which is now beginning to dawn? Or play for safety by hanging on to what one has, while attempting to justify the decision in terms of conventional ideas of 'success' – despite the fact that doing so will effectively exclude the possibility of ultimately fulfilling one's own inner potential?

It is a difficult decision, and one that is likely to be taken more on the basis of unconscious personal proclivities than of a careful weighing of the likely consequences. Curiously enough, clear thinking is the one thing that *is* needed at this juncture – and it is, of course, always possible that the Pyramid's portrayal of the various options may help to promote it.

One way or the other, however, the decision has to be taken, and the Pyramid duly spells out the likely results.

Yet not before it has traced in graphic detail the results of *not* taking the upward path at the age of twelve (14) in the first place.

True, the Pyramid seems to have little or nothing to say about the *immediate* consequences, other than to portray the inevitable, continuing decline which results – the headlong descent into the materialism of a world ruled entirely by linguistic categories and the assumptions based on them. What it does indicate, however,

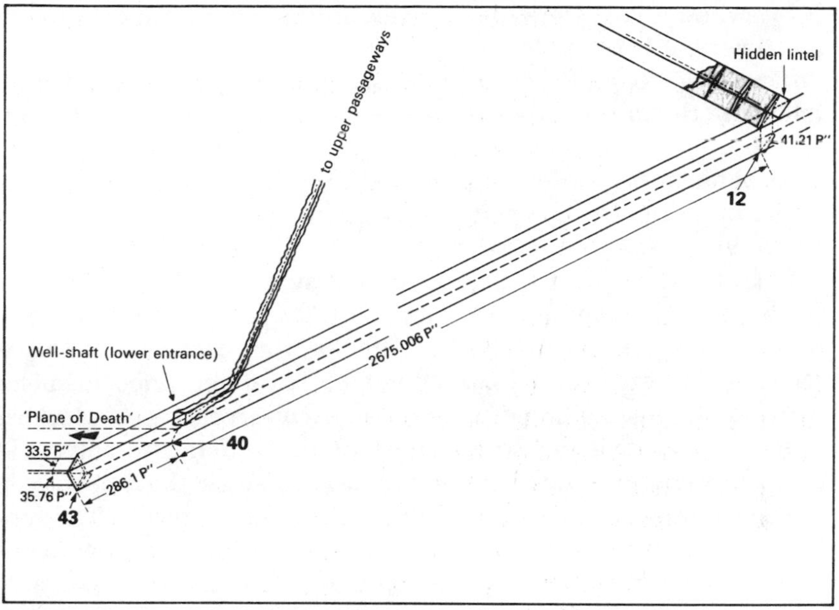

The individual's decline into language-based materialism continues, with 'rock-bottom' reached during the early forties. This truncated view of the Descending Passage shows the junctions with the Ascending Passage, Well-Shaft and Subterranean Chamber Passage.

is that the cumulative effects are likely to become critical by the age of around forty (46).

For at this point the descending floorline finally reaches the level of the Great Subterranean Chamber's roof, which we have already identified as the level of imbalance beyond which redemption is next to impossible. More than that, it continues down through it, finally reaching rock-bottom between the ages of forty-three (49) and forty-four (50).

From that event all sorts of dire consequences follow, but not only for those on this lowest of paths. We all have a physical and an intellectual aspect. We all use language. Moreover, it seems reasonable to suppose that the critical state of affairs symbolised by the Subterranean Passage is due not only to the particular form of consciousness involved, but also to the reaction between that form of consciousness and the individual's in-built psychological programming. Yet that programming applies to everybody. It is part of our common genetic inheritance. And so it is likely to apply *whatever the path chosen*.

Everybody, consequently, is likely to find this a critical time of life. Everybody is liable to experience to some degree the same difficult sequence of inner events. It is just that, to the individual following the lowest path, those events are likely to amount virtually to a life-and-death matter – involving, as they do, the very basis of his or her understanding of the world – whereas a follower of the higher pathways may see them in a very different light.

But what are those events?

Well, to start with there is the period symbolised by the Lesser Subterranean Chamber, with its carefully sculptured limestone 'roof-fall', which extends to the right of the passageway. Apparently it is a time of physical, linguistically determined idealism between the ages of forty-six (53) and forty-seven (54) – a forlorn attempt, it seems, to use left-hemisphere thinking to solve the problems which left-hemisphere thinking caused in the first place.

The Chamber's symbolism depicts the obvious result. The roof falls in. The whole initiative is destroyed by the very tools with which it has tried to attack the problem. The development may be encouraging to the extent that it suggests a certain awareness that something is wrong; but in terms of practical results it was always a non-starter.

Now there is worse to come. For at the notional age of forty-eight

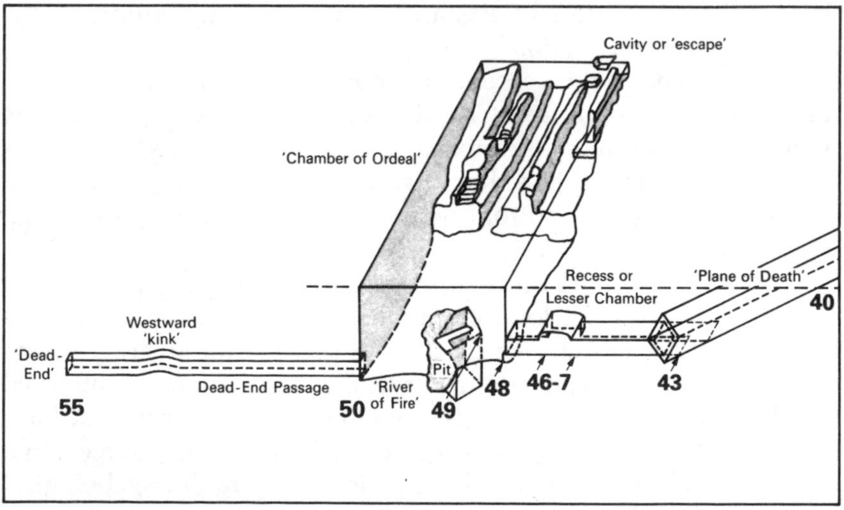

The Great Pyramid's subterranean complex depicts a period of some difficulty for the materially orientated, starting at age forty. The period between ages forty-eight and fifty seems to be marked out as especially critical.

(55) a thorough-going time of ordeal commences. Represented by the Great Subterranean Chamber itself, it is characterised by an initial period of minor 'ups and downs', followed first by two successive downturns and then by an almost total collapse at age forty-nine (56). A collapse, that is, into almost total lopsidedness and dissociation – even, perhaps, into psychosis and/or actual physical illness.

Yet the picture is not all gloom. For a start, a genuine effort at recognising what is happening and redressing one's inner balance may succeed in avoiding the worst effects of the collapse before it even begins. Evidently things do not have to go as far as psychosis and illness. Moreover the collapse itself (once it happens and if it happens) can help to bring about a drastic self-reappraisal. With everything apparently lost, after all, what else can there be to lose?

So it is actually in the very pit of deepest despair that real hope at last starts to dawn.

For the Chamber extends far to the west – further, in fact, than any of the Pyramid's other chambers, and certainly well beyond the Pyramid's centre-line. Turning to the right and mounting the gulley opposite the pit, one eventually comes within reach of roof-level. This time there is no roof-fall. Instead, sunk into the western wall, there is a small recess which apparently symbolises the lower end of the Well-Shaft.

Yet the *real* lower end of the Well-Shaft is to be found in the right-hand wall of the Descending Passage, just before the final descent through the so-called 'plane of death' – i.e. the level of the Great Subterranean Chamber's roof. Technically, in other words, it seems to apply to a time just before the age of forty (46). But the aperture is not a clean-cut doorway. Manifestly it is just a rough opening in the rock. The significance of this seems to be that it has no particular 'dating'. Instead, it refers only to a particular level – namely that of the Subterranean Chamber Roof.

The meaning seems to be this: thanks to whatever measure of integration the individual has managed to achieve at around the age of twenty-eight (32) in the conventional religious or idealistic sphere represented by the upper passageways – and, more specifically perhaps, thanks to whatever measure of integration *others* have managed to achieve at that age – a possible path of healing and integration is available to anybody who is prepared to turn to it (or indeed is forced to turn to it under the stress of physical events) during their passage through the 'valley of the shadow of

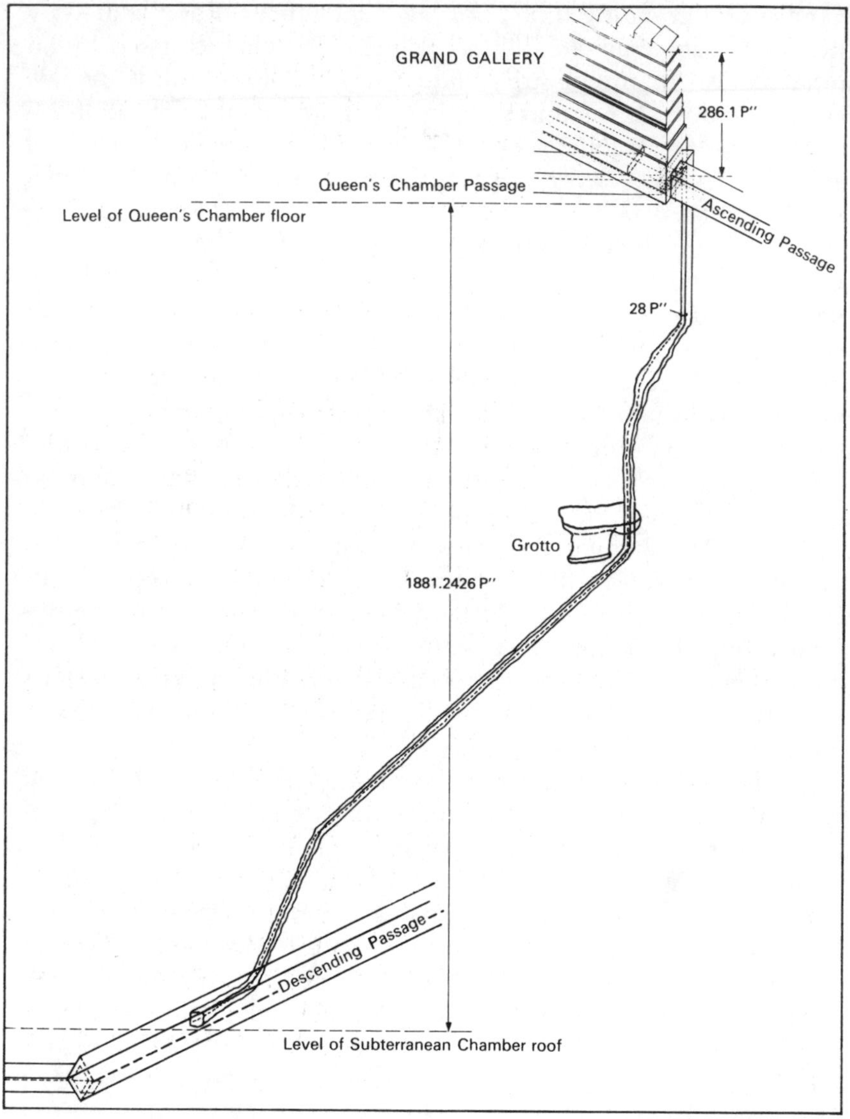

The tortuous Well-Shaft links the bottom end of the Grand Gallery to the lower end of the Descending Passage. It is bored not only through the bedrock but also through the lower courses of the Pyramid's masonry. Some distance above the natural 'grotto', however, it becomes a properly-constructed, square shaft culminating at Queen's Chamber floor-level in a low, horizontal tunnel originally terminating behind the Grand Gallery's western ramp. The lower entrance to the Well-Shaft comes just above the level of the Great Subterranean Chamber's roof.

death' of the Great Subterranean Chamber. In effect, anybody who is prepared to make the effort can, in symbol, regain in mid-life – and specifically during the late forties (mid-50s) – the point represented by the 'Crossing of the Pure Roads of Life' in the upper passageways (i.e. the bottom end of the Grand Gallery).

Even though it is likely to involve a total jettisoning of conventional wisdom and a corresponding – if temporary – imbalance in favour of the world of emotion and intuition.

But of course there is no absolute necessity to do so. Even the pit of despair is unlikely to last for ever. Healing of a sort will come. By the age of fifty (57) a good measure of physical and mental well-being is likely to be regained, even within the general context of imbalance towards the rational and material.

Yet there is no real future in this new lease of life. As the various features of the final Dead-End Passage suggest, it leads only to a restricted physical existence of virtual semi-consciousness up to the age of fifty-five (62), when the path represented by the passage finishes – or rather, simply stops. And while the measurements do not actually say that anybody following it will be dead by that age, they make it quite clear that he or she might as well be.

Although those who pass this way have the *physical* basis of perfection and planetary harmony within their grasp (the squared-off end of the limestone Dead-End passage is exactly the same distance from the entrance as the summit-platform is above the Pyramid's base), their state of chronic inner imbalance places the larger experience of cosmic oneness forever beyond them.

All of which suggests that whatever happens at the early age of around twelve (14) is of truly crucial importance for the rest of life, and that those responsible for bringing up the young have a critical responsibility for encouraging the development of a well-balanced outlook at this age. Emotions, intuition and the deeper aspects of awareness all need to be sensitively cultivated – not least, perhaps, through the arts – and not merely the physical body, the intellect and the largely social mask which we call the 'personality'. To neglect that responsibility is, in effect, to consign the children, and with them our own posterity, to hell on earth.

If then, our present world seems already to reflect that hell with almost unprecedented vividness, may we not see in that fact an apt commentary – if not an actual judgement – on our traditional forms of upbringing and education? And having seen, shall we not act?

11
Pathways to the Light

Yet Hell is not inevitable. Salvation can be achieved. To the bleak picture of personal gloom and despair that I have just been painting the upper passageways offer a much more encouraging alternative. Even by the age of twenty-eight (32), as we noted earlier, a positive explosion of genuine insight and illumination is likely to have occurred within anybody who has chosen to follow the uphill path of ritualised endeavour represented by the Ascending Passage. Yet this very development poses problems of its own – not the least of them being the practical question of what to *do* with that illumination.

One possibility, as we saw on p. 187, is represented by the Well-Shaft. It involves devoting oneself totally to this newly-discovered, all-inclusive mode of consciousness *whatever the consequences*. Yet the results of this course of action are likely to be personally disastrous. Conventional society, as we also noted above, cannot tolerate the practical application of such a revolution of consciousness within its midst. The two are, for obvious reasons, totally incompatible.

So, while the example and the recorded insights of anybody who *does* make such a commitment are likely to prove invaluable to others going through the familiar 'mid-life crisis', the experience is not one to be recommended as a developmental route for the individual twenty-eight (or 32) year old. Which is no doubt why the Pyramid offers two other courses of action.

In the one case – that of the limestone Queen's Chamber Passage – it proposes a continuation of the path represented by the Ascending Passage, but without its characteristic dimension of upward endeavour. Rest, in other words, on your ritual laurels. Simply be constant in your chosen religion or idealistic philosophy. And eventually, through sheer persistence in what is, in effect, the physical and linguistic realm, your path may culminate in the attainment of sufficient balance and wholeness to permit at least a measure of emergence.

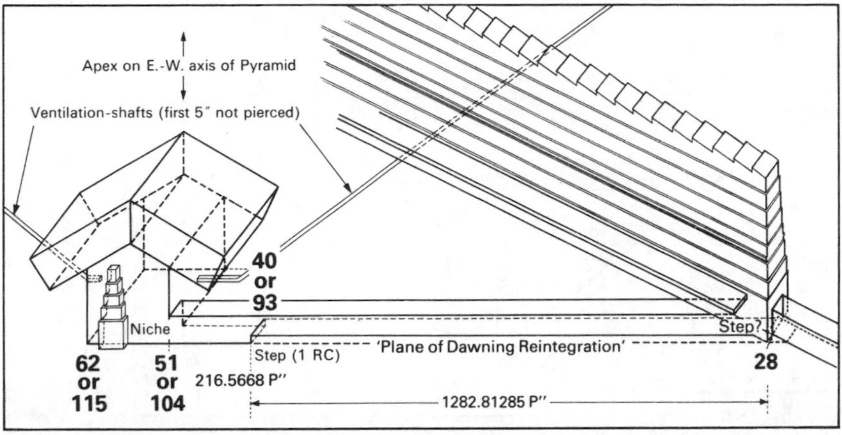

The Queen's Chamber and its passage depict a relatively static physical path which nevertheless results in a gradual, if painful, emergence from the limitations of materially orientated consciousness.

Such, at least, seems to be the message of the characteristic features of the Queen's Chamber – notably its seven 'sides' and its airshafts, whose outer ends correspond more or less exactly to the level of emergence or transcendence – i.e. the half-height of the Pyramid's summit-platform. Note, however, that the chamber actually fails to extend far enough to the west to reach the Pyramid's north-south centre-line: *total* inner balance, it seems, remains beyond one's grasp.

As the diagram reveals, the initial step along this road occurs at the age of forty (46) – i.e. at virtually the same time as the experience of chronic and more or less irreversible psychological imbalance in the Descending Passage. Clearly it is events connected with the familiar 'mid-life crisis' which also tend to provoke the crucial developments depicted in the Queen's Chamber Passage.

Specifically, the latter's height now increases to 67.5946 P", or just over twice 33.5 P". Possibly this symbolises the fact that the new psychological climate experienced at this stage in the individual's evolution is more than sufficient to produce a transformation of consciousness.

Precisely how is not spelt out, but perhaps what happens at this stage is that the underlying symbols of one's chosen religion or philosophy at last start (however unconsciously) to 'bite' deep within the psyche, so tending to bridge the gap between that long-neglected area of consciousness and the relatively superficial

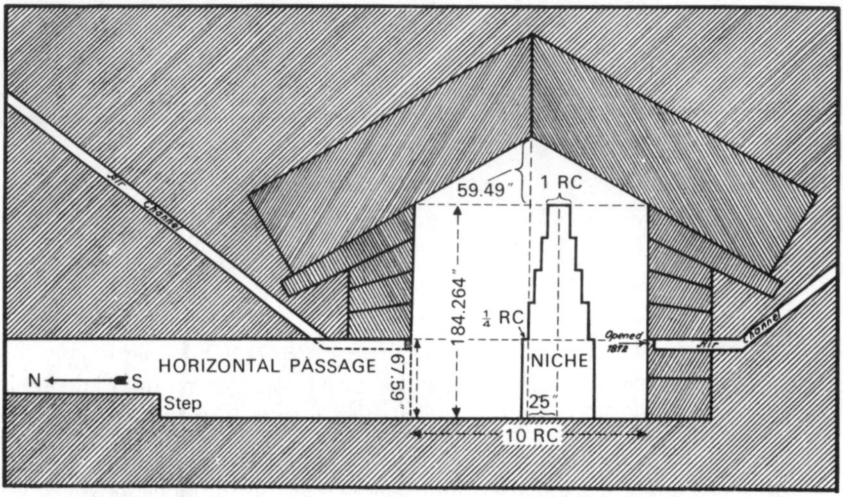

Cross-section of the Queen's Chamber, looking east, showing significant measurements. Note airshaft-blockages and eccentricity of niche.

rational mind, which has hitherto been concerned only with the corresponding apparatus of linguistic dogma and argument.

At all events, the result seems to be a period of relative fulfilment and culmination between the ages of fifty-one (59) and sixty-two (71). And during it sufficient integration is achieved to permit some kind of emergence into wholeness, and thus at the same time a measure of newly attained oneness with the cosmos.

Vague terms, admittedly, yet necessarily so. Our language, as we saw earlier, was devised – indeed largely responsible – for our *conventional* form of consciousness. It deals exclusively with the lopsided world of our everyday perceptions. By its very nature it is not designed to venture outside the confines of received rationality, and when it tries to – as in the case of 'religious' language, for example – it immediately tends to falsify, to define that which has no rational limits, to fix that which is essentially fluid, to give (in Shakespeare's words) 'to airy nothing / A local habitation and a name'.

Possibly, then, a certain amount of linguistic vagueness is no bad idea at this point, at least where the nature of 'emergence' and 'wholeness' is concerned. Similar considerations apply to the means whereby they are to be attained – for the rounded lower corners of the airshafts suggest that whatever emergence, or transcendence, is achieved at this stage is likely to be based on at least some degree of consciousness-expansion. It may even be that we are meant to think of the Queen's Chamber as having a granite floor from the mid-passage step onwards, very much after the style of the King's Chamber Complex above it – and this would have a similar symbolic significance.

'Emergence', 'transcendence', 'wholeness', 'consciousness-expansion', then – we are going to have to be content with such terms until we actually achieve the new type of consciousness for ourselves. Only then are we likely to know exactly what is involved. Rather as with walking or riding a bicycle, we cannot necessarily explain in detail the inner mechanics of the process – but we shall certainly know when we are doing it. All we *can* be sure about is that it will involve aspects of awareness that lie well outside the rational form of consciousness with which we normally confront the world – modes of experience that have more in common with the world of our dreams and our moments of intense ecstasy.

On matters such as dating, however, much greater precision is normally possible. Yet at this point we are faced with something of a conundrum. For there are clear indications that the Queen's Chamber dispensation needs in some sense to be experienced *five times* if the measure of perfection is to be achieved on which eventual emergence or transcendence depends. The axis of the *five-storeyed* Niche in the chamber's limestone eastern wall, after all – the most easterly feature of the whole passage-system, incidentally – lies exactly one sacred cubit, or 25 P″, *beyond* the axis of the chamber itself. Apparently, then, some kind of five-fold experience has to be undergone in the chamber – and an experience of the most physical kind, at that. The fact that the first *five* inches of the airshafts were left uncut by the builders similarly suggests some kind of five-fold experience – or possibly it means simply that, in symbol, the path of emergence symbolised by the airshafts is not open until perfection has been achieved within the chamber.

A notion which we may also see reflected in the chamber's patently 'unfinished' state.

Again, the fact that the chamber has a northern (i.e. backward-facing) airshaft as well as a southern one suggests a to-and-fro process involving a form of 'regression' prior to re-experiencing the events involved all over again. And the fact that the nomenclature of the ancient Egyptian *Book of the Dead* seems to identify the Queen's Chamber Passage as the *Path of the Coming Forth of the Regenerated Soul,* and the chamber itself not merely as the *Chamber of Regeneration*, but also as that *of Rebirth* or *of the Moon*, similarly seems to hint at a long-drawn-out process involving some kind of cyclic repetition.

Apparently, then, this period of culmination – this prolonged psychological 'high' resulting from the interaction of a lifetime of religious or philosophical endeavour with the typical inner turmoil of mid-life – needs to last not eleven (12) years *but fifty-five (60)*, if its symbolic purpose is to be achieved.

At this point we discover a gratifying convergence between the two sets of apparently paradoxical 'alternative' datings for this whole complex.

Those given above are in fact based on the assumption that the small downward 'nick' at the beginning of the Queen's Chamber Passage (compare diagram page 171) is intended to be read as a 'step' which duly modifies the timescale of the first part of the passage in combination with the later, mid-passage step. As I have pointed out in *The Great Pyramid Decoded*, however, this feature is nowadays little more than a slight hump that has evidently been worn down into its present shape by the feet of centuries. Whether it was ever exactly as portrayed in the diagram, therefore, cannot be established with any certainty. Possibly it was merely designed as a retaining notch for the stone slabs which originally concealed the entrance to the Queen's Chamber Passage and provided a continuation of the floor of the Ascending Passage into the Grand Gallery.

If so, the timescale of the Queen's Chamber Passage is governed only by its mid-passage step – and this has the effect of lengthning the time involved vey considerably.

The result is distinctly sobering.

In the 'personal' context, it means that the mid-passage step itself marks an age of no less than ninety-three (107), while the period covered by the Queen's Chamber itself lasts, not from age fifty-one (59) to sixty two (71), but from one hundred and four (120) to one hundred and fifteen (122). Astonishing as this paticular age-bracket may seem, it has be admitted that it fits very satisfactorily the notion of a fifty-five year (60 year) occupation of the chamber from age fifty-one (59).

Clearly, then, the odds are stacked heavily *against* ever achieving emergence via the route of conventional religion and philosophy, if the Pyramid's apparent message is valid. It *can* be done, certainly, but only dint of dogged persistence and a remarkable degree of

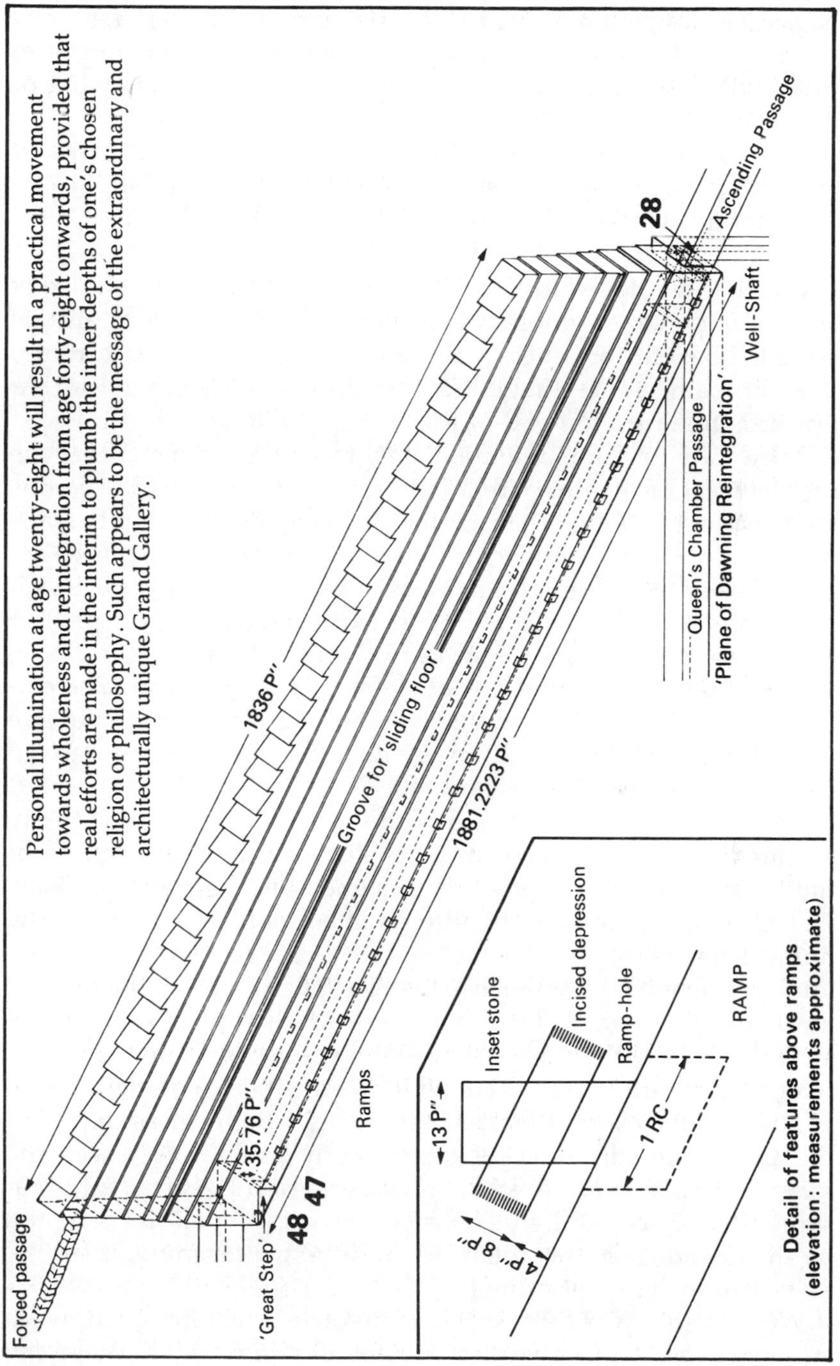

Personal illumination at age twenty-eight will result in a practical movement towards wholeness and reintegration from age forty-eight onwards, provided that real efforts are made in the interim to plumb the inner depths of one's chosen religion or philosophy. Such appears to be the message of the extraordinary and architecturally unique Grand Gallery.

physical health, strength and longevity – consistent, perhaps, with an initially well-adjusted psyche and a consequent freedom from psychologically induced disease. One is reminded somewhat of the ancient sages of India and China.

So we should do well not to count on such good fortune, and instead return to the 'Crossing of the Pure Roads of Life' to see what other routes are open to us.

Given that we have already ruled out the Well-Shaft as a likely avenue of personal progress – despite its patent idealism and its potential benefit for others – there remains only one such route. It is the path of the Grand Gallery itself, as it leads us further upwards from the top end of the Ascending Passage.

Yet we are, of course, immediately faced with the fact that the first few feet of the floor are missing. Possibly we should see this merely as a function of the fact that the Queen's Chamber Passage has been opened. Possibly, in other words, the floor can be regarded as symbolically 'still in place' if we have resisted the temptation of embarking on the Queen's Chamber Passage's path of religious and philosophical stasis in the first place.

Nevertheless the influence of those around us who *have* embarked on it is not to be underestimated. Perhaps, in symbol, we should not count too much on the ability of the bridging slabs to bear our own particular weight.

And, indeed, the symbolism of the Grand Gallery seems to say as much. For half-way up each of its side walls it offers, right from the outset, a groove apparently designed to take a sliding floor. At the same time the clearly differentiated roof-slabs mark out the number forty (8 x 5) – or possibly thirty-nine (13 x 3) – while the total roof-length is remarkably close to 153 x 12 P". True, the present measurement, over a distance of some fifty yards, is a fraction of an inch short of the ideal figure. Yet even without this apparent reference to 'the suspended enlightenment of mankind' ('suspended' to the extent that it is a roof, not a floor, measurement), the symbolism still indicates quite clearly that the results of the inner illumination achieved at around age twenty-eight (32) are in some way 'suspended – i.e. postponed – if the path represented by the Grand Gallery is followed; and the matter must, it seems, be settled by age thirty-one (35).

What is this path? Basically, it involves a continued upward struggle *within the framework of traditional religion and/or philosophy.*

But note the word 'upward'. It is not a mere matter of sticking to one's familiar beliefs and practices. Spurred onward by one's own inner illumination and by the autonomous, intuitive insights which it brings, one now starts to push outwards beyond the old, familiar limits, to delve ever more deeply into the underlying meanings of received doctrines and rituals, to seek the truths which underlie the mere facts. Having entered the realm of illusion, one has to pass all the way through it before one can hope to come out again on the other side. And so exoteric religion becomes esotericised: superficial philosophy gives way to actual personal change, however slow and for whatever dubious motives. For the time being at least, there is no attempt to repeat the original 'peak experience' of direct illumination itself.

No doubt this is just as well. The very attempt to do anything of the kind, after all, is normally more than sufficient to ensure that it never happens at all. In Blake's celebrated words:

> He who bends to himself a Joy
> Doth the wingéd life destroy;
> But he who kisses the Joy as it flies
> Lives in Eternity's sunrise.

All that is needed, in fact, is to wait for the seed that was sown earlier to germinate and sprout of its own accord. And this – according to the Pyramid at least – is likely to happen from about the forty-eighth (55th) year onwards, provided the upward struggle is persisted with.

As ever, it seems, the forties are the truly crucial time.

For it is at this point that the Great Step comes into play at the top end of the Gallery. With its height of 35.76 P″ reflecting, like the original distance to the axis of the Well-Shaft, the result of the earlier move towards inner integration and wholeness, it seems to represent a kind of 'landing-pad' for the suspended illumination of the last twenty years or so to come back into operation. No doubt that is why it also corresponds to the top of the fiftieth (10 x 5) course of masonry, as well as to the east-west centre-line of the Pyramid itself, thus apparently symbolising the beginning of the age of completion or perfection – or indeed of renewed illumination.

Certainly by the age of forty-eight (55) the period of suspended illumination represented by the Grand Gallery's roof is at an end,

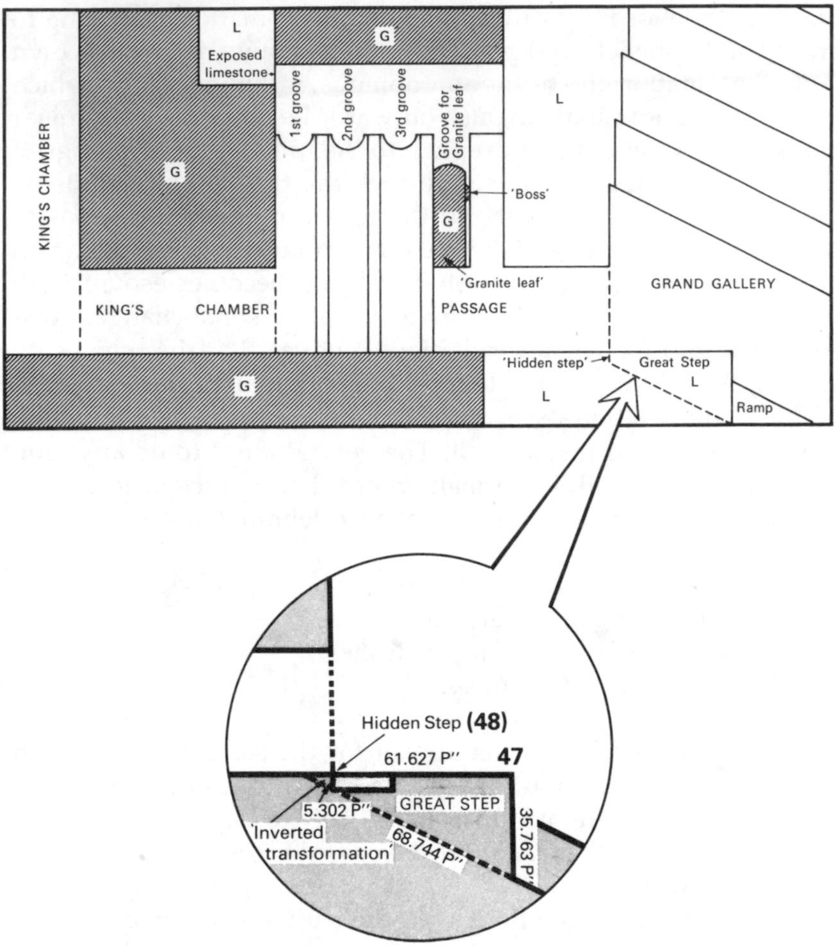

The 'Great Step' in inner evolution at the top end of the Grand Gallery involves the active resurfacing of direct personal illumination at age forty-seven. But it is necessary to resist any reactionist tendency at age forty-eight if this development is to result in eventual reintegration. G = granite; L = limestone.

and the new dispensation represented by the King's Chamber Complex is in full swing. And unless one can somehow enter the lowest of the Construction Chambers *directly,* via the rough limestone tunnel leading from the top section of the Grand Gallery – possibly some kind of materially orientated route conditioned directly by one's own illumination – one is in for a period of radical, and possibly even painful, inner transformation.

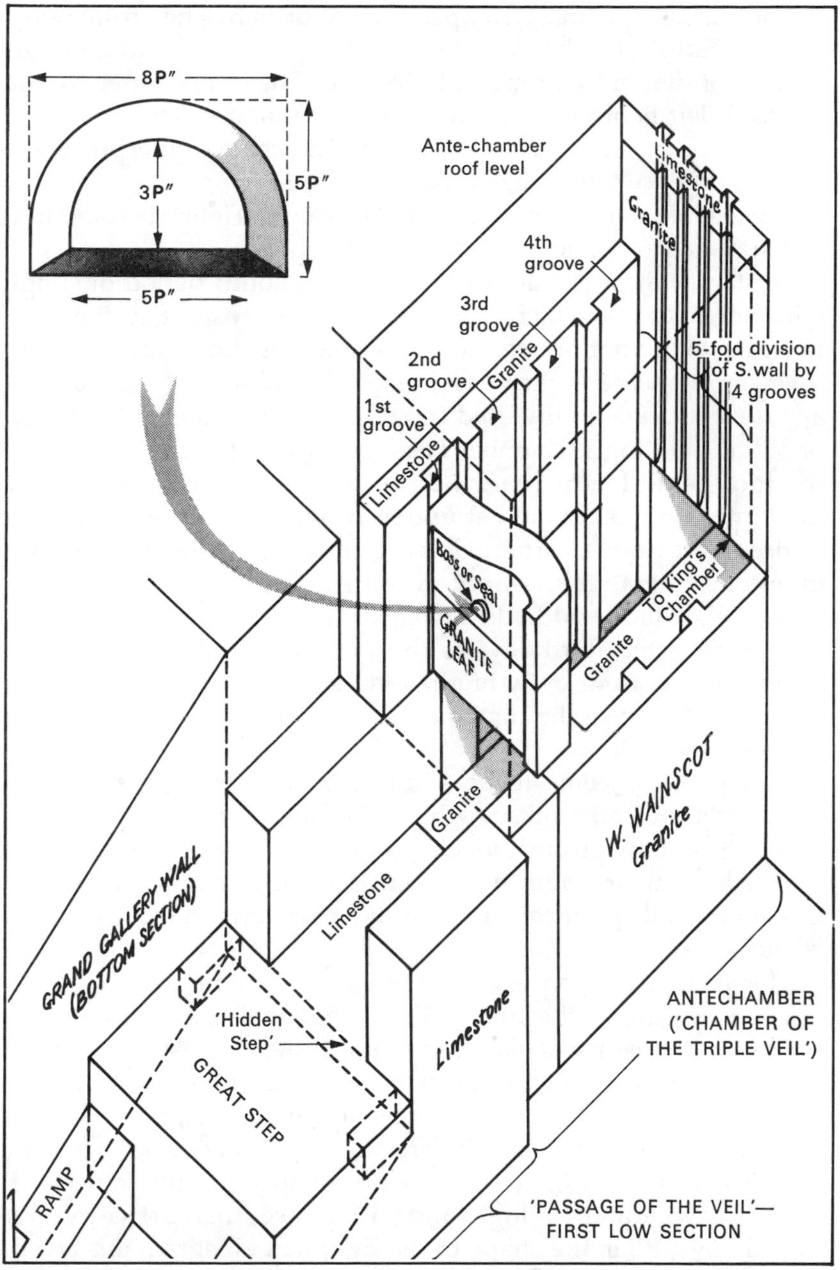

The Antechamber's 'age of transformation' in isometric projection. The inset shows the details of the so-called 'Boss' or 'Seal', whose shape resembles the ancient Egyptian ideogram for 'bread'.

For now at last the final, lofty plateau has been reached from which ultimate human fulfilment is destined to be achieved. But no longer by dint of determined upward struggle. The era of inner conflict is finally left behind. From now on it is a matter not so much of grasping as of letting go. Given only the chance, the process of final emergence will largely take care of itself.

The trouble is that, for most of us, learning to let go is something of a traumatic experience.

To start with, it is true, there is a nine-month period of simply lying low, during which the sole task is to resist any tendency towards what might be termed 'de-transformation'; that is to say, reversion to some earlier psychological paradigm. (Compare the apparent 'triangle of inverted transformation' at the Hidden Step, or sill of the King's Chamber Passage.) Then, towards the end of the forty-ninth (56th) year, the process of inner change towards final integration starts to get under away. At first there is little to notice apart from a certain clearing of the air – the change from limestone to granite masonry in the Antechamber occurs only at roof-level, which suddenly increases at this point. But with the forty-ninth (56th) birthday, as the granite floor begins, the very ground-rules of our daily life have to start changing. And within three months or so the metamorphic process of inner integration begins in earnest.

This process seems to be symbolised above all by the Antechamber's four portcullises which (like all portcullises) are, so to speak, 'sent down from above' – i.e. they represent developments which have their origin in the 'suspended', or hidden, parts of ourselves, and specifically in what we have termed the 'hyperconscious'.

The ancient archetypes, it seems, are on the march.

The surfacing of the first of them, notionally at age forty-nine (56), may not be particularly obvious. Provided that we symbolically 'bow beneath it', we can pass on relatively unscathed, since the portcullis in question never reaches the floor. Yet the Granite Leaf, as it is called, bears before it, 33.5 P″ above its base, the so-called Seal or Boss – a horseshoe-shaped protuberance 1 P″ thick, 8 P″ wide and 5 P″ high, and with an eventual surface measuring 5 P″ by 3 P″, in the shape of the Egyptian ideogram for 'bread'. Some kind of hyperconscious, transformative 'bread sent down from above', possibly? Certainly some new kind of nourishment – the result, it seems, of perfect illumination gained at the heart of reality – is about to well up out of the unconscious.

So it is no surprise to find that the three further developments in hyperconsciousness which follow at fifty (57), fifty-one (59) and fifty-three (60) are inherently much more demanding, not to say

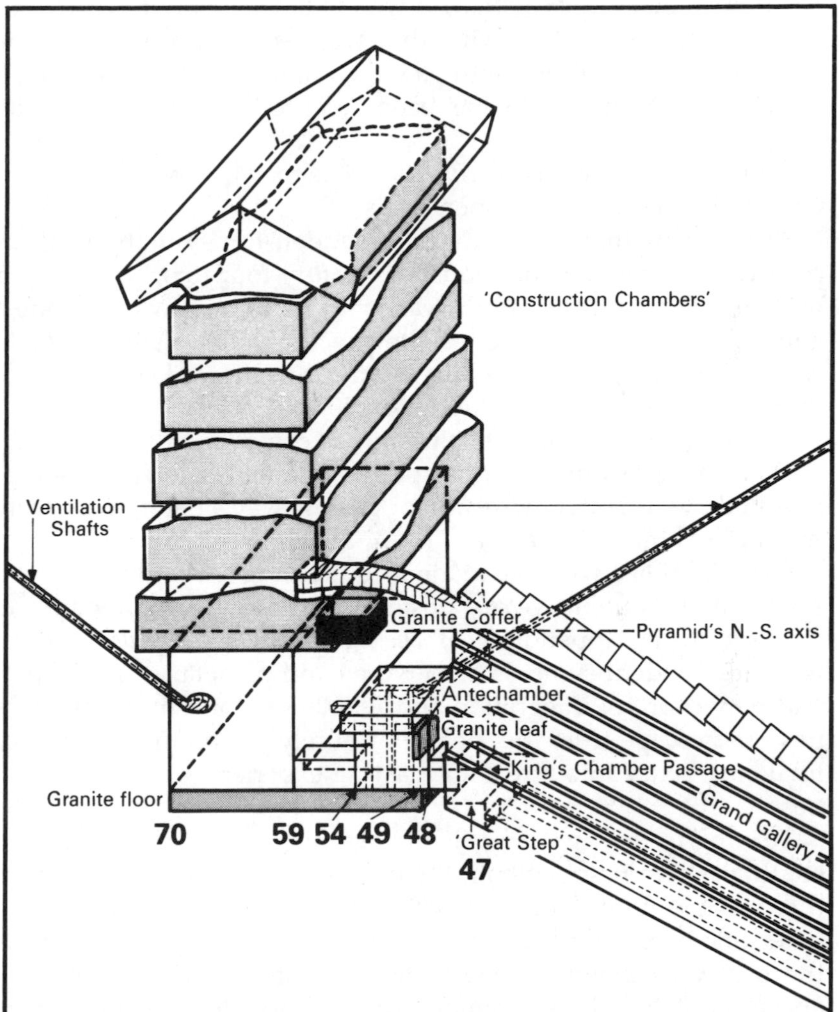

In the King's Chamber and its five superincumbent Relieving, or Construction Chambers, fully integrated consciousness is finally achieved. Consequent emergence is symbolised both by the open coffer and by the twin airshafts. The curious twists and turns of the northern (right-hand) shaft are not shown in the diagram.

any kind – then a dramatic rebirth ensues, and our final emergence into the light is the only possible result.

For society, unwilling though it may be to permit such a revolution in its young people, can have very little to say against such overwhelming. The Pyramid does not individually identify them, but it does make it clear that, if we are successfully to reach our goal, it is almost literally vital that we respond positively to the inner, psychological promptings which they represent. Perhaps it is as well that, once each has been accepted, there is apparently no going back.

For now the portcullises are down. The road behind us is closed. Only the path ahead lies open to us.

And so it is that there ensues a sudden transmutation of our physically orientated consciousness at fifty-four (62), represented by the Antechamber's south wall with its four upward 'scoops' and its top 12 P″ of limestone. The psychic chemicals have finally worked their magic. The mixture having duly brewed and bubbled, there is a sudden, all-enveloping explosion.

The long-sought inner revolution has come.

There remains only a further period of quiet assimilation – represented by the last, low section of passageway – before we finally reach our culminating age at fifty-nine (68).

For now at last we have made it to the King's Chamber dispensation. At this point we are positively surrounded (compare the data set out in Appendix F of *The Great Pyramid Decoded*) by the most resplendent symbols of personal and planetary culmination and perfection, of integration and wholeness, of hyperconsciousness and escape from the 'death' of purely left-brain thinking, of final emergence into a real and lasting experience of cosmic oneness.

Turning to the right and finally reaching the Pyramid's north-south axis, we first symbolically occupy the lidless granite coffer (i.e. we 'die' to our state thus far), and then emerge from it, to enter one or the other of the chamber's two airshafts. If we take the backward-facing northern one, with its square cross-section and multiple bends, we symbolically fall prey to prevarication as we attempt, even at this late stage, to adopt a somewhat devious, materially orientated path of emergence. But if by the age of seventy (80) we take the straight, southern airshaft, with its womb-like entrance and circular cross-section – if, in other words, we fully accept the demands of inner wholeness without preconditions of

a development in its relatively unthreatening septuagenarians.

And so total perfection reigns. For, whether the five Construction Chambers represent five further quantum-leaps of consciousness or merely point to the truly ultimate nature of the wholeness and

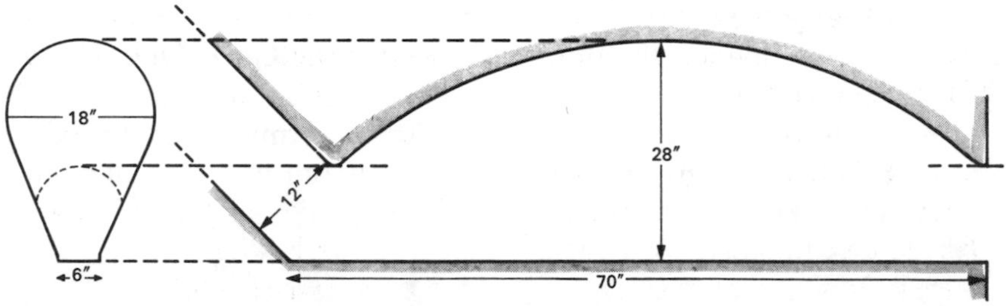

The King's Chamber's south ventilator-opening is curiously reminiscent both of an old-fashioned brick oven and of the belly of a pregnant woman. Together with the circular airshaft at its southern end, it apparently represents a path of rebirth involving the eventual emergence of human consciousness into the full light of reality. Measurements approximate.

integration that has been achieved, the level finally attained is that of perfect balance and wholeness – a balance and wholeness which must of necessity mean (if the Pyramid's basic symbolism is to be believed) that Planet Earth, too, is once again seen to be whole and perfect, and in total harmony with the universe of which (did we but realise it) it has never ceased to be an integral part.

The journey is over. The individual's destiny is achieved. The inherent wholeness and nobility of human nature is fulfilled. The symbolic postulant is united with the light, the equally symbolic soul of the 'dead' with the divinity that is its birthright, and by the same token the perceived universe, too, finally re-achieves the perfection which our traditional, warped form of human consciousness has for too long denied it.

Yet the universe does not cease to be the universe, any more than the physical individual ceases to be a physical individual. It is not reality that has changed, but our comprehension of it. And if that reality seems to have become far greater and more all-embracing than we have ever suspected it to be, it is because our consciousness has become so too.

That is the true triumph – the triumph of total self-discovery. And it is the overwhelming sense of that triumph that is duly reflected in the culminating words of the Osirian ritual of the *Book of the Dead:*

> Hail thou, my Father of Light . . . I am whole as my Father, the self-begotten God . . . Do thou establish me as the Master of the Grave . . .
>
> I have opened the doors . . . well is the Great One who is in the coffin.
>
> The tortoise dies; Ra lives! O Amun, Amun, Amun, who art in heaven, give thy face to the body of thy Son. Make him well in Hades.
>
> It is finished.

12
House of Initiation

Whether by accident or design, then – and it is for the reader to draw his or her own conclusions in this regard – the internal design of the Great Pyramid seems to portray with remarkable aptness not only the history and likely prospects of civilised humanity as a whole, but also the inner development of the individual. Moreover, this 'personal' blueprint is necessarily quite independent of the psychological theories of the last century or so of our own era, and so may have real potential value as a kind of verificatory 'second opinion'.

From parental conditioning and the descent into language-based materialism demanded by society, to the dire consequences for the psyche during mid-life and afterwards, the path of the 'normal' individual is mapped out with chilling inevitability. But there is a more hopeful alternative. A path of religious or philosophical idealism becomes available as early as adolescence. Diligently pursued, it leads to a time both of sudden insights and of crucial decisions at age twenty-eight, when a choice has to be made between deliberate self-sacrifice, a long period of doctrinal rigidity, or some two decades of continued inner searching. In this last case, the earlier insights tend to resurface in active form during the late forties and go on to produce a period of total transformation. Out of this transformation comes a thorough-going integration of the psyche leading, by the age of seventy, to final emergence into personal wholeness and a newly discovered cosmic identity.

Now it has long been known to Pyramidologists that the Pyramid's chambers and passageways trace out in their north-south elevation a pattern startlingly reminiscent of a male human figure wearing a five-fold crown and facing towards the west (i.e. towards the Pyramid's centre-line). Apart from remarking that this is a remarkably apt symbol for what each human individual clearly needs to attain – namely a retreat from the unbalanced, left-brain-orientated form of consciousness that is typical of our current, male-dominated society, in favour of the adoption of a much more

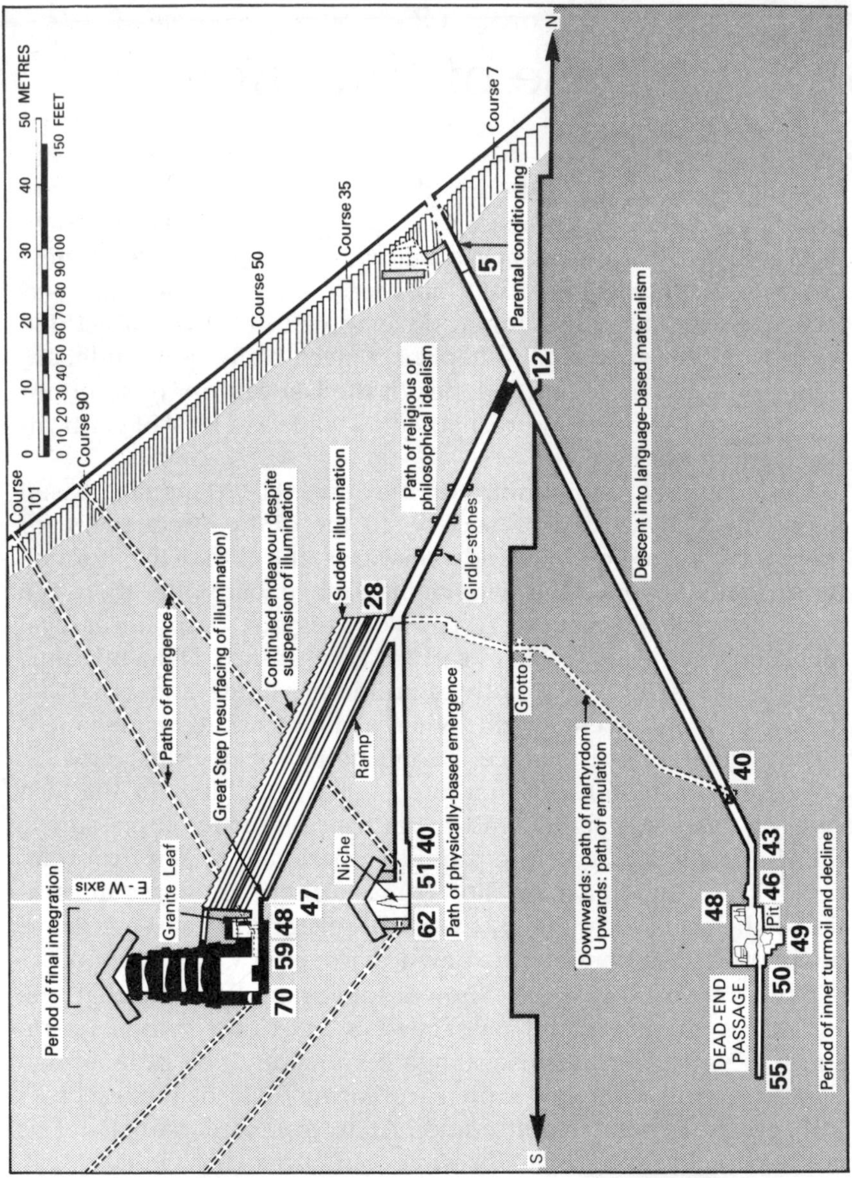

Summary chart of the Great Pyramid's life-plan for the individual. Figures refer to notional ages.

balanced outlook – we may conceivably see in this outline some indication of how the building's designer himself saw the various paths that I have just delineated. They seem, in other words, quite literally to represent his own *outline* of the processes involved.

Thus, the physically-orientated subterranean route begs to be identified as the *Way of the Feet;* the redemptive Well-Shaft as the *Way of the Genitals* (or *of Reproduction);* the uphill path of the Ascending Passage and Grand Gallery (and possibly the Entrance Passage too) as the *Way of the Spine;* The Queen's Chamber dispensation as the *Way of the Stomach;* and that of the King's Chamber, crowned as it is with its five-fold Construction Chambers, as the *Way of Whole and Perfect Mind.*

The terms seem appropriate. *The Way of the Feet* suggests the blind pursuit of uninformed material ends; the *Way of Reproduction* a path which promotes not our own advantage, but that of others who take their rise from us; the *Way of the Spine* a route of rising endeavour that demands (as we say) 'backbone'; the *Way of the Stomach* a side-road that attaches more importance to immediate feelings of satisfaction than to long-term goals; and the *Way of Whole and Perfect Mind* a crowning route to immortality that involves

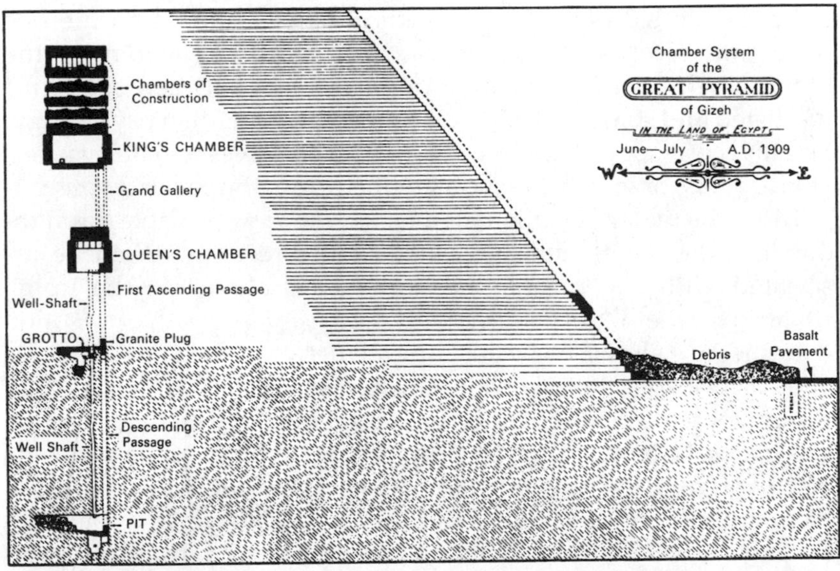

The north-south elevation of the Pyramid's passage-system reveals the outline of a 'stone man' – apparently the designer's own summary-chart of the various choices and routes facing both humanity as a whole and each individual human being.

the eventual development of a whole psyche and a totally integrated form of consciousness.

Such, indeed, appear to be the options available to us in terms of our earlier readout, and so we may well choose to take note of the suggested nomenclature as a convenient shorthand for discussing and referring to them.

Meanwhile the diagram offers us a further bonus. For the tongue of the ghostly 'stone man' quite clearly corresponds to the King's Chamber coffer, which is the only specific feature in the entire passage-system that lies fairly and squarely on the Pyramid's north-south centre-line. The whole question of life and death, of man's 'aliveness' and 'deadness', in other words, is seen to hinge uniquely on his tongue – i.e. on his use or misuse of language.

This, it will be remembered, was one of the points which I took to be virtually axiomatic to my whole interpretation from the very beginning in connection with the Pyramid's directional symbolism. So it would seem that our introduction of the left brain/right brain hypothesis, with all its inevitable linguistic implications, was a shot in the dark which, in the event, truly hit the mark.

It is, of course, for the reader to make whatever associations seem to be demanded between the readout I have offered on the one hand and received psychological and spiritual wisdom on the other. There are, for example, possible links between the terms just listed and some of the typical concepts of Freudian psychology. Equally, correspondences may suggest themselves with the various Hindu *yogas*, or with the associated doctrine of the seven *chakras*.

Thus, the materially orientated *Path of the Feet*, available throughout life (though tending in a downhill direction), could be associated with *karma yoga*, the path of simple work; the uphill ritualism of the *Way of the Spine* with *bhakti yoga*, the path of devotion – in this case shown to be appropriate between the ages of twelve and forty-seven; the relatively unaspiring *Way of the Stomach*, still firmly rooted in materiality, with *raja yoga*, the path of mental self-mastery, here shown as primarily for twenty-eight year olds and over; and the *Way of Whole and Perfect Mind* with *jñana yoga*, the path of spiritual knowledge or *gnosis*, which is apparently available, given adequate training and preparation, from age forty-seven onwards.

Alternatively, the ramrod-straight floorline of the *Way of the Spine* could be associated with the semi-magical pursuit of *kundalini yoga*, its seven so-called spinal *chakras*, or vital energy-centres, perhaps corresponding to the Granite Plug, the three great girdle stones, the beginning of the Grand Gallery, the Great Step at its upper end, and the eventual intersection of the Ascending Passage floor-line with the three final, full-length portcullises in the Antechamber (compare diagram p. 210). All of which would suggest that the ideal (or possibly the designed) ages for the opening of the various *chakras* – i.e. the awakening and control of the respective energies with which they are generally associated – are, in ascending order, 12, 19, 21, 24, 28, 47 and 49-54.[1]

Applying the conventional interpretations, this could conceivably suggest that age twelve is an appropriate time to awaken the dormant energies of adolescence and to teach the growing child to come to terms with them. By around age nineteen, sexuality, self-assertion and aggression should have been aroused and similarly channelled into healthy and creative forms of expression. Twenty-one is an appropriate age for taking on board wider interactions of every kind – physical, intellectual, social and commercial; twenty-four the ideal time for adding to all this activity the important dimension of deeply-felt humanity and selfless love – whether marital or otherwise. By twenty-eight speech becomes the activity of the moment – the voice, it may be, of command, of experience, advice and teaching, even (if the previous work has been successfully applied and built on) the exalted tongue of prophecy in its broadest sense. So eventually, with the attainment of age forty-seven, all kinds of spiritual and psychic abilities start to dawn, preparatory to the final gaining of total, cosmic consciousness from age forty-nine onwards.

Once again, the proposed links seem appropriate. Certainly they seem compatible with our earlier readout. Moreover, there is another possible 'esoteric' connection. For the Well-Shaft – essentially, as we have seen, a path of self-sacrifice in the cause of wholeness – seems, in the diagram, to link the feet directly with

[1] Comparison of the diagrams on pp. 210 and 211 reveals that the *Way of the Spine* ought strictly to be seen as including the descending Entrance Passage as well. In this case, with the entrance itself roughly on the level of the third Girdle Stone (and thus notionally of the so-called Heart Chakra), the layout could be seen as indicating that all four lower *chakras* are already open at birth – possibly through the direct umbilical connection of child with mother. The upper two are then progressively closed down until, at age twelve, only the bottom two remain open, leaving the growing child to reconstruct his or her own house of experiential consciousness on what, in Freudian terms, might be described as an essentially anal and genital foundation.

the genitals and stomach. It might thus be deduced that the feet have a potential healing link with the basic physical drives and the 'gut-feelings' or emotions. In which case one is immediately reminded of the parallel claims of acupuncture and other, related healing techniques such as acupressure, reflexology and the so-called 'metamorphic technique'.

All this is as may be, and the reader is entitled to pursue such associations just as far as he or she wishes. My own task has been simply to decipher what the Pyramid appears to say *on its own terms,* quite independently of such external considerations. And out of it all one fact does appear to be abundantly clear.

To the extent that you are prepared to allow it, the Great Pyramid is truly – as the deliberately two-edged title of this book would have it – 'your personal guide'. Not only does it offer a kind of psychological life-map setting out all your likely inner choices in advance. It also has potential value in a more immediate context. For, by carefully positioning yourself according to your age in whichever of the passageways most closely accords with your chosen way of life, you are also in a position to use the building as a kind of 'personal oracle' – i.e. as a guide to what psychic events you should expect to befall you next, and to how you might most profitably respond when they do.

But if all this is the case, then we seem to have achieved something rather remarkable. We have, in effect, recovered the basic sense of whatever initiations were originally carried out in connection with the building – if not actually inside it. For their very basis must, as we saw earlier, have been the quest to experience in advance all the various stages of life (and perhaps also of planetary history) in such a way as to permit those participating to 'steal a march on' their contemporaries, and so qualify to lead them into the future.

Always assuming, of course, not merely that such initiations ever occurred in the first place, but that they were serious efforts at personal transformation and not mere magico-religious rigmaroles.

The successful initiate, in other words, would have attained the wisdom of a seventy-year-old while remaining physically young and vigorous enough to do something substantial about putting it into practice for the benefit of humanity at large.

Quite how ritualised the actual procedure was, or through what words and symbols it was experienced, we can of course never know, though the words of the Egyptian *Book of the Dead* may give us at least some inkling of what was involved. The passage-nomenclature listed in chapter 6 is an obvious case in point.

We may reasonably assume, however, that the postulant was led in succession through all the various passages and chambers, whether physically or in symbol only, while being submitted to a whole series of experiences startling enough to impress upon him or her the archetypal sequence of developments which – as it now seems – typifies man's individual and collective life on this planet. The initial psychic imbalance, the decline into language-based materialism, the opening up of the alternative, 'upward' path of ritualism, the dire consequences of neglecting it, the later need to choose a path whose advantages might not immediately appear obvious, its likely consequences and the need for continued resolution in the latter stages – all must have been symbolised in terms dramatic enough to involve not merely the intellect, but the emotions and physical senses too. And who knows which of the esoteric concepts and techniques to which we have just been referring might not also have had their place in that shattering initiatory sequence?

The process cannot have been without its dangers. Not every psyche is strong enough to contemplate and cope with all life's transitions and crises in advance. Deliberately awakening the hitherto-dormant primal drives of the human organism – the process to which esotericists generally refer when they speak of 'opening the *chakras*' – brings with it serious risks of burn-out. As the case of Hitler demonstrates, the premature release of the long-enchained Krakens of the unconscious, unattended by the most careful preparation and control, can unleash vast destruction both on the inner and the outer levels. Even if the obvious precautions were taken, many a would-be initiate must still have been psychologically scarred for life or even destroyed by the experience.

In any such process there are dangers, too, of concealed egotism – of undertaking the strenuous inner curriculum purely in order to gain power, status and self-esteem. And no doubt for that very reason the point must have been rubbed home again and again that what was at stake was the future, not merely of the postulant, but of humanity itself. As the Pyramid's symbolism makes quite clear, what applies to the individual also applies to society as a whole . . .

The point is extraordinarily important – and especially so for the light which each sphere of interest consequently throws upon the other. In particular, it permits us to gain a much better perspective on the various stages of world history by seeing them *as phases in the life of the typical individual* (compare the two summary-diagrams on pages 165 and 210). Which, to the extent that we *are* all one individual – the individual being that is humanity – is no more than appropriate.

From this point of view, civilised humanity at the time of the Exodus was just starting its idealistic, adolescent phase. By the time of Christ, it had reached sufficient adult maturity to permit the surfacing – if not the acceptance – of insights which were likely to prove inherently destructive of its own basic tenets. The turmoil of the Middle Ages and Renaissance was, in effect, the beginning of humanity's 'mid-life crisis', which was to reach its climactic period in 1914. And we today, who are living through the very depths of that crisis – with all its typical 'madness', its abandoning of long-respected traditions, its self-destructive tendencies – must expect to have to throw overboard all our inherited assumptions about who we are and where we are going before the fever will finally depart, leaving us chastened, but totally transformed. And heirs to a racial 'old age' of astonishing and undreamt-of possibilities.

Chief among those inherited assumptions, no doubt, will be the idea, quintessentially typical of our time, that we are, at basis, a collection of separate individuals and warring interests – an idea that ultimately has its root in language and thus reflects with great aptness both the nature and the cause of our *personal* disintegration, which similarly has its roots in our tendency to divide our experience into disconnected bits.

The very future of our race, it seems, depends on our final acceptance of a new, holistic form of consciousness.

From whatever point of view, then, there is by this point in our investigation ample evidence to suggest that the Great Pyramid's most vital symbolic role is to link the development of the individual psyche with the ultimate destiny of Planet Earth itself. Not only is this apparent from the interchangeability of the 'historical' and the 'initiatory' approaches to interpreting the building. The link is also basic to the Pyramid's whole geometric symbolism, as I established much earlier when elaborating its interpretative code. Earth's lack of harmony with the cosmos in general is, it seems, a *direct function of* humanity's own lack of psychic harmony. Once that inner harmony is restored, not only will man's psychological and social problems be solved at a stroke, but Planet Earth itself will also be seen to be whole and perfect, and totally in tune with the universe of which it has always been part.

The Great Pyramid, in consequence, has a powerful catalytic function to perform, if only we are prepared to let it. Possibly that is the true reason behind its enormous bulk and resplendent technology. It is deliberately designed in such a way as to make it impossible to ignore. Not only has it *become* a tourist-attraction. Rather like the great Gothic cathedrals of Europe, it was actually *built* as one. Its prime function is to draw people to experience its catalytic mysteries.

It is truly a house of initiation in every sense, but that is not to say that the Great Pyramid was never used for anything else. Theodolite it may have been, astronomical observatory, in one sense or another, it almost certainly was. And there can be scarcely any doubt that pyramid-construction – even if not that of the Great Pyramid itself – lay at the very basis of the sudden rise of Egyptian civilisation in the third millennium BC. Indeed, of all the various subsidiary theories proposed, only the long-familiar tombic, treasury and granary theories seem decidedly *un*likely.

Initiation, however, seems in one sense or the other always to have been the primary function – whether initiation of the soul of the dead, the psyche of the living or the mind of humanity *en masse*. And all three cases are of course essentially one and the same. They are merely particular manifestations of a single evolutionary dynamic that is characteristic of *genus homo* – a fundamental, archetypal programme which controls the inner growth no less of the human race in general than of each individual member of it in particular.

It was presumably in response – whether conscious or unconscious – to this archetypal imperative that (if the various esoteric traditions are to be believed) the mere physical act of tracing out humanity's psychic destiny – whether individual or collective – in the Great Pyramid was expected to confer initiateship on those individuals chosen to perform it. Somehow it would impress upon the serious student the unchanging paradigm of the evolution of human consciousness. Additional symbolic adjuncts there may well have been, but in one way or the other the experience was expected to help prepare participants for the subsequent phases not only of their own life, but also of the history of their planet. Just as a baby has to open up its neural pathways through physical actions before it can learn to walk, and as a child needs to learn through symbolic play the rudiments of adult relationships, so too those privileged to undergo the Pyramid experience would find that it facilitated their own development – not to mention that of humanity as a whole.

Indeed, only the planetary aspect of the process can possibly have justified the conferring of such initiateship in the first place.

It is this magic which, in the past, is said to have worked on Moses, on Plato, on Heraclitus, on Pythagoras, on John the Baptist and on Jesus of Nazareth. Today, too, perhaps, it still exerts itself, all unsuspected, on the thousands of tourists who continue to converge upon the mighty edifice day after day – provided, that is, that they duly explore *all* its passageways.

Yourself, perhaps, included.

Indeed, it is intriguing to note how many of the modern world's major political leaders too, from Napoleon onwards, have at some time or other had occasion to explore the Pyramid's interior. As conquerors or private citizens they have simply been drawn by curiosity. As state guests they have found the visit more or less obligatory. And who knows what echoes of that experience have subsequently reverberated through the world of national and international politics?

Who knows, indeed, whether the fact that virtually none of them has ever visited the *lower* passageways has not made them that much worse-prepared to cope with 'lower passage' events, and thus more prone to be overwhelmed by the dire physical developments involved?

Meanwhile the mountain has, in a sense, managed to come to Mahomet. For through the medium of words and pictures others far and wide across the world can now participate in the initiatory process at second hand. And so the possibility arises that some at least of the magic may rub off on them as well.

Perhaps it will. Perhaps you have been one of those beneficiaries. Perhaps your own reading of this book and others like it, your own self-immersion in the stages of its symbolism, will itself help to spark off a minor miracle within your consciousness. Perhaps, indeed, my own writing of it, and my own work on the site will have similar effects on me.

It may be many years before either of us will know.

But if it does, then our own first-hand experience will testify to the fact that the Pyramid's designer and the astonishing monument that he created all those centuries ago are truly working their magic yet.

Postscript

Even as we go to press, news is coming in of the discovery of a hitherto-unsuspected underground chamber some six feet east of the Sphinx. Using sensitive sonic scanners, a Japanese team from Waseda University claims to have established that the cavity contains objects made of stone, wood and rope. An archaeological conference in Cairo has been proposed for October 1987 to discuss what should be done about the find – as also about the Great Pyramid's fifth boat-pit, which has now been subjected to similar remote scanning, and apparently contains, as hoped for, the remains of a further wooden ship. An underground tunnel near the Great Pyramid has also been detected (*Christian Science Monitor*, 6 July 1987).

Whether the newly-discovered chamber in front of the Sphinx turns out to be the Atlantean 'hall of records' whose discovery 'between . . . the Sphinx and the river' was long ago predicted by Edgar Cayce (see page 111) – or, more likely, one of the anticipated 'connecting chambers' near its paws – only time and excavation will tell. The fact that the Nile water-table at this point lies only some six feet below the surface may have an important influence on what is discovered and when. But any 'Atlantean' discoveries on the site must inevitably throw important new light on the origin, purpose and dating of the Great Pyramid itself.

Meanwhile, calculations in a quite different area of research are already leading to startling new revelations about one of these questions at least – namely the likely date of the Pyramid's construction.

The reader will recall that the full-design Pyramid's ground-plan (page 141) contains direct references to the length in days of the mean solar tropical, anomalistic and sidereal years. *But in all three cases the figures differ slightly from present-day values*. Now it is known that the lengths of all three types of year change slowly with the passage of time. Moreover, it seems clear that the Pyramid's architect would have built into his design *the values current in his day*.

They would, in effect, be his 'time-signature'.

Given accurate figures for the rate of change, then, it should be possible to calculate the date of the Pryamid's design and/or construction from present-day astronomical values.

The most promising type of year for this calculation appears, at first sight, to be the mean solar tropical year, since its length is repeatedly reflected in the design to a value of 365.2423499 days (to seven places of decimals). The current figure, by contrast, is known to be 365.242191. Since, until recently, the accepted rate of change was −.00000161 days per century, the calculation was therefore a simple one. *And the upshot was that the Great Pyramid was apparently designed around 7884 BC.*

However, with the continual updating of astronomical information, this formula is currently regarded as obsolete. In its place, a much more complicated mathematical procedure is now involved which, so far, it has not been possible (to my knowledge, at least) to extend far enough back in time to check this proposed dating at all reliably.

As for the anomalistic year, this might offer us a simpler and more direct approach, but for the fact that the architect clearly chose not to express it explicitly in his design. Points. C, G, K and O in the diagram on page 141, in other words, would not in fact be visible in the exterior masonry. Consequently it would seem unfair to quote the architect as saying what, in effect, he did not say.

This leaves the sidereal year – the time taken by the earth to complete one revolution about the sun, relative to the stars themselves. Being much the simplest of the three to calculate back into the past, this seems to offer us the most reliable approach to the question that is currently available. Here the architect's figure, expressly repeated in the Pyramid's exterior design, is 365.2563565, to compare with the present-day value of 365.25636556. The rate of change, meanwhile, is a steady +.00000011 days per century.

When, then, on this basis, did the architect live, and when, in consequence, must his building have been designed and/or built? The answer bids fair to shatter current archaeological assumptions, and to back up to an astonishing degree the general theory, propounded in chapter 5, that the Great Pyramid is much older than has hitherto been supposed.

For the date, on current figures, works out at 6250 BC, give or take some four hundred years – *nearly four millennia earlier than the date currently accepted by historians.*

The Pyramid's likely age, in other words, is almost doubled at a stroke.

Might it yet be, then, that the proposed 'Atlantean' initiative (whatever its real nature) and the construction of the Great Pyramid will at some point meet in time, as the figures are further refined, to form the basis of a new history of the birth of Western civilisation?

APPENDIX A

The Great Pyramid: Technical Data

Abbreviations used throughout the Appendices are as follows:

P″	Primitive Inch (To convert to Imperial inches, multiply by 1.00106)		
RC	Royal Cubit		
SC	Sacred Cubit		
in	inches	mm	millimetres
ft	feet	cm	centimetres
y	yards	m	metres
t	tons	te	tonnes
a	acres	ha	hectares

x°, x′, x″ degrees, minutes, seconds

1. SITE

Geographical co-ordinates	29°58′51″N 31°09′00″E
Elevation above mean sea-level at Alexandria	198 ft 2½ in (60.41 m)
Site geology	Nummulitic limestone anticline on eastern edge of Giza plateau
Geographical situation (local)	(a) 10 miles SW of centre of Cairo (b) At hub of Nile Delta quadrant – i.e. ancient kingdom of Lower Egypt (see map overleaf)
Geographical situation (planetary)	(a) At approximate 'centre of gravity' of world's entire landmass (cf. any equal-area projection) (b) On world's longest land-contact meridian (c) On world's longest land-contact earth-circuit rhumb-line

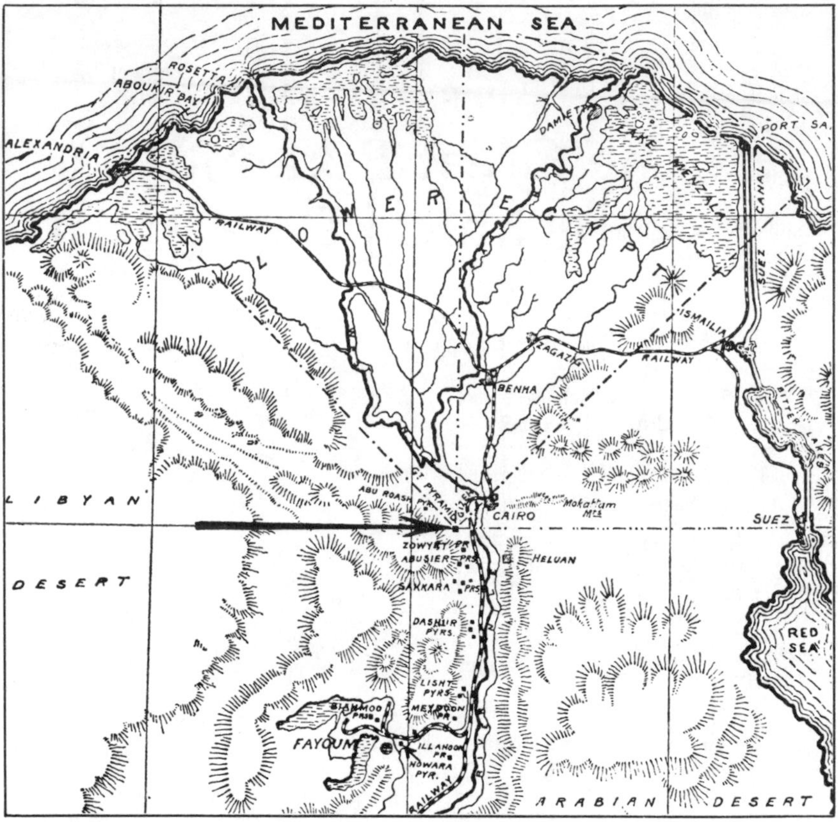

The Nile Delta Quadrant, centred on the Great Pyramid (arrowed), and measured 45° either side of True North, encompasses the ancient kingdom of Lower Egypt. Meanwhile, stretching far away to the south, the other main groups of pyramids form a veritable necropolis along the west bank of the Nile.

2. ORIGINAL PYRAMID (AS BUILT)

(Measurements calculated correct to 8 significant digits or less, on the basis of the figures noted as having been published by Rutherford.)

Composition	Mainly limestone (see details under 'Core Masonry' and 'Casing')		
Total volume (assuming flat base)	157,788,858,900 P″³	91,603,715 cu ft	2,593,944 m³
Estimated minimum total weight	–	6,637,500 t	6,745,000 te
Height of theoretical apex	5767.4780 P″	481 ft 1.59 in	146.64954 m
Average slope-height	7333.6612 P″	611 ft 9.4358 in	186.47284 m
Total surface area	132,879,096 P″²	21.228857 a	8.5910483 ha

Average area of each face	33,219,774 P''^2	5.3072144 a	2.1477621 ha
Base area	82,075,142 P''^2	13.112382 a	5.3064144 ha
Base-perimeter	36,238.133 P″	3023 ft 0.545 in	921.42621 m
Average length of side	9059.5332 P″	755 ft 9.1374 in	230.35655 m
Length of sides (Cole):			
W side	9059.5508 P″	755 ft 9.1551 in	230.357 m
N side	9055.3820 P″	755 ft 4.9818 in	230.251 m
E side	9060.8880 P″	755 ft 10.4937 in	230.391 m
S side	9063.3656 P″	756 ft 0.9739 in	230.454 m*
Orientation of sides:			
W side	0°02′30″ west of true north (i.e. 359°57′30″T)		
N side	0°02′28″ north of true east (i.e. 089°57′32″T)		
E side	0°05′30″ west of true north (i.e. 359°54′30″T)		
S side	0°01′57″ north of true east (i.e. 089°58′03″T)		
Deviation of base-corners from true right-angle (Cole)†:			
NW corner	− 0°00′02″		
NE corner	+ 0°03′02″		
SE corner	− 0°03′33″		
SW corner	+ 0°00′33″		
Slope-angle (ave.)	51°51′14.3″		
Arris slope-angle (ave.)	41°59′50″		
Passage slope angle	26°18′9.7″		
Displacement of passage axis eastward of centre-line (Rutherford)	286.10213 P″	23 ft 10.4054 in	7.2747124 m
Present orientation of N-S axis	0°05′16″ west of true north (i.e. 359° 54′44″T)		

Core-masonry (see diagram p. 24)

General composition	Mainly nummulitic (coarse) limestone blocks of indeterminate origin, but probably quarried from the valley of the Sphinx		
Total volume (est.)	146,724,610, 000, P''^3	85,180,407 cu ft	2,412,005m^3
Estimated minimum total weight	–	6,172,240 t	6,271,330 te
Number of courses to summit-platform	203 (resulting in 203 vertical 'steps' on each face)		
Heights and thicknesses of courses	See diagram overleaf for current post subsidence data		
Number of blocks (est. Petrie)	2,300,000		

* Thus, Cole's average length of side works out at 230.36325 metres, 755 ft 9.4011 in or 9059.7966 P″ (compare with the above figure derived from Rutherford). This degree of correlation over a distance of more than 250 yards is distinctly impressive.

† According to L. C. Stecchini, in Peter Tompkins: *Secrets of the Great Pyramid,* these apparent 'errors' seem to have been quite deliberate.

Present mean thicknesses and heights above the Pyramid's base of individual courses of core-masonry after Petrie, based on measurements at the south-west and north-east corners. (To convert to metres and British inches, multiply by .02542687 and 1.001059 respectively).

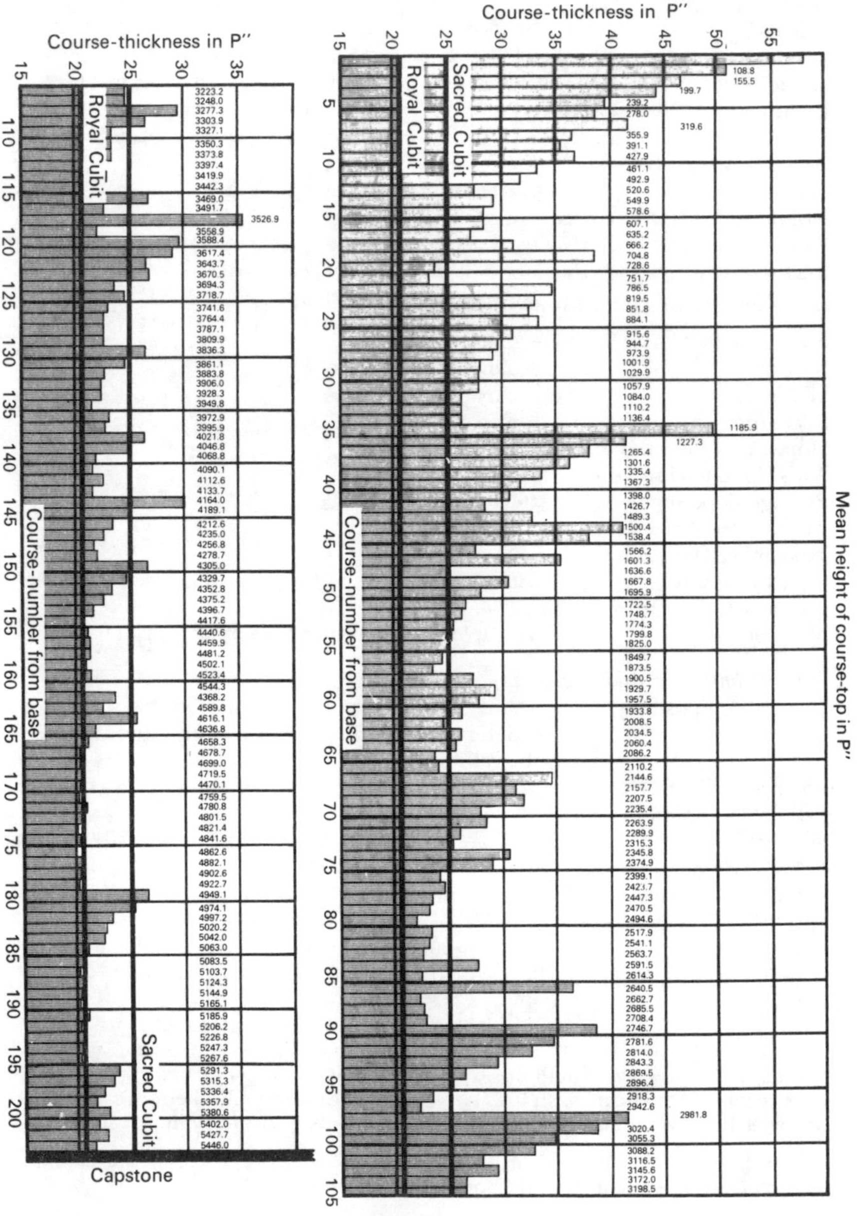

Consequent average weight of blocks	–	2.68 t	2.72 te
Estimated weight of heaviest known block (granite beam in King's Chamber roof)	–	72 t	73 te
Depth of concavity on each face	35.76277 P″	2 ft 11.8007 in	90.9330 cm
Height of inset-triangle on each face	1162.6024 P″	96 ft 11.8350 in	29.56147 m
Height of 35th course axis	1162.6024 P″	96 ft 11.8350 in	29.56147 m
Extreme height of summit-platform now exposed	5448.7360 P″	454 ft 6.5123 in	138.54489 m
Original elevation of entrance-passage	26°18′9.7″ (i.e. 3°40′41.3″ below celestial pole)		
Composition of passage-masonry	(*a*) Most of the King's Chamber complex, and the three plugging blocks at the bottom of the Ascending Passage, are of red granite from Syene (Aswân), 500 miles to the south. (*b*) Otherwise, limestone blocks from Tura and Masara (Moqattam Hills), 10 miles distant on the east bank of the Nile.		
Casing			
Composition	Polished blocks of white, high-grade limestone from Tura and Masara (Moqattam Hills), 10 miles distant on the east bank of the Nile.		
Method of securing	Fine aluminosilicate cement		
Average thickness of joints (Petrie)	.02 P″	.02 in	.5 mm
General configuration	Exterior flat on all four faces: inner side married to stepped and concave core-masonry (q.v.)		
Accuracy of levelling (Petrie)	1 in 7,500 (.013%)		
Minimum thickness at centre of each face (Rutherford)	71.5255 P″	5 ft 11.6013 in	181.868 cm
Minimum thickness at edge of each face (Rutherford)	35.7628 P″	2 ft 11.8007 in	90.9339 cm
Slope-angle	51°51′14.3″		
Present whereabouts	(*a*) Some blocks of the bottom course remain in place at the centre of each face. (*b*) Most larger blocks now form part of Cairo's dams, bridges and mosques – notably the Sultan Hasan Mosque. (*c*) Some smaller blocks of the upper courses, recovered from the site-debris, are lodged in various museums (e.g. British Museum, London; Royal Scottish Observatory, Edinburgh).		

3. *Full-Design Pyramid (Theoretical)*

(All except angular measurements given to 8 significant digits only: dimensions in P″ calculated after Rutherford unless otherwise stated.)

Total volume (assuming flat base)*	161,555,680,000 P''^3	93,790,493 cu ft	2,655,867.9 m^3
Estimated minimum total weight	–	6,796,136 t	6,905,239 te
Height of apex	5813.0125 P″	484 ft 11.175 in	147.80734 m
Slope height	7391.5610 P″	616 ft 7.3969 in	187.94506 m
Height of summit-platform	See under 'Capstone: level of base'		
Perimeter of summit-platform	See under 'Capstone: base-perimeter'		
Full square base perimeter (Rutherford)	36524.235 P″	3046 ft 10.96 in	928.7009 m
Total base-area	83,376,234 P''^2	13.320246 a	5.3904534 ha
Minimum total surface area (disregarding concavity)	134,985,555 P''^2	21.565387 a	8.727237 ha
Minimum area of each face (disregarding concavity)	33,746,388 P''^2	5.3913467 a	2.181809 ha
Depth of concavity on each face (Rutherford)	35.76277 P″	2 ft 11.8007 in	90.93391 cm
Height of inset-triangle on each face	1162.6024 P″	96 ft 11.8351 in	29.56147 m
Height of 35th course axis	1162.6024 P″	96 ft 11.8351 in	29.56147 m
Straight length of side, corner to corner (Rutherford)	9131.0587 P″ (365.24235 SC)	761 ft 8.7388 in	232.17523 m
Actual length of base-side, measured via concavity	9131.4089 P″	761 ft 9.0893 in	232.18406 m
Square base-perimeter excess over original Pyramid (as built)	286.10213 P″	23 ft 10.4054 in	7.2747124 m
Length of base-diagonal	12,913.27 P″	1,077 ft 2.957 in	328.34536 m
Sum of base-diagonals	25,826.53 P″	2,154 ft 5.914 in	656.69072 m
Minimum thickness of casing throughout (Rutherford)	71.5255 P″	5 ft 11.6014 in	181.8678 cm
Slope-angle	51°51′14.31″		
Arris slope angle	41°59′50.01″		
Passage slope-angle	26°18′9.73″		
Displacement of passage axis eastward of centre-line (Rutherford)	286.10213 P″	23′10.4054″	7.2747124 m

* The total size of the rocky outcrop underneath the Pyramid's centre is, of course, unknown, though it rises to at least the level of the 7th course of masonry.

Capstone

Composition	Probably gold-sheathed granite from Syene (Aswân)		
Estimated minimum weight	–	1,704 t	1,731 te
Volume	39,756,863 P″³	23,080 cu ft 1198.5 cu in	653.57638 m³
Height	364.2765 P″	30 ft 4.6627 in	9.2624515 m
Slope-height	463.1974 P″	38 ft 7.6884 in	11.777710 m
Length of base-side (Rutherford)	572.2043 P″	47 ft 8.8109 in	14.549425 m
Base-perimeter	2288.8170 P″ (= 8 x 286.10213P″)	190 ft 11.243 in	58.19770 m
Base-area	327,417.70 P″²	2278 sq ft 80.28 sq in	211.68576 m²
Intended level of base (summit-platform) above Pyramid's base	5448.7360 P″	454 ft 6.5123 in	138.54489 m
Corresponding course-number	203		
Thus, course-number represented by capstone	204		
Slope-angle	51°51′14.31″		
Arris slope-angle	41°59′50.01″		

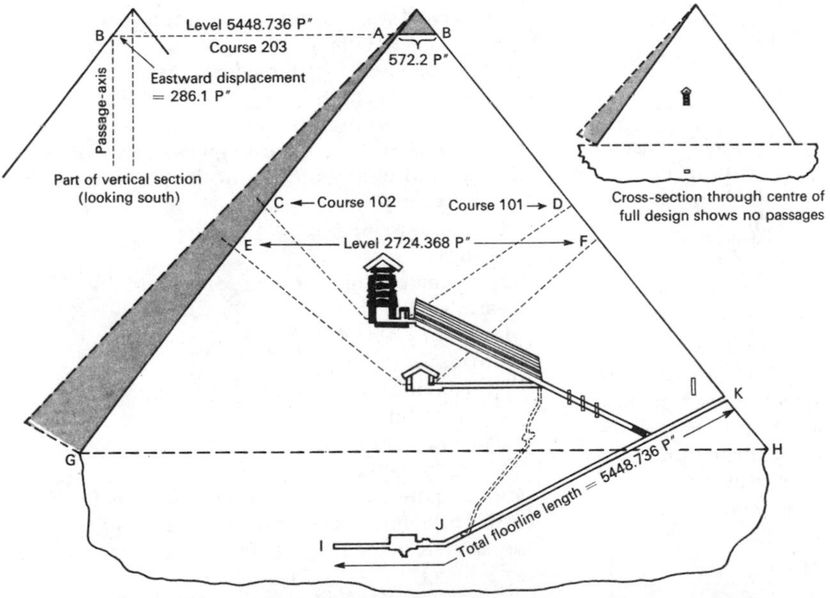

Vertical section through the Great Pyramid at the passage-axis, 286.1 P″ east of the building's centre-line, looking west. This summary-diagram demonstrates the direct relationships between the Pyramid's missing capstone, the eccentricity of the passage-axis, the heights of the four ventilator-outlets and the overall floorline-length of the lower passageways.

Note: By all accounts, the Pyramid's capstone was never added. The surviving historical records tell the story of a steadily disintegrating 'false apex' of small limestone blocks, presumably added in its place.

The level of the capstone's intended base (see diagram) is attested (a) by the floor-length from the entrance of the Descending Passage to the termination of the Dead End Passage, (b) by the heights and course-numbers of the various airshaft-outlets and (c) by the fact that a vertical cross-section of the Pyramid at the passage-axis defines the edge of it.

Whether or not the capstone was ever cut and transported is unknown. If so, it may be buried somewhere in the vicinity of the Pyramid, possibly in connection with Cayce's proposed 'Hall of Records' (compare footnote p. 111, and *The Great Pyramid Decoded* pp. 207-8). Many pyramidologists see this stone as the biblical 'stone which the builders rejected': its eventual installation, they claim, will symbolise, or even accompany, the long-awaited Second Coming.

Geographical / astronomical / geometrical correlations

1 sacred cubit	= 25.0265 British inches (63.56725 cm)
	= one ten-millionth of earth's mean polar radius
1 primitive inch	= 1.00106 British inches (2.54268 cm)
	= 1/250,000,000 of earth's mean polar radius
In the diagram, AB	= 365.242 sacred cubits
	= number of days in mean solar tropical year
AD_1H_1B	= 365.256 sacred cubits
	= number of days in earth's sidereal year
AmB	= 365.259 sacred cubits
	= number of days in earth's anomalistic year

(The Pyramid's base-perimeter measured in P″ necessarily gives exactly the same figures multiplied by 100: even measured in any other unit, it still demonstrates the ratios between the three types of year.)

VOU/OK	= 1826.2117/470860.606
	= 0.0038785
	= approximate minimum value of eccentricity of earth's orbit
WOC/OK	= 9131.0587/470860.606
	= 0.0193923
	= approximate maximum value of eccentricity of earth's orbit
OK	= 7.4393819 statute miles
	= 185, 984, 548 miles/25,000,000
	= approximately 1/25,000,000 of mean diameter of earth's orbit (giving a theoretical mean distance of the earth from the sun's centre of 92,992,274 miles)
AY + BX	= 25,826.53 P″
	= approximate duration in years of the cycle of the equinoxes
AXYB (plan)/CX(section)	= 36524.235/5813.0125
	= 6.2831853
	= 3.1415926 x 2
	= 2 π (ratio of any circle's radius to its circumference)

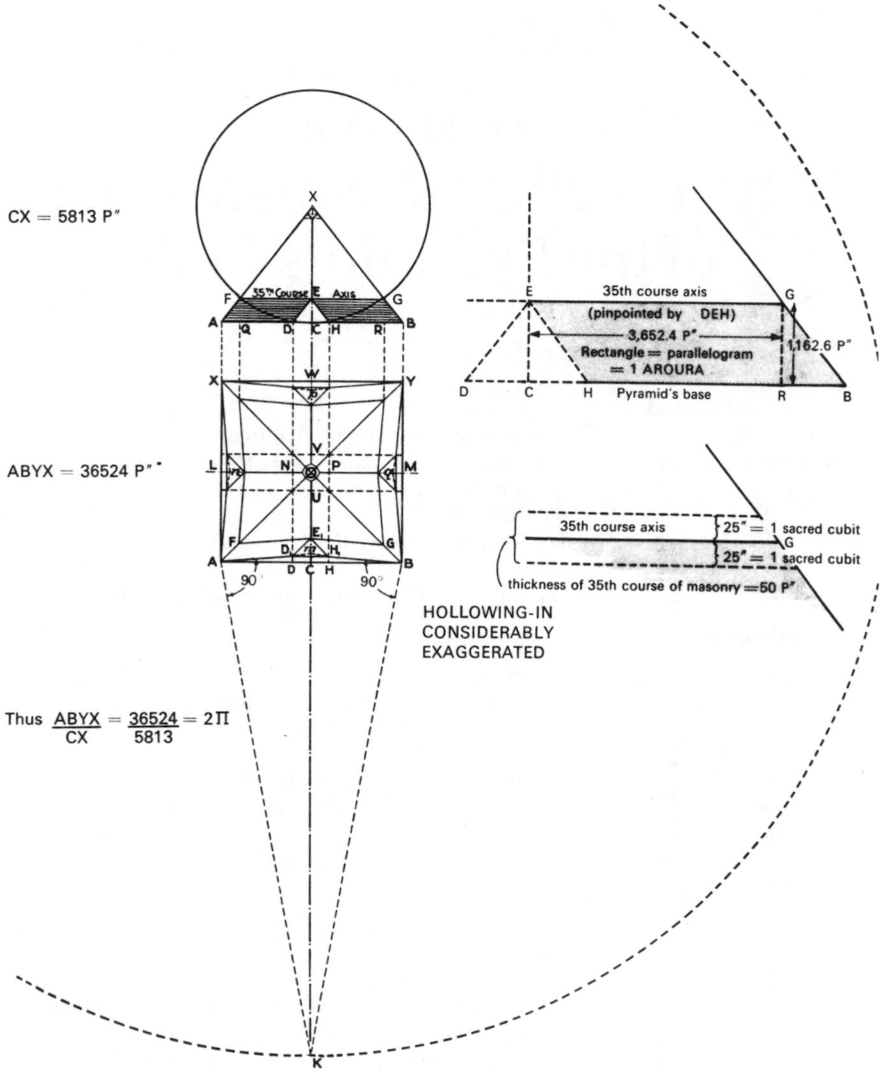

The basic geometry of the Pyramid's elevation and ground-plan, as designed, showing its direct links with the standard Egyptian unit of area, the *aroura*.

Interior Measurements

A diagram showing the Pyramid's main internal dimensions, and a comprehensive list of the principle passage-measurements in primitive inches (correct to four places of decimals), may be found in Appendix F of *The Great Pyramid Decoded*. To convert to primitive inches, multiply by 1.001060125: to convert to metres, multiply by .025426978.

APPENDIX B

Hypothetical Reconstruction of the Pyramid's Code

General

The Great Pyramid	= Planet Earth
The capstone	= completion, perfection, illumination
The passage-system	= the path of humanity, as yet 'dead' to the potentialities of consciousness latent within the psyche
Pyramid's N/S axis	= the achievement of balance and harmony
Pyramid's one-third height	= the achievement of balance and harmony

Directional symbolism

Southwards	= progress through time
Off-centredness	= lack of psychic balance and harmony
Downwards Leftwards Eastwards	= imbalance towards intellect and rationality at the expense of feeling and intuition
Upwards Rightwards Westwards	= return towards psychic balance and harmony

Passage features

Sloping passages at 26°18′9.7″	= evolution of human consciousness through time ('planetary' readout only)
Horizontal passages	= 'insets' portraying man's attainment of particular levels of consciousness (see Levels)
Steps	= changes of timescale
(a) up	= change of timescale giving more years per P″
(b) down	= changes of timescale giving less years per P″
(c) vertical	= changes of timescale based on relationship between height of step and nearest base-unit of previous timescale
(d) non-vertical or irregular	= changes of timescale arrived at trigonometrically by projecting old, 'sloping' scale onto new, horizontal floor
Limestone	= physical, material (see 4, square)

Granite	= supraphysical, pertaining to extended dimensions of awareness; 'hyperconsciousness'
Chambers	= ages of culmination
Chambers, gabled	= ages of wholeness and inner integration
Chambers, flat-roofed	= preparatory ages short of final perfection
Ventilation-shafts	= paths of life, emergence and transformation
'Telescopic' structures	= forms of society or consciousness symbolically 'blasted apart' by force from within
Portcullises	= interventions on the part of hyperconsciousness
Scored lines	= datum for chronograph
Levels	
Subterranean Chamber roof	= plane of despair, darkness and 'death'; total lack of wholeness and balance
Queen's Chamber floor	= plane of dawning reintegration
Queen's Chamber airshaft outlets (Pyramid's ½-height)	= plane of emergence from inner 'deadness'
Summit-platform	= plane of potential re-achievement of cosmic wholeness; imminent perfection and fulfilment
Geometrical symbolism	
1 P″	= one year (sloping passages only)*
20.6066 P″ (1RC)	= mortality, physicality, earthly experience: birth or death
25 P″ (1SC)	= total perfection (5^2)
29.84 P″	= death
33.5 P″	= transformation, transformer
35.763 P″	= physical/social effect of earlier consciousness-change (see 286.1 P″)
37.995 P″	= death
41.21 P″	= mortality
286.1 P″	= shift of consciousness, imbalance towards the rational (see Leftwards, Eastwards, Downwards) or, in the reverse direction, return to psychic integration
1881.2 P″	= quantum-jump of consciousness separating planes of 'death', dawning reintegration and emergence
5448.736 P″	= incompleteness, leading to imminent possibility of perfection and fulfilment
26°18′9.7″	= evolutionary progress or decline
51°51′14.3″	= ultimate wholeness and perfection
Square or rectangle	= physical or material (see 4, Limestone)
Circle	= extended dimensions of consciousness (see 3, π, Granite)
Circle superimposed on square of equal area	= total integration of physical experience with extended consciousness

* Applicable to 'planetary' readout only: for the corresponding 'personal' timescale refer to chapter 10.

Arithmetical symbolism

1	= heart of reality
2	= productive
3	= perfect, whole, pertaining to extended dimensions of consciousness (see Circle, Granite)
π	= as for 3
4	= physical, material, physicality (see Square, Limestone)
5	= completion, perfection; illumination (see Capstone)
6	= incompleteness, imperfection; preparation
7	= inner or psychic culmination, integration or perfection
8	= manifestation, result
9 (3^2)	= utter perfection
10	= age, era
11	= realisation, achievement
12	= man, humankind
13	= human 'metadimensional' aspect or 'higher self'; collective hyperconscious
19	= death, mortality
25 (5^2)	= total perfection and illumination
153	= enlightened, transformed, whole
+	= plus, added to
−	= minus
x	= of, times
÷	= through, by per (agent)
Square root	= the essence of, the inception of, the seed of
Squared $(^2)$	= *par excellence*, complete, utter

Bibliography

Adams, W. Marsham: *The Book of the Master of the Hidden Places* (Aquarian, 1980)
Benavides, R.: *Dramatic Prophecies of the Great Pyramid* (trans. of eleventh ed., Editores Mexicanos Unidos, 1970)
Budge, Sir E. A. W.: *The Egyptian Book of the Dead* (Routledge, 1960)
Cayce, H. L.: *The Edward Cayce Reader* [*et alia*] (Paperback Library, 1969)
Cottrell, L.: *The Lost Pharaohs* (Pan, 1960)
Davidson, D. and Aldersmith, H.: *The Great Pyramid: Its Divine Message* (Williams and Norgate, 1925)
Davidson, D.: *The Judgement of the Nations in the Great Pyramid's Prophecy* (Covenant, 1940)
Edgar, J. and M.: *The Great Pyramid Passages and Chambers* (Bone & Hulley, 1925)
Edgar, M.: *The Great Pyramid; Its Scientific Features* (Maclure, Macdonald and Co., 1924)
Edwards, I. E. S.: *The Pyramids of Egypt* (Penguin, 1949)
Fakhry, A.: *The Pyramids* (University of Chicago, 1969)
Gardiner, Sir A. H.: *Egyptian Grammar* (third ed., Oxford University Press, 1957)
Hawkins, G. S.: *Stonehenge Decoded* (Souvenir, 1966)
Ivimy, J.: *The Sphinx and the Megaliths* (Turnstone, 1974)
Kingsland, W.: *The Great Pyramid in Fact and in Theory* (Rider, 1932)
Lemesurier, P.: *The Armageddon Script* (Element, 1981)
Lemesurier, P.: *Gospel of the Stars* (Element, 1977)
Lemesurier, P.: *The Great Pyramid Decoded* (Element, 1977)
Lunan, D.: *Man and the Stars* (Souvenir, 1974)
McCollum, R., Fraccaro, G. and Robinson, E.: *The Giza Pyramids: Final Decoding* (Pyramid of Aquarius, 1978)
Mendelssohn, K.: *The Riddle of the Pyramids* (Cardinal, 1976)
Michell, J.: *City of Revelation* (Abacus, 1973)
Petrie, Sir W. M. F.: *The Pyramids and Temples of Gizeh* (1883)
Pochan, A.: *L'Enigme de la Grande Pyramide* (Laffont, 1971)
Rutherford, A.: *Pyramidology*, Books 1-4 (Institute of Pyramidology, 1957 onwards)
Schul, B. and Pettit, E.: *The Psychic Power of Pyramids* (Coronet, 1977)
Schul, B. and Pettit, E.: *The Secret Power of Pyramids* (Coronet, 1975)
Sitchin, Z.: *The Stairway to Heaven* (Avon, 1980)
Smith, W.: *The Secret Forces of the Pyramids* (Sphere, 1977)
Smyth, C. Piazzi: *Our Inheritance in the Great Pyramid* (Straham, 1864)
Thom, A.: *Megalithic Sites in Britain* (O.U.P., 1967)
Tompkins, P.: *Secrets of the Great Pyramid* (Allen Lane, 1973)
Toth, M. and Nielsen, G.: *Pyramid Power* (Warner, 1976)
Valentine, T.: *The Great Pyramid: Man's Monument to Man* (Granada, 1977)

Index

Figures in italics refer to illustrations and diagrams.